Interpreting in Multilingual, Multicultural Contexts

Studies in
Interpretation

Melanie Metzger and Earl Fleetwood, General Editors

Interpreting in Multilingual, Multicultural Contexts

Rachel Locker McKee and Jeffrey E. Davis, Editors

GALLAUDET UNIVERSITY PRESS

Washington, D.C.

Studies in Interpretation
A Series Edited by Melanie Metzger and Earl Fleetwood

Gallaudet University Press
Washington, DC 20002
http://gupress.gallaudet.edu

© 2010 by Gallaudet University
All rights reserved. Published 2010
Printed in the United States of America

ISBN 978-1-56368-445-6
    1-56368-445-4
ISSN 1545-7613

Interior design by Richard Hendel

The weaving on the front cover is by Veranoa Hetet, Te Ati Awa,
Ngati Tuwharetoa, and Ngati Maniapoto

♾ The paper used in this publication meets the minimum requirements of American
National Standard for Information Sciences—Permanence of Paper for Printed Library
Materials, ANSI Z39.48–1984.

Contents

Introduction

Rachel Locker McKee and Jeffrey E. Davis

Kotahi te kowhao o te ngira i kuhuna ai te miro ma, te miro pango, me te miro whero. There is but a single eye of the needle through which the threads of white, black and red must pass. (Mead & Grove, 2001, p. 246)

In this Māori homily, the white, black, and red threads of traditional weaving are used as a metaphor for the joining together of people from different cultures to form a strong social fabric. In this volume, we cast the sign language interpreter as the "eye of the needle" through which a plurality of languages, cultures, and identities of various hues are delicately passed to weave positive human connections.

FROM DUALISM TO PLURALISM

Linguistic proof that signed languages are distinct from spoken languages has supported a narrative of oppositional contrast between Deaf cultural identity and social norms and those of hearing people. In turn, the discourse of the sign language interpreting profession has tended to characterize consumers and languages in a binary distinction as Deaf or hearing, at times perhaps implying that these social categories are homogeneous, mutually exclusive, and all-encompassing primary identities. While the Deaf-hearing contrast is obviously central in defining the context of our work, this dualism potentially dulls our perception of the multiplicity and fluidity of identities, allegiances, and language resources that Deaf and hearing participants (and interpreters) bring to interpreted interactions. This volume probes the multiplex nature of interpreted interaction involving Deaf and hearing people of diverse linguistic and cultural backgrounds, and the contextualized interpreting practices and considerations that transpire from this diversity.

Contemporary studies of variation within and contact between signing communities are building a more detailed picture of the linguistically heterogeneous profile of Deaf communities and showing how variation in language use correlates with dimensions of social identity and context (Branson and Miller, 1998; Brentari, 2001; Lucas & Valli, 1989; Lucas, Bayley, & Valli, 2001; Metzger, 2000; Quinto-Pozos, 2007). Social scientists have also drawn attention to the spectrum of ethnic and social identities within Deaf communities, observing how Deaf elements of identity interact with other contextual variables such as family, race, place, and ethnicity to manifest in plural constructions of "Deaf" (Ahmad, Darr, Jones, & Nisar, 1998; Aramburo, 1989; Breivik, 2005; Christensen & Delgado, 1993; Foster & Kinuthia, 2003; McKay-Cody, 1998/1999; Monaghan, Schmaling, Nakamura, & Turner, 2003; Parasnis, 1996; Paris & Wood, 2002; Smiler & McKee, 2007).

Demographic data in the United States show that ethnicity in the Deaf population is rapidly diversifying (Leigh, 2008, p. 24). Leigh emphasizes that Deaf people are increasingly likely to interact with up to four communities: the majority hearing community, the larger deaf community, the ethnic hearing community of their family, and their ethnic deaf peers. In each of these contexts, Deaf and hearing people use language and other means of self-representation in fluctuating ways to construct identity and connection with each other. The multiplicity of identities in the Deaf world challenges the sociolinguistic repertoire of interpreters who are called upon to mediate communication across multiplex combinations of culture and language.

It is widely noted that the interpreter workforce is less diverse than the profile of Deaf populations: The majority of sign language interpreters in Western countries tend to be white, majority-culture females, and sign language interpreters are more commonly bilingual than tri- or multilingual. It can therefore be difficult for consumers from diverse backgrounds to find an interpreter with overlapping social characteristics and thought-worlds, or the ability to work in a third language that would connect them to the minority language community of their family. Few training programs and professional accreditation systems address multilingual/multicultural competencies in sign language interpreting; the National Multicultural Interpreting Project (Mooney, 2006) is an example of a pedagogical initiative in the United States that focused on preparing interpreters for the demands of cultural diversity in their work.

The first section in the volume focuses on the growing specialization of American Sign Language (ASL), English, and Spanish trilingual interpreting in the United States. Some contexts involving two spoken languages and two sign languages require quadrilingual interpreting (e.g., Mexican Sign Language (LSM), ASL, English, and Spanish). In Chapter 1, Ramsey and Peña explore the convergence of the Mexico-U.S. border with the Deaf-hearing border and the complex dynamics of this physically close but culturally distant interaction mediated by tri- and quadrilingual interpreters. In particular, they examine sociocultural and competency considerations for three- and four-language interpreting in this context, including disparity of language status and interpreting education between these countries.

In Chapter 2, Quinto-Pozos, Casanova de Canales, and Treviño describe an innovative trilingual (ASL, English, Spanish) Video Relay Service (VRS). Their chapter reviews the history of the trilingual VRS, discusses some of the linguistic challenges presented by the consumer cultures and the medium, analyzes evaluation data from practitioners and stakeholders in the service, and considers implications of this data.

Although the need to provide proficient interpreters qualified to work between ASL, English, and Spanish is well established, only recently has a formal trilingual interpreter certification process been successfully developed. In Chapter 3, González, Gatto, and Bichsel review the development and testing of a recently implemented trilingual (ASL, English, Spanish) interpreter certification process; they explain the processes of ensuring standardization, fairness, and psychometric validity of the test in measuring appropriateness and accuracy with respect to linguistic and cultural elements of candidates' interpretation.

MEDIATING MINORITY VOICES AND IDENTITIES

Acknowledging cultural diversity in Deaf communities highlights that the voice of some minorities is marginalized within the Deaf world and doubly so in hearing society (Anderson & Bowe, 1972; Dively, 2001; James & Woll, 2004; Padden & Humphries, 2005; Smiler, 2004). As witnesses to the inequities arising from differences in hearing status, class, ethnicity, and language, interpreters are often intrinsically concerned with empowering the voice of these Deaf consumers. In practice, interpreters sometimes agonize about how to respond ethically to underlying issues of social disadvantage in situations (particularly crises) involving minority group consumers who are culturally marginal in any community; they may struggle to reconcile their responses to these challenges with the textbook interpreter role. In a slightly different vein, interpreters of minority identity may choose to align themselves with the goals of indigenous and ethnic minority Deaf people to access their hearing community's sphere of cultural and political activities. The goal of interpreted transactions for Deaf participants in such contexts may be principally negotiating ethnic identity and solidarity, and gaining access to heritage cultural capital. Accordingly, the interpreter's ability to codeswitch between three languages or varieties is critical to enabling Deaf participants "to opt for a language that would symbolize the rights and obligations they wish to enforce in the exchange in question and index the appropriate identities" (Pavlenko & Blackledge, 2004, p. 8).

We agree with Dean and Pollard's (2005) assertion that "revealing situated practice" is a vital source of evidence for refining models of professional practice that are based in particular, and diverse, realities rather than universal idealizations. In situated practice, how does an interpreter's personal alignment with cultural norms and power relations shape their ethical framework and their manner of working? How do the cultural positions and agendas of ethnic minority Deaf and hearing people shape their expectations of an interpreter in situations of contact? These issues have been somewhat explored in relation to African American Deaf and interpreters in the United States (e.g., Jones, 1986; Mathers & White, 1986) but remain relatively under-researched.

The need to stimulate and disseminate further practice-based evidence prompted our invitation for contributions on the theme of interpreting in indigenous and minority language community contexts. This second group of chapters focuses on interpreters working with people of indigenous origin, addressing issues of role and responsibilities, the challenges of bridging wide gaps in cultural competencies and discourse norms, and the use of indigenous sign varieties. In Chapter 4, McKee and Awheto examine the way in which a trilingual Māori interpreter in New Zealand negotiates a role in response to the divergent schemas of participants, her own cultural alignment, and the sociocultural conditions framing the event. This chapter highlights that the role and ethics considered normative for a professional interpreter are not culturally neutral, and that contextualized practice in culturally diverse situations may be differently motivated and manifested.

Davis and McKay-Cody, Chapter 5, report on ethnographic fieldwork and observations from over two decades of collaborating, interpreting, and participating in multicultural and multilingual North American Indian communities. They describe the traditional and contemporary varieties of sign language used among North American Indian communities, and suggest strategies, best practices, and links to resources for interpreters working with Deaf people in these communities.

Indigenous Deaf people in legal settings can be doubly disadvantaged by their distance from the cultural parameters of "the system"; this is a context in which facilitating understanding about cultural-linguistic background is critical to the process of interpreting and achieving fair outcomes. In Chapter 6, Fayd'herbe and Teuma bring their professional experience in interpreting and forensic psychology to a discussion of issues in affording due process to Indigenous Deaf people of Far North Queensland, Australia. They discuss cultural differences and language competencies of these clients, outline practical interpreter strategies for working in a forensic team, and illustrate the risks of denial of due process by reference to relevant cases.

TRANSNATIONAL INTERPRETING

International exchange between members of different sign language communities has increased rapidly due to factors including improved Deaf access to higher education (leading to professionalization and international academic exchange), greater mobility, and the formalization of global Deaf advocacy activities. Increasing trans-national exchange between Deaf people over the last 20 years has presented sign language interpreters with challenges akin to those of spoken language interpreters who have traditionally worked in elite, multilingual domains such as conferences, business, and politics. Furthermore, borderless technologies such as video relay and remote interpreting services have changed the boundaries of when, where, and how Deaf and hearing parties can use their respective languages to interact via interpreters.

An emerging area of expertise is interpreting across multiple signed and spoken languages at international conferences. In Chapter 7, Supalla, Clark, Neumann Solow, and Muller de Quadros address the requirements of ensuring quality of interpreted access for Deaf and hearing academics participating in a conference. The authors describe the development, implementation, and outcomes of a protocol for conference interpreting designed to bring Deaf participants, including minority sign language participants, from the margins of the conference into full involvement. Finally, in Chapter 8, de Wit discusses challenges and skills relevant to interpreting in multilingual, multimodal European conference settings, and suggests practical strategies for furthering these, such as the acquisition of additional languages, teamwork, and mentoring into the specialist skill-set required.

Most of the chapters in this book draw strongly upon practitioner and consumer insight as a source of data. In each instance, authors describe a localized situation and explore its implications for interpreting practice in the wider field. We believe this is a valuable contribution to an emerging area in the research literature. Commenting upon methods of sociolinguistic research, Coupland (2007, p. 28) states that "Single-case analyses are more likely to allow adequate sensitivity to context and contextualization" and may allow generalization to the possibilities in a given situation rather than to "what people typically do." Since the practices of interpreters in culturally and linguistically complex situations are as yet little-documented, this volume aims to highlight the state of current practice and perspectives via case studies of practice from various contexts, in order to stimulate directions for further research and dialogue.

Collaborative authorship of all but one of the chapters seems to reflect an intuition that alliances between culturally and academically diverse professionals, consumers, and researchers are important in constructing new knowledge about interpreting, and in re-balancing power relations. All chapters emphasize the importance of dialogue and cooperative initiatives, and reflect an orientation towards the practitioner as researcher. We would like to think that the collaborative nature of the work in this volume enacts the following advice from the National Multicultural Interpreting Project (2000):

> Without true and authentic multicultural partnerships with both Deaf and Hearing interpreters from a diversity of backgrounds, experiences and cultural competencies, we will not be able to effectively meet these challenges. With the development of increased access to technology, transportation, and organizational networking, we no longer have to function as "Super Interpreters" who must understand all languages, know all cultures and be all things to all communities. With the development of multicultural partnerships, agencies, teams, and training programs, we can develop the true respect and appreciation for our colleagues in this dynamic field. (p. 4)

In many respects the fundamental challenge of interpreting in multiethnic contexts is like that in any interpreting situation: to bridge a gap of linguistic and cultural expression between hearing and Deaf people who need to communicate with each other, while managing the logistics of bimodal communication. At the same time, there are particular contextual issues for interpreters in multilingual/multiethnic situations relating to cultural assumptions about relationships and roles within the interaction, differences in power, the impact of participants' social identities and alliances, interpreter training and competence, and negotiating teamwork. The degree of distance between the languages and thought-worlds of participants in such situations sometimes requires interpreters to span very wide gulfs or to build multiple bridges between a diverse set of participants.

This volume particularly addresses the experience of interpreters in those "wide gap" situations, in order to identify challenges, strategies and consequences, and to stimulate consideration of how this kind of work abides with more "mainstream" models of practice.

REFERENCES

Ahmad, W., Darr, A., Jones, L., & Nisar, G. (1998). *Deafness and ethnicity: Services, policy and politics.* Bristol, UK: Policy Press.

Anderson, G. B., & Bowe, F. G. (1972). Racism within the Deaf community. *American Annals of the Deaf, 117,* 617–19.

Aramburo, A. J. (1989). Sociolinguistic aspects of the Black Deaf community. In C. Lucas (Ed.), *The sociolinguistics of the Deaf community.* New York: Academic Press.

Branson, J., & Miller, D. (1998). Nationalism and the linguistic rights of Deaf communities: Linguistic imperialism and the recognition and development of sign languages. *Journal of Sociolinguistics, 2*(1), 3–34.

Breivik, J. K. (2005). *Deaf identities in the making.* Washington, DC: Gallaudet University Press.

Brentari, D. (Ed.). (2001). *Foreign vocabulary in sign languages: A cross-linguistic investigation of word formation.* Mahwah, NJ: Lawrence Erlbaum.

Christensen, K. M., & Delgado, G. L. (Eds.). (1993). *Multicultural issues in deafness.* White Plains, NY: Longman.

Coupland, N. (2007). *Style: Language variation and identity.* Cambridge: Cambridge University Press.

Dean, R., & Pollard, R. (2005). Consumers and service effectiveness in interpreting work: A practice profession perspective. In M. Marschark,

R. Peterson, & E. A. Winston (Eds.), *Interpreting and interpreter education: Directions for research and practice.* New York: Oxford University Press.

Dively, V. L. (2001). Contemporary native Deaf experience: Overdue smoke rising. In L. Bragg (Ed.), *Deaf world. A historical reader and primary sourcebook* (pp. 390–405). New York: New York University Press.

Foster, S., & Kinuthia, W. (2003). Deaf persons of Asian American, Hispanic American, and African American backgrounds: A study of intra-individual diversity and identity. *Journal of Deaf Studies and Deaf Education, 8*(3), 271–90.

James, M., & Woll, B. (2004). Black Deaf or Deaf Black? In A. Pavlenko & A. Blackledge (Eds.), *Negotiation of identities in multilingual contexts* (pp.125–60). Bristol, UK: Multilingual Matters.

Jones, P. (1986). Issues involving Black interpreters and Black Deaf. In M. McIntire (Ed.), *Interpreting: The art of cross-cultural mediation proceedings of the 9th national convention of the Registry of Interpreters for the Deaf* (pp. 61–68). Silver Spring, MD: RID Publications.

Leigh, I. W. (2008). Who am I? Deaf identity issues. In K. Lindgren, D. DeLuca, & D. J. Napoli (Eds.), *Signs and voices: Deaf culture, identity, language and the arts.* Washington, DC: Gallaudet University Press.

Lucas, C., & Valli, C. (1989). Language contact in the American Deaf community. In C. Lucas (Ed.), *The sociolinguistics of the Deaf community* (pp. 11–41). San Diego: Academic Press.

Lucas, C., Bayley, R., & Valli, C. (2001). *Sociolinguistic variation in American Sign Language: Sociolinguistics in deaf communities.* Washington, DC: Gallaudet University Press.

McKay-Cody, M. (1998/1999). The well-hidden people in Deaf and Native Communities. In M. Garretson (Ed.), *Unrealized visions: Vol. 48. NAD Deaf American monograph series,* (pp. 49–51). Silver Spring, MD: NAD Publications.

Mathers, C., & White, P. (1986). Cross-cultural cross-racial mediation. In M. McIntire (Ed.), *Interpreting: The art of cross-cultural mediation proceedings of the 9th national convention of the Registry of Interpreters for the Deaf* (pp. 97–106). Silver Spring, MD: RID Publications.

Mead, H. M, .& Grove, N. (2001). *Ngā pepeha a ngā tipuna.* Wellington, New Zealand: Victoria University Press.

Metzger, M. (Ed.). (2000). *Bilingualism and identities in Deaf communities.* Washington, DC: Gallaudet University Press.

Monaghan, L., Schmaling, C., Nakamura, K., & Turner, G. (Eds.). (2003). *Many ways to be Deaf.* Washington, DC: Gallaudet University Press.

Mooney, M. (2006). Interpreter training in less frequently taught languages. Changing the curriculum paradigm to multilingual and multicultural as applied to interpreter education programs. In C. Roy (Ed.), *New approaches to interpreter education* (pp. 139–52). Washington, DC: Gallaudet University Press.

National Multicultural Interpreting Project (NMIP) Curriculum. (2000). *Decision making in culturally and linguistically diverse communities: Creating authentic teams (section VIII), lecture notes.* Retrieved from http://www.asl.neu.edu/TIEM.online/curriculum_nmip.html.

Padden, C., & Humphries, T. (2005). *Inside Deaf culture.* Cambridge, MA: Harvard University Press.

Parasnis, I. (1996). *Cultural and language diversity and the deaf experience.* Cambridge: Cambridge University Press.

Paris, D. G., & Wood, S. K. (2002). *Step into the circle: The heartbeat of American Indian, Alsaka Native, and First Nations Deaf communities.* Salem, OR: AGO Publications.

Pavlenko, A., & Blackledge, A. (Eds.). (2004). *Negotiation of identities in multilingual contexts.* Bristol, UK: Multilingual Matters.

Quinto-Pozos, D. (Ed.). (2007). *Signed languages in contact: Vol. 13. Sociolinguistics in Deaf communities series.* Washington, DC: Gallaudet University Press.

Smiler, K. (2004). *Māori Deaf: Perceptions of cultural and linguistic identity of Māori members of the New Zealand Deaf community.* Unpublished master's thesis, Victoria University of Wellington, New Zealand.

Smiler, K., & McKee, R. (2007). Perceptions of Māori Deaf identity in New Zealand. *Journal of Deaf Studies and Deaf Education, 12,* 93–111.

Part I Expanding Frontiers: ASL-English-Spanish Interpreting in the United States

Sign Language Interpreting

at the Border of the Two Californias

Claire Ramsey and Sergio Peña

The U.S.-Mexico border is a complex geopolitical phenomenon. Looking south, North Americans see a chaotic and colorful culture, potential streams of illegal immigrants and security threats as well as a thriving marketplace, an abundant pool of cheap labor, and easy-to-reach beach vacation destinations. Mexicans looking north, in contrast, see educational and economic opportunity as well as bigotry, a violent and inexplicably cold culture, and hypocrisy in a nation of immigrants that stifles new immigration. Little that takes place at the Tijuana, Baja California, Mexico–San Ysidro, California, United States border is neutral from a political perspective. To cross *la linea* is to move in a matter of seconds between two Californias in high contrast.

Deaf people's lives in the border region are subject to the same influences. San Diego, California, the eighth largest city in the United States, sits almost directly on the border. Even so, most of the hearing and Deaf population has minimal intentional contact with the political border and barely acknowledge it. Nonetheless, those who navigate the border from Mexico into the United States and back know that on the north side of the line being Mexican carries a huge range of meanings, and that being both Mexican and Deaf amplifies and adds complexity to those meanings. On the south side of the line lie national and cultural familiarity, but being a signing Deaf person still places one in a singular category that receives very little attention. The sign language interpreters who work in the border zone must understand these facts and meanings, as well as master ways to adapt to them, explain them, and to apply their multicultural and multilingual life experiences to bridge the legendary variability they encounter in their work.

A small group of hearing and Deaf sign language interpreters lives on the Mexican side of the border, working in four languages and at least two cultures. We estimate that in Tijuana and Rosarito (the town directly south of Tijuana) this group totals 20, approximately half hearing and

3

half Deaf. Their services are needed in Mexico but they spend more time on the U.S. side of the border where they provide community interpreting (for example, at weddings, funerals, or other large group events), as well as interpreting in medical, legal, and social services settings. Although the pool of trilingual interpreters (Spanish, English, and American Sign Language [ASL]) on the U.S. side of the border is relatively large, we have not been successful in identifying in Southern California any "border interpreters" who use all four languages professionally. At this time, four-language interpreters from Mexico are imported to the United States when their services are needed.

In general, four-language interpreters do not work with Deaf Mexican immigrants to the U.S. While there are *Lengua de Señas Mexicana* (LSM)-dominant Deaf immigrants in the U.S. border region who may periodically need interpreting services, border interpreters more commonly travel from Mexico to the United States to interpret for Deaf people who have also crossed the line for a specific and temporary purpose—a medical appointment, a meeting to resolve a legal or social services issue, or a social or community event. The Deaf LSM-signer may be the client or the patient, or may be a family member of the client or patient. Although issues of power imbalance, marginalization relative to dominant groups, and racial or language prejudice apply equally to temporary visitors from Mexico and to immigrants and permanent residents with Mexican origins, the interpreters we describe here generally work with monolingual hearing speakers of English in the United States who know neither Spanish, LSM, or ASL but who interact for various reasons with Deaf people from Mexico, whose dominant language is LSM.

Interpreters at the border work with two national signed languages, ASL and LSM, at least two varieties of signing found at the border (a locally recognized but undescribed variety referred to as "Tijuana Sign Language," and ASL as it is signed by returned Mexicans schooled in the United States), and two spoken languages, English and Spanish. Other languages occur in Mexico as well, and make appearances at the border. Mexico's *Instituto Nacional de Lenguas Indígenas* (Insituto Nacional de Lenguas Indígenas, 2007), the national institute of indigenous languages, officially recognizes over 60 national languages of Mexico, including, as of 2004, LSM. National languages other than LSM and Spanish, for example Purépecha, Nahuatl, or Mixe-Zoque are use in the border region. Last, other types of signing also appear, including varieties of a second group of signed languages of Mexico, Yucatec Maya Sign Language (e.g.,

Escobedo Delgado, 2008; Johnson, 1991), idiosyncratic home signs, and signs emerging from Rancho Sordo Mudo, in nearby Valle de Guadalupe, Baja California, a Christian residential school for the deaf whose residents avail themselves of signing resources that include both ASL and LSM (Rancho Sordo Mudo, 2008).

In addition, border interpreters fluently manipulate the symbols and meanings of Mexican, Mexican-American, and American hearing and Deaf cultures in a range of domains. All of the border interpreters we know of, the 20 Deaf and hearing people referred to above, are Mexicans. They possess native knowledge, developed over lifetimes, of Mexican ways of life, with special knowledge about the United States that only Mexicans who live on the border have acquired. In addition, a few are hearing members of Deaf families, whose life experiences include personal knowledge of Deaf life in Mexico. Finally, most have traveled to the United States for interpreting courses and workshops, and have interacted with U.S. interpreters. And, like many border residents of Mexico, they have spent time in the United States, have years of exposure to U.S. television and other media, and have developed knowledge about and interpretations of the United States that help them understand and adjust to cultural differences that influence interpreted situations.

Here we consider the development of hearing border interpreters, the professional and educational resources they have created or located for themselves on both sides of the border, and the language variability among Deaf signers to which they must adjust in their work. We also suggest areas that merit the systematic attention of researchers. Readers should note that at this point in our study of border interpreters we have no data about Deaf border interpreters in either Mexico or California beyond the knowledge that they periodically work as intermediary interpreters. The state of, and the course of development of Deaf signers' range of signed and spoken language knowledge is a question that deserves researchers' attention.

POSITIONALITY OF THE AUTHORS

For this chapter, because so much is unknown about four-language, California–Baja California international border interpreting, we decided to use one author's history to document issues in *la interpretación en la frontera* (border interpreting) as well as our respective histories as participants in border life. Accordingly, we do not offer a conventional account of research methods, particularly data collection. We generated our data by laying out and examining our experiences as border-dwellers and multilinguals, our observations in the region, and our firsthand participation in the context we describe. As a result, we acknowledge that readers should know who we are, and for this reason we present our positionality as authors in the place of a more detailed explanation of our research methods. Clarifying our positionality is especially important because there is little published knowledge upon which we can rely to supply a credible basis for our comments. What's more, using a narrative structure complements both our respective skills and our history as friends and colleagues. The first time Ramsey interviewed Peña was in 1996, and many conversations, and formal and informal interviews have followed. We have a cordial working relationship and we share a deep interest in the many fascinations of living on the Mexico-U.S. border.

Ramsey's mother tongue is English. She grew up in Seattle, Washington, and is from an American and Canadian family, all English-speaking. Her mother is a second generation American of Norwegian descent. Her father's family arrived in the United States in the late 19th century from the British Isles. She was schooled in the United States, with the exception of a period of study abroad in Bogotá, Colombia. She began to learn Spanish in third grade, ASL in her 20s, and LSM in the late 1990s, and resided at the U.S.-Mexico border from 1991 to 1997. In 2003 she returned to the California–Baja California region, and maintains a residence in Mexico City where she spends about 16 weeks a year. Ramsey has been studying Deaf signers and Deaf education at the border of *las dos californias* (e.g., Ramsey, 2000; Ramsey & Noriega, 2000) and in Mexico City (Ramsey & Ruiz Bedolla, 2004, 2006) for nearly 10 years, using life histories as a primary data source. The objective of her ongoing research in Mexico is to produce a rich description of the sociolinguistic context of LSM, in particular so that the language might emerge from stigma, be transmitted to deaf infants, and used as a medium of instruction in Mexican deaf education.

Peña was born in Los Angeles, California, and is a lifelong resident of Tijuana, Baja California, Mexico, schooled in Tijuana and San Diego. He is an interpreter and interpreter educator on both sides of the border. His mother tongue is Spanish. He learned LSM as a 5-year-old, and English and ASL in middle school. He earned his bachelor's degree at San Diego State University, and in 2007 founded an interpreter education program at *Universidad Autónoma de Baja California* in Tijuana. As of 2008, this program is the first and only university-based sign language interpreting program in Mexico. Peña is a good historian, particularly because his schooling history and postsecondary education have placed him in both the United States and Mexico. Through years of participation in life on both sides of the border, he can step back and reflect on his observations of Mexicans and Americans, both Deaf and hearing. He shares Ramsey's objective of promoting increased awareness and better understanding of signed language and its use in Mexico.

Our report then grows out of a felicitous collaboration. Ramsey knows how to ask questions and propose topics for discussion, and Peña is a gifted narrator as well as a highly sought-after interpreting practitioner. Although we have spent hours in conversation about signed languages, cultures, deaf education, and interpreting over at least a decade, to prepare this paper we decided to meet and videotape a conversation. No interview protocol was used. Ramsey asked questions about language and cultural differences Peña had observed, which generated conversation about languages, cultures, conditions for Deaf people in the two countries, and conditions for interpreters and interpreter education in the two countries. Not surprisingly, our conversation was carried out in a mix of English, Spanish, ASL, and LSM.

BACKGROUND TO THE TOPIC OF BORDER INTERPRETERS

We have been unable to locate any published description or analysis of sign language interpreters working in four languages at the U.S.-Mexico border. Other topics that consider borders, signed languages, and interpreting have been examined by Quinto-Pozos and colleagues (e.g., Quinto-Pozos et al., this volume; Quinto-Pozos, 2008). In addition, in the United States, the National Multicultural Interpreter Project (e.g., NMIP, 2000) developed curriculum in response to the needs of interpreters working in the United States in settings which are bi- or multicultural, and may or may not be multilingual. To clearly understand the language variation presented by Deaf signers in the border area of interest here, the history of Deaf Education in Mexico, particularly its role in the transmission and continuity of LSM (Ramsey & Ruiz Bedolla, 2006; Ramsey & Quinto-Pozos, in press) is also relevant. Although these topics are under investigation, a great deal more work will be needed to grasp their applied and theoretical impacts. This work will be important. Knowledge about four-language interpretation across international borders will contribute to the literature on sign language interpretation and sign language socio-linguistics, as well as to the rich research base about life on borders.

DEVELOPMENT OF FOUR-LANGUAGE INTERPRETERS AT THE CALIFORNIA-BAJA CALIFORNIA BORDER

There are two key questions about four-language interpreters, especially if we wish to consider the possibility of preparing interpreters to fill this specific niche. First, how do four-language interpreters develop their language abilities, or in broader terms, under what circumstances do hearing people come to learn two spoken and two signed languages? And, second, where and how do they develop and practice their interpreting abilities? Readers should note that here and throughout we distinguish between language abilities and interpreting abilities.

Developing Multilingual Fluency

In most cases, although intuitively it makes sense to think of bilingual and multilingual people as particularly skilled individuals, fluency in two or more languages is not simply an individual intellectual accomplishment. Instead, ranges of language knowledge and fluency reflect social contexts, features of which are manifested in the behavior of individuals. People become bilingual or multilingual and maintain a range of languages because they need them to carry out their lives. Grosjean (1985) defines a bilingual as a person who needs and uses two (or more) languages in everyday life. Peña's observations over many years of using four languages daily are even more detailed. From his perspective there comes a turning point where one no longer knows or remembers which languages are used in everyday life. Peña describes his multilingualism as an intrapersonal and cognitive phenomenon rather than a meta-level awareness of knowing a second, or third language. Clearly this level of integration of one's languages is an ideal starting place for skills in interpretation.

So we can easily claim that interpreters *need* language knowledge, but the nature of language knowledge is such that its development is not rapid, and that multilingualism grows into a fluent integrated intellectual and interpersonal experience. For many adult learners, it is also far from easy. In fact, we set out on our paths to multilingualism when we were children, with no thought of future careers using languages. These paths were also very much a matter of being in a certain place at a certain time.

It is not unusual for Mexicans who live in the border area, on either side, to acquire Spanish natively as well as some functional fluency in English early in life, sometimes simultaneously beginning in infancy. United States citizens at the border who are not of Latino heritage, in contrast, rarely acquire fluent Spanish. Related to this is the observation that even if they study Spanish, few U.S. students gain functional fluency in the languages that they study to meet high school graduation or postsecondary admission requirements. Baker (2001) claims that fewer than 20% of U.S. students actually become bilingual as a result of language study. In addition, although over 300 languages are spoken in the United States (National Virtual Translation Center [NVTC], 2007) ideologically the United States is a monolingual English-speaking society. In essence, despite the national reality of widespread multilingualism, most English-speaking U.S. citizens do not consider themselves residents of a multilingual society or affected by the multilingualism that exists in the nation, so using languages other than English is relatively rare for them. Most importantly, few native speakers of English need two or more languages in everyday life.

Still, hypothetically we are all potentially bilingual. Both Grosjean (1985) and Baker (2001) describe bilingualism as a fluid phenomenon that changes over the life course and is not static. That is, needs for languages arise and speakers adapt, even to the point of learning new languages in adulthood. (See Smith, 2002, for a convincing discussion of language development examined within sociolinguistic networks in U.S. ex-patriots working abroad.)

Peña learned English when his family sent him to middle school in San Diego. Ramsey began to learn Spanish in elementary school as a result of the changes in U.S. education after Sputnik was launched, but did not "need" to use and maintain Spanish until much later in life when she was a student in Latin America. The characteristic we have in common in our spoken language fluencies is an early start, in childhood. We both added signed languages to our repertoires after we acquired at least one spoken language. Peña came into contact with LSM when he was 5 years old, and met a Deaf boy his age at church. He came into contact with ASL later in his life when he attended school in San Diego. Ramsey learned ASL as a young adult prior to entering an interpreter training program and she began learning LSM in 1996, when she first lived at the San Diego/Tijuana border in a class that Peña taught.

Early Exposure to Languages and Four-language Interpreting

What are the implications of the language histories of adult specialists like we are for four-language interpreting in general? Relatively early bilingualism is a common characteristic among the small group of four-language interpreters in the border region. More specifically, exposure to a signed language came from having one or more signing Deaf parents or having a signing Deaf childhood friend. This is what we refer to when we say that the four-language interpreters we know of were exposed to and as a result needed two or more of their languages at the "right time," that is in childhood or adolescence.

Again, we emphasize that language exposure grew from specific social contexts. Neither of us was a particularly clever or studious language learner as a child, although both of us were taken with language, as some children are, and curious about words, spelling, and other languages. It is possible that our personalities or our ways of being in the social world may have predisposed us to take particular advantage of the language exposure we experienced. Research on children and second language learning at school indicates that some personal characteristics may incline children towards more productive learning of a second language. They include "sociability, communicative need, risk-taking, and self-confidence" (Wong-Fillmore, 1991, p. 49). Still, few children can conceive of future careers as interpreters of Spanish, English, ASL, and LSM, so career planning early in life does not appear to be a recruitment strategy, even though early exposure to and an early need for more than one language are the characteristics that most distinguish current four-language interpreters in the border region.

In reality, in the United States many young adults and adults who wish to become sign language interpreters begin with fluency in only one language: spoken English. In Mexico, where interpreter education has only recently been available, and is not widespread, the applicant pool is similar. Given the amount of time required to develop language fluency (note that we have not yet discussed skills required for interpretation), and school-based language teaching's general lack of success, how can the field locate potential four-language interpreters? For now, four-language interpreters start out as at least trilingual. Yet even for this group, language training must be intense. Immersion might be the most efficient strategy for gaining initial fluency, although we do not know anything about the nature of four-language interpreters as language learners. It is possible that this group contains people who have extraordinary language learning abilities, or specific, particularly efficient strategies for learning languages. Learning and building fluency in four languages, which should precede the development of interpreting skills, is a long-term project. Still, given the dearth of information available about four-language interpreters' levels of language fluency, communicative competence, processing strategies, and trajectories of development, in our view the viability of four-language interpretation as a specialty will continue to rest on expanding the abilities of those who present strong fluency in the languages used at the border.

The Border as a Location for Language Exposure

We also see that, in addition to the timing of their language exposure, four-language interpreters need to be at the right place. For example, the border of the two Californias is a reasonable location for developing several languages in response to the need to use them. There is a sizeable literature on border phenomena, particularly about *las dos californias* (e.g., King's [2004] discussion of the "literary space" of the borderlands). Still it would be naïve to suggest that four-language interpreters are needed only at the geographic border. Indeed, discussions about the border can no longer be limited to the geographic U.S.-Mexico border. Movement of Mexicans into North America takes place at land border crossings in places like San Ysidro, California, and El Paso, Texas, among many. But the south-to-north migration has generated a diaspora, and Mexican people reside all over the United States, far from the physical border. Every bus station or airport in the United States is a potential border crossing, from California and Arizona to Nebraska and Maine (see Wortham, Hamann, & Murillo, 2001, on the Latino diaspora). The diaspora also flows in both directions. Mexican Deaf people educated in the United States who sign ASL often return to Mexico, but maintain ASL as they add LSM to their language repertoires. Accordingly, the need for four-language interpreters can occur any place in either country. Although we are physically located at the U.S.-Mexico border, we know of four-language interpreters who have worked in states far from the geographical border, from Georgia and North Carolina in the United States to Mexico City in Mexico. This observation has potential importance for planning education for four-language interpreters.

INTERPRETATION AS A PROFESSION IN
THE UNITED STATES AND MEXICO

Research knowledge about the border is based most strongly on the north side of the line. As a result North Americans' view of the border region, its extent, and its meaning from the Mexican perspective is relatively "shallow" (Curiel, 2008, p. 404). The implications of this observation are that for now at least, interpreting at the border of *las dos californias* is inevitably framed within a U.S. perspective. Indeed, academic research, preparation of interpreters, funding for provision of interpreting services, and education of interpreters is now common in the United States but relatively uncommon in Mexico. The profession is highly developed in the United States, and Deaf people and increasingly hearing people have a sophisticated level of awareness about interpreting. Professionalization has just taken root in Mexico. In September 2008 the Mexican *Comisión de Normatividad y Certificación Laboral* and the *Consejo Nacional para Personas con Discapaciad* convened a *Grupo Técnico de Especialistas de Señas*,[1] in which Peña participated, to lay out the details of an LSM/ Spanish interpreting certification. Obviously, simply importing U.S. methods of examining interpreting and designing education of interpreters, and U.S. models of ethics and funding for interpreters will likely not turn out to be a completely useful strategy for fostering sign language interpreting in Mexico or for understanding and fostering four-language interpreters. And, despite more advanced practice in sign language interpreting in the United States, neither the culture of the border and the diaspora, nor the culture of Mexicans, are well understood north of the line. As noted, there is virtually no literature on this topic, in either the United States or in Mexico. Additionally, on the ground, interpreters of Mexican origin, like other Mexicans, are highly likely to comprehend and parse North American–Mexican interactions more accurately than non-Latino U.S. interpreters do. This is of course common in contexts where equilibrium in power relations is off balance. The less powerful have to understand

---

1. The *Comisión de Normatividad y Certificación Laboral* translates as Commission for Labor Rules, Regulations and Certification. The *Consejo Nacional para Personas con Discapaciad* translates to the National Council for Persons With Disabilities. The *Grupo Técnico de Especialistas de Señas* is the technical group of specialists in signing.

the more powerful in order to survive and participate in interactions. The more powerful do not have the same need for understanding their less powerful neighbors. Inevitably, this imbalance also affects the work of border interpreters, and understanding it is critical to their work.

In sum, providing foundations for development of four-language interpreters presents challenges. First, building language abilities at the level required for quality interpreting requires many years of intense practice. In general, traditional classroom teaching is not likely to provide sufficient functional practice to achieve these levels. Although current U.S. interpreter education occurs most commonly in two year programs, no one believes that is sufficient. Yet, the interpreting field does not recruit children, and the amount of time and the intensity of language practice required to develop multilingual abilities far surpasses two years. Clearly, development of four-language interpreters will have to extend beyond current practice in training interpreters. Additionally, although the geographic border is the most likely place to locate potential four-language interpreter candidates, the "border" exists all over the United States and all over Mexico. Experience suggests that four-language interpreters are needed both at and far from physical borders. Last, current thinking about interpreting at the border may be heavily influenced by U.S. style professionalization and practice, even though the interpreters themselves, and their Deaf clients, are overwhelmingly of Mexican heritage. The imbalance between nations in academic research interest in signed languages and in interpretation has created a wider knowledge gap about four-language interpreting than the knowledge gap about sign language interpreting in Mexico in general, which is also vast. All of these issues deserve research attention, in the interest of expanding our knowledge base and recasting sign language interpreting so that the unique needs of life at the border can also be addressed by the field.

PROFESSIONAL AND EDUCATIONAL RESOURCES IN THE CALIFORNIA–BAJA CALIFORNIA BORDER REGION

It is clear to us that four-language interpreters are not only rare within the ranks of sign language interpreters, but that people with language abilities at the level required for interpretation in two languages, much less four, are quite unusual and develop their abilities as a result of circumstances that begin relatively early in life. Importantly, these circumstances are not necessarily related to formal schooling. In contrast, interpretation abilities do not easily develop in the absence of instruction, and are typically transmitted and practiced in training or preparation programs, where mentorship from more experienced practitioners plays a role. Although to our knowledge no practical training or education for four-language interpreters is currently available in either Mexico or the United States, interpreters at the borders of the two Californias avail themselves of nearby professional and educational opportunities, and in Mexico have initiated some new educational opportunities.

Peña, for example, along with other two- and four-language interpreters based in northern Mexico, attended an interpreter education program at a community college in San Diego county in the United States. Others have taken ASL courses in the United States, while some U.S.-based interpreters have taken LSM courses from Mexican signers in either San Diego or Tijuana. College-level courses and programs, and professional-level workshops and conferences are currently more available and more numerous in the United States than in Mexico.

Recently, however, Peña has been involved with the initiation of two diploma[2] programs at the *Universidad Autónoma de Baja California* (UABC) in the Languages Department. The first, *Diplomado en Lengua de Señas Mexicana*, is a 185-hour program that covers Deaf community issues, and offers instruction and practice in LSM grammar and vocabulary. This university developed this program in collaboration with Graciela Rascón, a Deaf woman from Tijuana, founder and head of *Asociación en Apoyo de Sordos, A.C.* (APSOR). APSOR organizes and supervises the program, and Peña coordinates it. He proposed and received university approval for the second, *Diplomado en Interpretación de Lengua de Señas Mexicana*. This diplomado consists of 185 hours of practice and instruction, and a minimum of 15 hours of practical experience, and is under Peña's supervision and direction. The faculty in the Languages Department was very responsive to Peña's original proposal to start a program. As a result of Deaf Community, interpreter organization, and university collaboration, UABC offers the first and so far only post-secondary program to prepare sign language interpreters in Mexico.

---

2. In Mexico a *diplomado* program is a non-degree program that includes a set of courses, often offered evenings or weekends, that transmit a specific body of knowledge or practical abilities.

See http://interpretesbc.blogspot.com/2008/01/diplomados-lsm.html, the web site of the *Asociación de Intérpretes y Traductores de Lengua de Señas de Baja California A.C.* (the Baja California Association of Interpreters and Translators of Sign Language) for further information and for links to several other regional interpreter associations in Mexico. Note that not all of Mexico's 31 states have interpreter associations.

In addition to enrolling in courses and workshops at U.S. community colleges, Baja California interpreters find training and instruction through professional associations like *Asociación de Intérpretes y Traductores de Lengua de Señas de Baja California A.C.* and Mano a Mano, a U.S-based organization of trilingual (ASL, Spanish, English) interpreters.[3] Both offer workshops and interpreter education events. Nonetheless, for interpreters or prospective border interpreters who seek preparation and skills training, much depends on location. In Mexico these opportunities are still rare, infrequent, and for many, at a distance that makes the expense of seeking training difficult to manage.

WHAT IS REQUIRED TO DO THE JOB: INTERPRETING AND EXPLAINING MEXICO, THE UNITED STATES, AND THE BORDER

Our final point is an obvious one, but one that we wish to discuss in detail. Interpreters must be experts in the details and variations of the languages they use. Although it is a truism to add that they must also be able to move between cultures with skill, here we want to bring the truism to life. The fact is that we can know a language without also having deep knowledge of the cultural factors that influence its users. And, especially at the border, we can know the languages without locating them in the complex world of the border. At the border of the two Californias, without exaggeration we suggest that the knowledge and ability to cross the line and bring clarity to one group about the other is often more critical than language and interpretation skills. Without the former, the latter is not useful. We began this paper with descriptions of the stereotypes that Mexicans hold about Americans, and that Americans hold about Mexicans. We also commented that, given the lines of political and economic power that weave across the border, Mexicans may

3. http://www.manoamano-unidos.org/.

know more about the United States than Americans know about Mexico. Border interpreters, of course, have to make constant observations of all groups that meet at the border. Not only this, they must place their knowledge into the contexts of social institutions, cultural values, and ways of life in the two countries. And, they must have meta-level awareness of their knowledge, especially because they will often need to recognize expectable misunderstandings, and explain them to others. Here we lay out key information that border interpreters must deploy in order to do their jobs.

First, throughout Mexico interpreting across LSM and Spanish is a relatively new phenomenon. Although an interpreter appears briefly on newscasts in parts of Mexico, the number of Deaf viewers is unknown, as is the degree to which the signed news is comprehensible to Deaf viewers. Although some report that it is not, no systematic study has been undertaken. In addition, it is rare to see an interpreter in a school, since this is a service that *Secretaria de la Educacion Publica* (SEP) schools (government-supported schools) do not provide. Government-supported schools offer students with disabilities access to schooling several ways. Students may simply attend any school along with hearing students, but without support services. In addition they may be in *grupos integrados*, integrated with hearing students with itinerant services of *Unidades de Servicios de Apoyo a la Educación Regular* (abbreviated to USAERs or Support Service Units to Regular Education), paraprofessionals who provide a set number of hours per week of services to support integration of able-bodied and disabled students. Others may enroll in or be referred to *Centros de la Atencion Multiple* (CAMs), schools that serve only students with disabilities. (See Fletcher, Dejud, Klingler, & Mariscal, 2003; and Fletcher & Artiles, 2005 for more details on special education in Mexico, USAERs, and CAMs). In general if a Deaf student has an interpreter in a SEP school, the interpreter is paid by parents or other sources. As a result, because there are few interpreters to be seen in Mexico, few people, Deaf and hearing, are familiar with interpreters' work. This generates an additional set of issues that a border interpreter may have to delineate for consumers.

Still, in our experience, if there is a place in Mexico where Deaf and hearing people are likely to have experience with professional interpreters, it is at the border with the United States. Even in Mexico City, an international megalopolis, few Deaf people have had experience with interpreters who are not family members. Indeed, across Mexico, we believe that the bulk of sign language interpreting is still carried out by hearing signers who accompany their Deaf family members to appointments with doctors, who explain what the hearing neighbors are saying, who sign the dialogue from television shows, or summarize the plots of movies viewed on DVDs. As Deaf Mexicans are invited to or gain entry to events organized for hearing people (e.g., conferences, religious gatherings, or meetings of teachers who work with Deaf children) they are beginning to expect signed access. However, their models for what interpreters do often rest on the highly engaged, highly contextualized personalized communication assistance their close family members have provided. This assistance is clearly, perhaps correctly, viewed as help for the Deaf person, rather than brokering of the communication where one party is not favored over another. Accordingly, one task that border interpreters face is explaining their roles and the limitations of their roles to their Deaf Mexican clients. This is especially important since the U.S. systems that Deaf Mexicans deal with most frequently—medicine, social services, and the courts—commonly assume that interpreters will maintain a professional distance during interactions.

The diffusion of professional interpreting services at the border is changing rapidly. Between the time we began this paper and its final submission six months later, a new niche for quadri-language interpreters opened, with substantial impact on Deaf LSM signers. Begun in October 2008, and formally unveiled on November 28, 2008 (The National Day of the Deaf in Mexico), the first VRS service in Mexico became available. Quinto-Pozos et al. (this volume) describe trilingual Spanish-English-ASL interpreting over video relay based in the U.S. The service in Tijuana, Tijuana SVR offers video relay calls (which are currently free) between Mexico and the United States, and within Mexico.[4] Deaf LSM signers go to the relay offices in Tijuana, where Deaf and hearing ASL/LSM interpreters are available to make and relay calls to hearing people in either English or Spanish. In addition to typical relay services, Deaf people have begun to request access to taped courses, generally in English, which are interpreted using the video telephone system into LSM or ASL. The inauguration of this kind of service will not only create demand for bicultural interpreters with four-language fluency, it will also eventually distribute

---

4. www.tijuanasvr.blogspot.com.

the experience of working with professional interpreters across a much greater proportion of Mexico's Deaf population.

Beyond the various challenges four-language interpreters confront, an additional common challenge for sign language interpreters within Mexico, which is even more complex at the border, is the need to know one's clients' language repertoires and schooling histories. A high level of language variation is found among signers in Mexico. Much of this variation comes about because educational histories of Deaf people vary so greatly. Prior to the mid-1960s Deaf Mexicans who attended school typically went to the *Escuela Nacional para Sordomudos* (ENS), the national school for the deaf in Mexico City. Signing was tolerated at ENS, but Ramsey and Bedolla's (2004, 2006) informants report that few hearing teachers were fluent signers, and that the most common medium of instruction was spoken and written Spanish. In addition, during the period that ENS was open (the 1860s to the 1960s), many families who could afford to, sent their Deaf children to private clinics. Although clinics often called their programs schools, as in U.S. oral education in the mid-20th century, the instructional focus was speech and speech-reading training.

When ENS closed in the mid-1960s the oral clinics remained, but special schools and classes for deaf students, especially sign-tolerant schooling, became difficult to find. In large cities like Mexico City and Guadalajara, SEP day schools for deaf students existed. And, although special education has undergone integration-focused reform in Mexico (Fletcher et al. 2003; Fletcher and Artiles 2005) to some degree schools that exclusively serve Deaf students still exist, especially if the population of Deaf students is large enough to fill an entire CAM. In Mexico City, for example, CAM #38, serves a large population of Deaf students and does not admit students with other disabilities. Despite these exceptions, integration is now promoted very strongly in Mexico, and CAMs are generally viewed as offering a type of integrated education.[5] The former middle school for Deaf students in Guadalajara, is now a CAM which admits students with a range of disabilities. Following the oral model, "scientific" pronouncements of doctors and audiologists, and general societal preferences, LSM is widely viewed as unacceptable as a medium of instruction, even where signing outside the classroom is tolerated. The

5. Admittedly, integration of deaf students with students with other disabilities may seem as odd to readers as it does to the authors.

oral ideology is still extremely powerful in Mexican medical and educational circles.

Since the mid-1990s, some LSM-medium schools have opened, sometimes founded and directed at the grassroots level by Deaf people. Often they operate under the regulations of the parallel education system of Mexico, the *Instituto Nactional para Educacion para Adultos* or INEA, rather than under SEP regulations. In these schools Deaf adults occupy teaching roles, despite their lack of secondary and post-secondary preparation, because LSM fluency is viewed as more beneficial to students than content area specialties or post-secondary degrees. These schools commonly describe themselves as "bilingual." In addition, in some states the paraprofessionals provided by the USAERs either already know LSM, or are provided resources for learning it, so that they can provide sign-medium support to their case loads of Deaf students. In late 2008, the education department for Mexico City hired a team of linguists with expertise in LSM and nine other indigenous languages, and began a "mother tongue" *preparatoria* (high school) program to increase the opportunities available to non-Spanish dominant Mexicans (M. Salgado, personal communication, Jan. 16, 2009).

The provision of LSM-medium services is not a general policy, however, so resources that may be available in one city or state, may not exist in others. Between 2006 and 2008 Ramsey informally interviewed close to 100 teachers, Deaf students, and USAER personnel from all over Mexico about the LSM resources available to them. The responses ranged from no resources and LSM prohibition, to tolerance of LSM if the teacher or tutor already knew it, to encouragement to use an LSM dictionary provided by SEP, to support for LSM-medium teaching and active transmission of LSM to teachers and USAER personnel. However, the most common response was that resources were not available—neither LSM teachers, nor materials, nor Deaf signers—for teacher and parents of Deaf children. The distribution of LSM across the population of people who need it, families, children, teachers, and friends, is extremely uneven. As a result, interpreters must know about their clients' educational backgrounds and must take note of demographic details like ages of school attendance and location of schools in order to plan ways to best serve their Deaf clients.

In addition to the uneven distribution of LSM across different schooling contexts and different generations, in Mexico school attendance cannot be assumed (Hanson & Woodruff, 2003). This is the case in the general population, as well as in the Deaf population. The Mexican constitution guarantees nine years of obligatory, secular, public education for all citizens, that is, completion of *secundaria*, approximately grades six to nine or equivalent to U.S. middle school. However, for various reasons not all citizens can attain nine years. The Organisation for Economic Co-operation and Development (OECD 2006) collected 2004 secondary school attainment statistics for Mexico and reports that 27% of females and 24% of males between the ages of 25 to 34 had completed secondary school. In an older age group (ages 45 to 54) approximately 20% of the population completed secondary school. Not surprisingly, the younger generation completes secondary school at a higher rate than the older, but close to 75% of the population does not complete secondary school. Secondary school has been compulsory in Mexico since 1992, and the number of students attending *secundaria* has been rising since then, but there continues to be a high rate of non-compliance.

There are many explanations for these figures, but the primary reason is a straightforward lack of resources. In many parts of Mexico secondary schools are simply not available. In a nation that still struggles to provide schooling for its entire population, special education at the secondary level will be at least as scarce as secondary education for able-bodied hearing students. Accordingly, although it is not currently documented in Mexico, it is reasonable to extend what we know about school attainment in general to Deaf students. As a result, interpreters will work with Deaf clients who have no formal education or only a few years of schooling, those who have formal education but who do not know LSM, or those who are very late learners of LSM. Elsewhere, Ramsey (2006) notes that in the Mexican Deaf population having Deaf family members does not dependably mean that a signer will be an LSM native or even know LSM. We have met many Deaf signers in Mexico, across the age range, who do not know LSM, or who sign a very idiosyncratic mix of home signs and LSM. In contrast, between us we have met only two such signers in the United States, both quite elderly.

Finally, border interpreters must be prepared to work with Mexican Deaf people who went to school in the U.S. and who know ASL, or who sign an ASL-LSM hybrid. Quinto-Pozos (2008) describes features of one such hybrid, the result of ASL-LSM contact in the Rio Grande Valley in Texas. The contact features he describes are both subtle and notable. They include handshape interference (specifically between the F handshape used in LSM and the one used in ASL), mixing of mouthing from one spoken language with the other signed language (e.g. mouthing Spanish words while signing ASL), and mixing of nonmanual markers for wh-questions from one language with signs from the other (e.g. using LSM wh-question markers with ASL wh-questions). Indeed during data collection in Mexico City Ramsey mistakenly used the ASL furrowed-brow wh-marker with an LSM wh-question, which alarmed her Mexican informant sufficiently that after the elicitation session he asked some other signers why Ramsey was "angry" at him (LSM signers tilt their heads back to mark wh-questions). An LSM signer who recognized ASL interference in LSM not only explained the error, but coached Ramsey so she could avoid the error with the remaining informants. In addition to the features Quinto-Pozo notes, we have also noted fingerspelled English words inserted into LSM discourse, interference between the T handshape still used by some elderly LSM signers and the T handshape use in ASL, and ASL lexical items inserted into LSM structures. In short, serving the needs of Deaf signers who present this wide range of language fluency and educational experiences involves not only knowing where and when a Deaf signer attended school, but also from whom they gained access to LSM, if ever.

Beyond the challenges of language variation and diverse educational careers that their clients may present, border interpreters must assess everything they say and sign according to what they know are potential misreadings of language, behavior and social expectations. In many instances, in addition to helping Deaf and hearing people to understand each other, this means helping Mexicans deal with the American way of doing things, and vice versa. Sergio describes an experience common when Mexicans cross the border for an encounter with U.S. hearing people. In the United States when a nurse in a hospital, a funeral director, or a doctor doing an examination says "Family only" or "Immediate family only," Americans, Deaf and hearing, understand that "family" means consanguineous, conjugal, or nuclear family (parents and children). Americans understand that a funeral director means that only a few people should attend the burial when he says "Family only at the burial." He might even mean that there is no public parking at the cemetery, a meaning that is transparent to Americans, who apply the same understanding to rules for visiting patients in the hospital. If the personnel ask "Are you family?" or says "Family only" it means "consanguineous or conjugal family" and again the intended implication is that only a few people, and no friends, are permitted to go into the patient's room.

In contrast in Mexico, the term *familia* casts a much bigger net, and can include nuclear family, all living generations of one's relatives, relatives who are no longer alive, *comadres* and *compadres* (honorary family members who are the parents' closest friends), cousins, the friends one grew up with, and perhaps a few statues of saints or the Virgin of Guadalupe. One important practical reality of the Mexican definition of family is that an individual almost never confronts a circumstance of life alone, whether in sickness or in health, in life or in death. At the root of the Mexican view that life in the United States is cold and lonely is the observation that Americans conduct much of their lives alone. Mexicans do their activities of daily life accompanied by family members or trusted friends, someone to consult with about decisions, to help one across a busy street, to help carry shopping bags and babies, to chat with, and to conform to the social norm expressed as *Mantiene a su familia cercana* (Keep your family nearby). Life in Mexico, from making a purchase to visiting a school, is inherently sociable, and people take time to make social connections as they conduct their lives. Being alone, or worse, not being permitted to have family members with one, strikes most Mexicans as an incomprehensible way to do things. At times elderly Deaf women have warned Ramsey not to do fieldwork alone in Mexico City. They might make it clear that she is about to do something improper (e.g., attend a meeting of elderly men). More commonly, though, they worry that she will be out and about unaccompanied, which they translate as uncared for, unprotected, or simply without the comforts that a relative, friend, child, or husband could provide when one must be away from home. Being alone sends a message about the solitary person but sends an even stronger message about her kin, who are not performing their duties as family members.

With this background knowledge then, border interpreters can predict that simply signing "Family only" or "Are you family members?" to Mexicans in a context defined by U.S. cultural norms may not transmit the intended but indirect practical meaning, that is, "Only a few people are allowed." A cultural explanation will be needed, perhaps two cultural explanations, one to the Mexicans and the other to the Americans. And, as Peña reports about a funeral director's attempts to limit the number of people at a burial, even direct cultural explanations may not affect people's behavior:

> My job was to close that culture gap. I explained "It means the rest of you can't go along. The rules in the US are that only . . . can go." They

responded "But in Mexico we can." "But that's not how Mexicans do it." "That's not the custom in Mexico." "But I can park over there by that tree." So I had to really stretch out my explanation. And in the end, everyone went, of course.

Similar potential misunderstandings occur when Deaf people who have never had a professional interpreter provided for them have to find a role identity for a perfect stranger who knows how to sign. They are used to having their hearing child with them, who signs for them, gives them advice, and helps them solve their problems. What social role does this other signer fit into? Often Deaf Mexicans' first solution is to redefine the signer as a type of family member. As Peña reports:

> They still want the interpreter to be the family member, and tell them what to do. Someone who gives advice. You ARE part of the family. They think "Why would you know how to sign to me if you were not a family member? If you do not have Deaf family members, why in the world are you involved with us? You must automatically be my friend.

It is common to describe sign language interpreting as language work that is also cultural, although generally the cultures are those of Deaf people and hearing people in the same society. At the border of *las dos Californias* the range of possible complications is great, from language variation to misunderstandings that cross several cultures. To some degree, the differences occur because Deaf people in Mexico and the United States are at very different moments in their histories. While in the United States Deaf people have a sense of themselves as a relatively cohesive group which shares a history and a language, in Mexico this awareness is not widespread. In fact, although Deaf Mexicans admire American Deaf people for the U.S. Deaf associations with their long histories, many claim that Deaf Mexicans do not constitute one community, and express doubts that they will ever unite into one cohesive group.

Still, Deaf Mexicans are beginning to have opportunities to participate in public life, especially public life with hearing people. Interpreting services are not widely available, though, which means that few Deaf people have had the experience of using professional interpreters. Public education through middle school and high school are difficult for Deaf people to access, and LSM is still an uncommon medium of instruction, adding to the huge variation in access to LSM. Like all interpreters in Mexico, those who work at the border face challenges in all aspects of their work. As we commented above, the border may look like a geographic location. But crossing it entails observation of laws, respect for the rules of each country, and if one is crossing from south to north, hours of time waiting in line. Still, we agree that the geographic border is insignificant compared to the less tangible social and cultural borders that interpreters approach and cross each time the pick up their hands.

RESEARCH TOPICS

Our discussion here is brief and anecdotal because there is no research literature on LSM-Spanish interpreters in Mexico, much less on border interpreters who operate in four languages. We note several areas where research would be very helpful. First, we know that Deaf signers act as intermediaries in four-language interpreting situations, including VRS interpreting. In these cases, they may not know all four languages well, but may have the skill of grasping the message of an unschooled, idiosyncratic signer, and the cultural and language knowledge to express the intended meaning as well as place it in the multicultural Deaf, Mexican, and U.S. context. As noted, the Deaf intermediary interpereters we know of are Mexican citizens, resident in Mexico, with knowledge of ASL through contacts with Deaf people in the United States and sometimes as a result of some schooling in the United States. We know of no ASL-dominant Deaf intermediary interpreters who work on four-language interpreting teams. Indeed, there is a great deal of movement over the border of California and Baja California, and naturally Deaf people participate in it. As a result, knowledge of ASL arises in surprising places: a park in Mexico City, a restaurant in Guadalajara, and a church in Rosarito. It would be very useful to know how Deaf interpreters come to occupy the intermediary niche, what skills they develop from participating in interpretation in this way, and what skills they believe they need to do so.

Second, we would like to know more about the language learning strategies that highly successful language learners (like four-language interpreters) employ, especially outside of formal education settings. Third, although the lives of Deaf Mexicans are only beginning to be the focus of research attention, we believe the lives of Deaf Mexicans who live near the U.S.-Mexico border and interact with it also merit attention. There is a vast literature on Mexican migration and diaspora, and many Deaf Mexicans make similar journeys, including some who migrate to seek the education that is not available to them in Mexico.

Last, the very recent introduction of four-language video relay interpreting offers the unique opportunity to observe and document the introduction of interpreting services across at least four languages and across the international Mexico-U.S. border. This event is likely to affect interpreting practice and preparation of interpreters, to innovate and distribute LSM lexical items, discourse structures, and registers rapidly across a large population, and to increase awareness of LSM, Deaf people and professional interpreters, and merits the attention of researchers. In addition, we clearly need enhanced knowledge about interpreters who work in four languages at the U.S.-Mexico border, not only who they are and how they developed their abilities, but whether conditions at the Tijuana-San Diego border are similar to conditions in other urban border areas like El Paso-Ciudad Juarez or McAllen-Reynosa, particularly the extent of the need for four-language interpreters in border areas.

CONCLUSION

Knowledge about the lives of Deaf people in Mexico, about deaf education in Mexico, and about LSM is limited and has been slowly developing over the last decade. There is almost no documentation of the development of professional sign language interpreting in Mexico, much less the development and need for four-language interpreters in U.S.-Mexico border areas. This paper contributes to this knowledge base, by placing border interpreters within the larger context of the border, by describing the language development and interpreting skills acquisition of interpreters at the border, and by outlining the consequences for border interpreters of systems of Deaf education, access to LSM, and differences between Mexican and U.S. cultures. Because we are border dwellers and because we have observed the range of border phenomena over many years, we know better than most the limits of our knowledge. We encourage other interpreters and linguists to examine the rich possibilities of studying interactions of Deaf and hearing people across national boundaries.

REFERENCES

Baker, C. (2001). *Foundations of bilingual education and bilingualism* (3rd ed.). Bristol, U.K.: Multilingual Matters.

Curiel, B. (2008). Writing in the disciplinary borderlands. *Modern Fiction Studies, 54*(2), 404–12.

Escobedo Delgado, E. (2008, February). *Culture and sign language in a Mexican Mayan Deaf community.* Paper presented at the Cross-Linguistic Research and International Cooperation in Sign Language Linguistics Conference, International Centre for Sign Languages and Deaf Studies, University of Central Lancashire, Preston, U.K.

Fletcher, T., & Artiles, A. (2005). Inclusive education and equity in Latin America. In D. Mitchell (Ed.), *Contextualizing inclusive education: Evaluating old and new international perspectives* (pp. 202–30). London: Routledge.

Fletcher, T., Dejud, C., Klingler, C., & Mariscal, I. L. (2003). The changing paradigm of special education in Mexico: Voices from the field. *Bilingual Research Journal* 27(3), 409–30.

Grosjean, F. (1985). The bilingual as a competent but specific speaker-hearer. *Journal of Multilingual and Multicultural Development, 6,* 467–77.

Hanson, G., & Woodruff, C. (2003). Emigration and educational attainment in Mexico. Retrieved from http://irpshome.ucsd.edu/faculty/gohanson/working _papers.htm.

Insituto Nacional de Lenguas Indígenas. (2007). *Catálogo de las lenguas indígenas nacionales.* Retrieved from http://www.inali.gob.mx/ catalogo2007/.

Johnson, R. E. (1991). Sign language, culture & community in a traditional Yucatec Maya village. *Sign Language Studies, 73,* 461–74.

King, R. (2004). *Border confluences: Borderland narratives from the Mexican War to the present.* Tucson: University of Arizona Press.

National Virtual Translation Center. (2007). *Languages spoken in the U.S.* Retrieved from http://www.nvtc.gov/lotw/months/november/USlanguages .html.

National Multicultural Interpreter Project. (2000). *Decision making in culturally and linguistically diverse communities: Creating authentic teams.* Retrieved from http://www.asl.neu.edu/TIEM.online/curriculum_nmip.html.

Organisation for Economic Co-operation and Development. (2006). *Education at a glance 2006.* Educational attainment by gender and average years spent in formal education. Retrieved from http://www.oecd.org/document/52/0,33 43,en_2649_39263238_37328564_1_1_1,00.htm.

Quinto-Pozos, D. (2008). Sign language contact and interference: ASL and LSM. *Language in Society, 37,* 161–89.

Ramsey, C. (2000). On the borders: Families, culture and schooling for Mexican-heritage deaf children in a transnational region. In K. Christensen (Ed.), *Deaf Plus* (pp. 121–48). San Diego, CA: DawnSignPress.

Ramsey, C. (2006). *Final report to the National Science Foundation: Survey of Mexican Sign Language.* Unpublished manuscript.

Ramsey, C., & Noriega, J. A. (2000). *Niños milagrizados* [Miracle-ized Children]: Language attitudes, deaf education and miracle cures in Mexico. In M. Metzger (Ed.), *Bilingualism and identity in Deaf communities: Sociolinguistics in Deaf Communities. Vol. 6.* (pp. 117–41). Washington D.C.: Gallaudet University Press.

Ramsey, C., & Ruiz Bedolla, F. (2004, September). *The Mexican Sign Language network and language transmission across generations.* Poster presented at conference, Theoretical Issues in Sign Language Research 8, Barcelona.

Ramsey, C., & Ruiz Bedolla, F. (2006, December). *Seeking sign language in two contexts: With and without a school.* Poster presented at conference, Theoretical Issues in Sign Language Research 9, Florianopolis, Brazil.

Ramsey, C., & Quinto-Pozos, D. (in press). Transmission of Sign Language: Latin America. In D. Brentari (Ed.), *Sign Languages.* Cambridge: Cambridge University Press.

Rancho Sordo Mudo. (2008). Rancho Sordo Mudo: Home and School for Deaf Children of Mexico. http://www.ranchosordomudo.org/.

Smith, L. R. (2002). The social architecture of communicative competence: A methodology for social-network research in sociolinguistics. *International Journal of Sociology of Language 153*, 130–60.

Wong-Fillmore, L. (1991). Second-Language learning in children: A model of language learning in social context. In E. Bialystok (Ed.), *Language processing in bilingual children* (pp. 49–69). Cambridge: Cambridge University Press.

Wortham, S., Hamann, E. T., & Murillo, E. G. (2001). *Education in the new latino diaspora: Policy and the politics of identity.* Westport, CT: Ablex.

Trilingual Video Relay Service Interpreting in the United States

David Quinto-Pozos, Kristie Casanova de Canales, and Rafael Treviño

In the United States, the demand for a new type of interpreting—one that involves the use of three (or more) languages—is increasing rapidly. Sometimes, English is not used in these interpreted events at all—apart from its phonological, lexical, and grammatical influence on Spanish, ASL, or another signed language. The interpreting is often referred to as "Spanish VRS" (Video Relay Service), and it combines all the challenges and complexities of video relay service interpreting, some of which we describe below, with three common languages (English, Spanish, and ASL), multiple dialects of each language, and various cultures.

In this chapter we provide an account of Spanish VRS, which we will refer to as "Trilingual VRS" throughout. We use this term—even though some calls may not include the use of all three languages—because an interpreter in these settings needs to generally be prepared to work with the three languages. The term *Trilingual VRS* is used by some agencies, interpreters, and Deaf and Hard of Hearing clients, but another common way to refer to VRS interpreting with Spanish, as noted above, is *Spanish VRS*. Perhaps the focus on Spanish in this latter label is because that language is how this type of interpretation differs from the more common ASL-English interpretation.

Trilingual (Spanish-English-ASL) interpreting has been occurring in some areas of the United States for at least two decades. As one example, a government office in Texas that was known as the Texas Commission for the Deaf and Hard of Hearing established a Trilingual Task Force around 1994 to address questions and issues with regards to situations where Spanish figures prominently into an interpreted situation. For instance, signed language interpreters would find themselves with Spanish-speaking clients at visits to doctors' offices, in school meetings among parents, principals and other educators, and at social service agencies that offer services to the public. Over the next decade or more, that task force worked to collect information about trilingual interpreted situations in Texas and address the need for some type of assessment instrument for interpreters who work in those settings.[1] In addition to the situation in Texas, other states within the United States with relatively large populations of Spanish-speaking persons (e.g., California, Florida, New York, etc.) have been locations where Spanish has constituted a significant part of some interpreted situations. Even though such trilingual interpreting has occurred in the community for years, our focus in the present chapter is on VRS interpreting.

A brief history of VRS interpreting in the United States is provided as a background for our discussion before we describe various linguistic and cultural challenges of trilingual interpreting among these languages. Other challenges of this type of interpreting (e.g., issues with technology and training and support of trilingual interpreters) are also touched upon in order to provide the reader with a general understanding of the intricacies of this work. In addition to anecdotal accounts of Trilingual VRS, we provide information that was collected through surveys and interviews with various stakeholders in these settings. Our intent is to highlight some of the challenges inherent in this type of interpreting and provide some suggestions for how to improve services in the future.

A BRIEF HISTORY OF ENGLISH-ASL VRS AND TRILINGUAL VRS

VRS is a telecommunication service that takes advantage of the Internet to provide "real-time" communication between Deaf or hard of hearing consumers and hearing consumers.[2] VRS accomplishes this by using sign language interpreters, videophones, and high-speed Internet connections. In the United States, Video Relay telecommunications are regulated and funded by the Federal Communications Commission (FCC). Interstate VRS providers, or the companies that provide the services, receive additional

1. See Gatto et al. (this volume) for an account of the Spanish-English-ASL certification exam for interpreters that was developed by the University of Arizona's National Center on Interpretation.

2. Consumers of interpreting services are also regularly referred to as *clients* or video *callers*, in the case of video relay interpreting. We use these terms interchangeably within this chapter.

financial support from the Interstate Telecommunications Relay Service (TRS) Fund.

In July of 1993, Telecommunications Relay Service became available for the first time under Title IV of the Americans with Disabilities Act. Title IV defines TRS as "telephone transmission services that provide the ability for an individual who has a hearing impairment or speech impairment to engage in communication by wire or radio with a hearing individual in a manner that is functionally equivalent to the ability of an individual who does not have a hearing impairment or speech impairment to communicate using voice communication services by wire or radio" (ADA, 1990). A TRS fund was begun for interstate calls in the 1990s. Initially, TRS only applied to calls placed via teletype, or TTY, machines. However, VRS was being piloted in Texas as early as the mid-1990s (*Inside Gallaudet*, 2008). By March of 2000, the FCC concluded that VRS is a legitimate form of TRS.

Texas played an important role in both the development of English-ASL VRS and later, Trilingual VRS. In 1995, the initial trials of VRS began in Austin, Texas. Three years later, VRS was being tested statewide in both Washington and Texas. With the FCC's declaration of VRS as a form of TRS in 2000, the service became officially available to the state of Texas. Additionally in 2000, Texas petitioned for Trilingual VRS to be compensable from the Interstate TRS fund. This would allow providers to offer Video Relay services for calls between Deaf or hard of hearing TRS users and hearing (Spanish-speaking) TRS users, and to be compensated for such services.

The evolution of the role of VRS within TRS is an interesting one. Two years after recognizing VRS as a form of TRS, the FCC allowed for the reimbursement of such services: beginning in 2002, interstate VRS providers could be compensated for their services through the interstate TRS fund administration. The FCC declared that, while VRS was not required by the FCC, it was offered by several TRS providers. Further, any TRS providers offering VRS had to abide by FCC regulations. The approval of English-ASL VRS came about because of the need for a "functional equivalent." This refers to TRS that is "(near) real-time" and "more articulate" than text-to-speech TRS. In other words, text-to-speech relay services with TTYs were not very efficient (see Lane, Hoffmeister, & Bahan, 1996). However, in 2004, the FCC declared non-shared language TRS (i.e., Trilingual VRS) a value-added translation service, not to be compensable by the TRS fund. Community Services for the Deaf, the National Video

Relay Service Coalition, which includes such organizations as the National Association of the Deaf, the Registry of Interpreters for the Deaf, and Telecommunications for the Deaf, Inc., as well as 18 individuals submitted petitions challenging the FCC's decision.

Within the petitions were many arguments emphasizing the validity of Trilingual VRS as a form of TRS. The petitioners argued this form of TRS was not a value-added translation service, pointing out that the FCC already supported Spanish-to-Spanish TRS (based on a large and growing population of Spanish users). The petitions also pointed out Deaf Latino children's need for communication with family and community. Notably, a recent report of deaf children in the United States from Spanish-speaking households places the number at 7,948 (or nearly 22% of the deaf and hard of hearing children enrolled in educational programs from Parent-Infant through 12th grade) (Gallaudet Research Institute, 2008). This suggests that a substantial percentage of deaf children need Trilingual VRS to communicate with their Spanish-speaking family members when they are not in the same location. Additionally, the National Video Relay Service Coalition noted that, "in Puerto Rico, where Spanish is the primary language, failure to compensate for ASL-to-Spanish VRS leads to the result that Puerto Ricans who are deaf or hard of hearing using ASL must have their VRS conversations translated into English, a language that is either not spoken or is a second language for most Puerto Ricans" (Federal Register, 2005).

Just 10 months later, the FCC reversed its decision, declaring Trilingual VRS a compensable form of VRS. The August 2005 reversal apparently occurred for a few reasons. First, the FCC deemed that Trilingual VRS does meet the need of an identifiable segment of the population of persons with hearing and speech disabilities. Second, the Commission stated that recognition of Trilingual VRS is consistent with recognition of VRS as a form of TRS. Recognition of Trilingual VRS as a form of TRS was also deemed consistent with the FCC's focus on Spanish-language access in other contexts. Finally, the FCC concluded that recognition of Trilingual VRS as a form of TRS would not have an undue impact on the interstate TRS fund.

The final argument (that Trilingual VRS would not unduly impact the interstate TRS fund) was supported by several factors. When the FCC reversed its 2004 decision, Trilingual VRS calls constituted only one to two percent of all VRS calls. Unfortunately, at the time of the writing of this chapter, no updated statistics were available regarding the percentage of Trilingual VRS calls within VRS calls, in general. Another assurance regarding the impact of Trilingual VRS on the TRS fund was that the cost of such VRS services would be no more than the cost of English-ASL VRS. Additionally, the FCC found that "no information has been presented that demonstrates that [Trilingual VRS] is too costly relative to the benefit derived from [this service]" (Federal Communications Commission, 2008). Thus, the earlier decision was reversed in 2005, and Trilingual VRS was again supported by the FCC TRS fund.

By January 1, 2006, Trilingual VRS was deemed a compensable form of TRS under FCC regulations. The FCC stated that all TRS providers offering VRS (including Trilingual VRS) would be required to provide the service 24 hours a day, seven days a week, and to answer incoming calls within a set number of seconds so that VRS users would not have to wait unreasonably long periods of time (FCC, 2008).

CHARACTERIZING TRILINGUAL VRS INTERPRETING

Language Use in Trilingual VRS

A Trilingual VRS call can be initiated in various ways. Perhaps the most common method is for the Deaf caller to alert the VRS interpreter (who is ordinarily a bilingual ASL-English interpreter) that an interpreter who speaks Spanish will be needed for the call. At that point, the bilingual (ASL-English) interpreter will request a transfer of the call to a Trilingual VRS interpreter. The two interpreters will likely have verbal contact (i.e., so that the bilingual interpreter can explain the request) before the trilingual interpreter takes over. There may also, however, be instances in which a call is begun by a bilingual VRS interpreter and during the course of the call, it becomes evident that Spanish is being used by one of the callers and a Trilingual VRS interpreter would be optimal. In such a case, a transfer occurs—much like the first scenario described here. A call initiated by a Spanish-speaking caller would also result in a transfer to a Trilingual VRS interpreter if that call was answered by a bilingual interpreter. Some providers allow the caller to request a particular interpreter for the call—either bilingual or trilingual—and the requested interpreter will join that call depending on his or her availability at that moment. Finally, some VRS providers have established a dedicated line so that Deaf callers who require Trilingual VRS services can access such services directly.

As can be imagined, Trilingual VRS calls vary greatly in terms of language use of the callers, based on various factors such as the location of the callers (i.e., the regional dialects of the languages being used) and the languages with which the callers are familiar. One way to categorize calls is to consider the signed language(s) that is/are used by the Deaf caller, and that information suggests that there are at least two primary "types" of calls. Certainly, other classifications are possible, such as defining calls from the perspective of the hearing caller, but we feel that the representation in Figure 1 is useful for understanding language use in Trilingual VRS as viewed from the point of view of the Deaf caller's signed language repertoire.

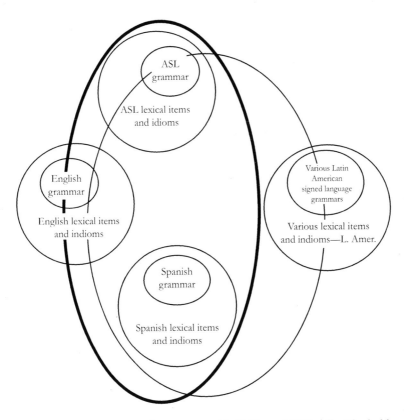

FIGURE 1. *Languages commonly represented in Trilingual VRS calls. The bold oval represents VRS calls with sign monolingual (ASL) Deaf caller. The lighter oval represents VRS calls with sign bi-/multi-lingual (e.g., ASL, LSM, LSV, etc.) Deaf caller.*

The first type is the call in which a mostly monolingual signed language user, namely ASL, is interacting with a Spanish speaker. This type of call is portrayed in Figure 1 with a bold oval encircling languages and aspects of languages that tend to be used in these calls. In particular, such calls are characterized primarily by use of ASL by the Deaf caller and Spanish by the hearing caller, although there can also exist elements of English in the language production of either caller. An example of such a call would be a Deaf ASL user who knows no or little Spanish but works with Deaf Latino students in a residential school for the Deaf. Such a Deaf employee might use Trilingual VRS to call a student's parents. If the parents speak only Spanish, the call could consist primarily of those two languages (Spanish and ASL), although there could be some elements of English in the interaction as well (such as English grammatical constructions and mouthing in the signing along with some lexical items or phrases from English in either caller's communication). This last point suggests that language mixing that is often referred to as code-switching or code-mixing between Spanish and English and/or ASL and English could be evident in such calls.

Hearing callers might include English or English-influenced items within their Spanish. For example, code-switching between Spanish and English—either inter- or intra-sententially—is common for some hearing callers, and this type of language use can be predicted for bilingual conversations in informal settings (or *registers*) as noted by Callahan (2003). There also exist many English-influenced lexical items that have become part of the linguistic repertoire of a large number of Spanish speakers. Along the U.S.-Mexico border, for instance, many people use Spanish words that demonstrate influence from English (and English words that show influence from Spanish, although our focus is not on this type of words here). These *loanwords* appear to have roots in their English semantic equivalents, but they are usually not considered among the standard vocabulary of Spanish as it is used across the globe. Some examples are *troca* for "truck" rather than the standard *camión* or *parquear* for "to park (your vehicle)" rather than the standard *estacionar*. Similarly, *calques* are also considered among the items that are borrowed from one language to another, and phrases such as "*escuela alta*" (literally, school tall) for 'high school' rather than the more common *secundaria* are used often. Such contact phenomena can also be seen in the English of Spanish speakers, and phrases such as 'get down from the car', a literal translation of *bajarse del carro* are also common.

Deaf callers may also code-switch or code-mix between ASL and English. Much work has been done on the interaction between ASL and English in the signed production of Deaf users of ASL. Lucas and Valli (1992) note that code-switching between a signed and a spoken language can and does occur, but it mostly differs from code-switching between two spoken languages because of one primary consideration: in signed code-switching or code-mixing (terms that are used interchangeably by some authors but have different meanings for others), elements from the two languages can occur simultaneously whereas the same switching across spoken languages primarily involves sequential switches. Davis (1989–1990) describes this phenomenon in detail with regard to the use of mouthing in ASL. In particular, mouthing can be described as the voiceless articulation of words as displayed on the mouth area of the signer, and Davis refers to the co-occurrence of English mouthing with an ASL sign as code-mixing. Quinto-Pozos (2008) notes that such mouthing that represents the spoken language of one country, Spanish for instance, can co-occur with signs from a signed language of another country, such as ASL. The same type of language mixing is true for some Trilingual VRS calls.

The second type of Trilingual VRS calls that are depicted in Figure 1 with a light oval encircling the languages are those that involve Deaf callers who sign elements of one (or more) Latin American signed languages in addition to elements of ASL. These calls occur with much less frequency than the first type of calls noted above. One example of such a call would be when a Deaf Peruvian immigrant to the United States uses Trilingual VRS to call a family member in South America. The sign language user could use a combination of ASL signs and perhaps signs from Peruvian Sign Language. It is possible to have one or more signed languages other than ASL (e.g., Mexican Sign Language, Colombian Sign Language, etc.) represented to varying degrees within Trilingual VRS calls. Ramsey and Peña (this volume) discuss quadrilingual interpreting (English-Spanish-ASL-Mexican Sign Language) along the U.S.-Mexico border, which exemplifies another case of the use of multiple signed languages in some interpreted situations.

It is also common to identify influence from English or Spanish within a Deaf caller's signed language. The influence can take a number of forms: the mouthing of spoken language words while signing, the use of initialized variants that highlight the first letter of the spoken language word within the handshape of the sign (see Quinto-Pozos, 2008), and perhaps having spoken language word-order influence the signed language grammar that is being produced.

Table 1 contains some of the linguistic features that would characterize the communication of each of the callers in both types of Trilingual VRS calls proposed here. Most Trilingual VRS interpreters in the United States are very familiar with the first type of caller, the Deaf person who primarily uses ASL and whose ASL is influenced at times only by English. The signed language used by this type of caller is taught in training programs

TABLE I. *Linguistic Features Characteristic of Typical Trilingual VRS Callers*

Caller	Grammar (ranges among)	Lexicon (ranges among)	Pronunciation (ranges among)
DEAF Primarily ASL	• ASL structure • Possible English influence	• ASL signs • Regional variants • English initialization • English fingerspelling • English idioms represented	• Native-like in ASL • Late acquisition characteristics
DEAF ASL + Other signed language(s)	• Mixing structure of ASL and another sign language • Possible Spanish and/or English influence	• Mixing lexicon of ASL and another sign language • Spanish and/or English initialization • Spanish and/or English fingerspelling • Spanish and/or English idioms represented	• Native-like in ASL • Late acquisition characteristics • "Foreign" accent in signing
HEARING Primarily Spanish	• Spanish structure • Possible English influence • Code-switching with English	• Spanish words • Regional variants • Code-switching with English • Spanish idioms • Possible English idioms	• Native-like speech • Dialectal/ regional sound patterns

across the United States and is used as the stimulus in certification and evaluation exams. The language of the second type of caller, however, is less familiar to many Trilingual VRS interpreters. Additionally, models of Deaf people who use ASL influenced by Spanish and other signed languages are scarce among training programs and are rarely, if ever, used in mainstream certification and evaluation exams. In regards to the hearing callers involved in Trilingual VRS calls, Spanish is usually the language of these parties. A Trilingual VRS interpreter can expect to be exposed to various dialects of Spanish from Latin America (and their corresponding sound patterns and other linguistic phenomena) and to constant code-switching between English and Spanish from callers who often reside in parts of the United States.

OTHER GENERAL CHARACTERISTICS OF VRS INTERPRETING

A number of characteristics differentiate VRS interpreting, and more specifically Trilingual VRS, from face-to-face interpreting between Deaf and hearing individuals. Certainly, there are challenges attributable to technologies that are used for such communication (e.g., pixilation of images on the screen and having to work with two-dimensional images of signers). Additionally, the lack of visual information about hearing callers presents various challenges for VRS interpreters (RID Video Interpreting Committee, 2008), and this may even be compounded for trilingual interpreting situations. The tendency for conversations to occur within intimate language registers also characterizes this type of interpreting. We focus on the latter issues within this next section.

Not having an image of a hearing consumer can be particularly challenging for an interpreter. If one considers the natural flow of conversation that is supported by visual cues and culture-specific turn-taking strategies, the VRS interpreter is faced with having to mediate turn-taking in the absence of visual information from one of the consumers. This can be particularly problematic if the hearing consumer is one who might normally elicit a high level of respect that could be influenced greatly by cultural conventions. For example, an older individual from a Spanish-speaking culture will ordinarily elicit specific forms from Spanish grammar (e.g., formal variants of Spanish pronouns and verb conjugations; discussed in more detail later in the chapter) that display deference toward that individual. As such, the Trilingual VRS interpreter is faced with the added challenge of knowing how to most appropriately mediate a conversation when non-visual cues are provided that the hearing caller is an elderly individual. Some information about age may be present in the audio signal (e.g., voice quality, lexical choices, etc.), but that is not always the case. So, an interpreter has to make decisions about the most appropriate linguistic choices (both grammatical and lexical) without having visual cues from the hearing caller. Whereas this also occurs in bilingual (English-ASL) VRS interpreting, the fact that English does not utilize distinctions between formal and informal variants of pronouns and verb conjugations makes it less of an issue for English-ASL VRS interpreting. Trilingual VRS interpreters, on the other hand, face the task of envisioning the social and cultural status of the hearing caller from context and some audio cues. This could lead to awkwardness and less-than-optimal interactions between the Deaf and hearing callers.

Related to this last point is the fact that many VRS calls involve intimate register use, and this may be more common for Trilingual VRS than for English-ASL VRS. The primary reason for this is that Trilingual VRS interpreters often interpret between Deaf and hearing family members. As evidence of this, we noted earlier that among the Federal Communications Commission's reasons for supporting Spanish-English-ASL VRS calls was the growing number of deaf children who use VRS services to communicate with their Spanish-speaking families. Those family members are located in various parts of the continental U.S. and territorial Puerto Rico and various countries within Latin America.

An example of such a situation would be a deaf child who has immigrated with his family to the United States from Guatemala. He may be calling his Spanish monolingual hearing grandmother in Guatemala for her birthday in order to send good wishes and share his experiences and achievements in the United States with her. They may talk about his hearing-extended family in Guatemala and what each is doing along with the recent happenings within his immediate family in the United States. In that conversation, it is likely that the "intimate register" would include references, made by the hearing grandmother and her deaf grandchild, that are well known by both of them. And, the familiarity with those topics might encourage abbreviations and incomplete references by the callers—aspects of those calls that are challenging for the interpreter. As part of the intimate register, topics of discussion often include family matters (e.g., general details about family members such as health, work, and relationships), cultural and religious practices, and responsibilities that are placed upon family members. Additionally, there is much lexical variation in the Spanish of the United States and Latin America for discussing such matters, which creates an additional challenge associated with interpreting in intimate registers in Trilingual VRS. There are also some dialectal differences that exist within the grammar of Spanish, and the pronominal system is one of the areas in which diversity is present.

Any VRS interpreter is faced with the task of comprehending the language use of the consumers—and a notable amount of language variation has been noted for the Deaf community in the United States (see Lucas & Valli, 1989; Lucas, Bayley, Rose, & Wulf, 2002). However, in the case of Trilingual VRS, there may exist more linguistic diversity than what is common in English-ASL VRS interpretation. An example of dialectal variation can be seen in pronoun use: while all Spanish-speaking countries and territories use both informal and formal pronoun variants (e.g., *tú* or *vos* [informal second person singular] and *usted* [formal second person singular]), the pragmatics of when to use these pronouns vary from country to country, and even within the same country in some instances. As noted, some countries employ the use of *vos* (informal second person singular), but *vos* is less common than *tú* and its use also varies. In some countries *vos* is as informal as *tú*, and in others it may be more formal than *tú*. Lastly, there exists the pronoun *vosotros* (informal second person plural), which is common in Spain but not in Latin America.

It is clear that Trilingual VRS presents some unique challenges for the interpreter who must navigate between various languages and cultures within an interpreting setting that has its own technological challenges. In what follows, we describe specific examples of such challenges within Trilingual VRS interpreting and we suggest ways to address the challenges.

EXAMINING CHALLENGES WITHIN TRILINGUAL VRS INTERPRETING

There are a number of challenges to VRS interpreting, and some that may be magnified in trilingual calls. Some of the challenges are based on some of the grammatical and other linguistic differences between the three languages being used, which are detailed later. Additionally, some of the challenges historically have been associated with the level of support for trilingual interpreters, although it appears that the latter may be changing in some cases. For the current work, we focus on a few linguistic challenges and some of the support-related issues that arise. Before providing information about the challenges, we present a brief account of our methodology for obtaining information from various stakeholders in the Trilingual VRS process: interpreters, agencies that employ such interpreters, and deaf callers who receive services from the interpreters.

Methodology

Information from interpreters and deaf/hard of hearing callers was obtained via written survey instruments. Admittedly, this method of data elicitation may not have been optimal for obtaining information from any of the callers who were not literate in English; future work will need to consider other methods for data collection as well. Each survey queried the respondents about their language knowledge and self-reported proficiency, but other questions across the two surveys differed. The survey for callers asked about their preference for interpreter pronunciation if the caller had a Spanish name (e.g., José, María, etc.), along with if and how they indicated to the interpreters their preferences. Likewise, one question inquired about whether or not the caller normally indicates to the interpreter preferences for the use of familiar versus formal forms (pronouns and verb conjugations) for each call. Other questions focused on callers' views of: two interpreters working together (referred to commonly as *teaming*), whether they preferred calls to be answered quickly over having optimally qualified interpreters, and other characteristics of the interpreter (e.g., interpreter friendliness, ASL skills, Spanish skills, appearance).

The interpreter survey was also quite extensive. Topics for the questions included language assessment (for Spanish), experience with trilingual interpreting, teaming, and the physical health of the interpreter's hands/arms. We also asked the interpreters to provide estimates about the number of trilingual calls per month and the average length of each call in which they participated. Finally, a series of questions about the linguistics of trilingual calls such as decisions about pronunciation, the use of gendered variants for certain nouns, and experiences with lexical differences across languages and within language dialects completed the survey for interpreters. Discussion of these linguistic points is provided in the next section.

The surveys for interpreters and callers were distributed through various means: conferences where these individuals were in attendance, through websites of various professional groups, through email distribution lists, and via the authors' personal contacts. A total of 13 surveys were completed by callers and 37 by interpreters.

Information from the TRS providers who participated in the study was obtained in a different manner. In particular, TRS providers were emailed and those that agreed to participate in a brief interview (via voice phone or video phone) were contacted at an agreed upon date and time. Questions about various topics were asked during the interviews, all of which concerned Trilingual VRS interpreting. Topics included length of time that the agency has offered such services, certification requirements for employment, assessments of Spanish skills, training, compensation, average length of call, and teaming. Questions about the number of trilingual interpreters employed at the agency, the most common countries included in such calls, and certification for such interpreters completed the interview. In total, four TRS providers were amenable to being interviewed and information reported in this chapter reflects reports of the experiences of representatives from those four agencies.

As appropriate, other information that is contained in this chapter will come from the personal experiences of the three authors. Each author is a nationally certified interpreter, and the second and third authors have also worked as trilingual interpreters in VRS settings. A wealth of knowledge is available from their experiences, but it will be provided among our anecdotal accounts in efforts to round out the information obtained empirically through the surveys and interviews described above. It is made clear if information comes from the data collection or from personal experiences.

Results

As with any type of interpretation or translation task, there are a number of challenges that an interpreter must confront on a regular basis. Some of the challenges stem from differences between the languages involved in the interpretation and others concern the availability of resources and support mechanisms—both for development of professional skills and for supporting optimal success of each Trilingual VRS call. Some of the linguistic challenges are detailed in this section, and they are followed in the next section by points about training and other support while conducting calls. The topics for our linguistic lens are lexical variants within each language, Spanish nouns that indicate the sex of the referent, formal versus informal pronominal and verbal forms, and pronunciation variants for various names and words from Spanish and English.

LEXICAL VARIANTS AND
UNFAMILIAR SIGNS/WORDS

Spanish is one of the world's most commonly spoken languages, and there are various dialects throughout the world. A substantial number of differences exist across varieties in pronunciation and phonology, lexical items, and idiomatic phrases, although there are comparably fewer differences in basic grammar across the varieties. Despite the differences across dialects, it is common for Spanish speakers to obtain mutual comprehension with conversation partners who speak different varieties of the language. For this chapter, we only consider one way in which differences across Spanish varieties can be challenging for Trilingual VRS interpreters—the existence of lexical variants across dialects. Although, future work should consider other differences as well.

Spanish speakers who have had contact with other speakers from outside of their geographical area can often provide examples of lexical differences. They will note that a word that they use for one concept or item is used to refer to something entirely different in another Spanish-speaking area, or they point out that other areas have word(s) that differ from their own for a certain object, action, etc. For example, the English word "cake" has various translation equivalents across Latin America: *pastel, torta, biscocho*, and *queque*. Additionally, the Spanish noun *tortilla* refers to an egg and potato dish in Spain and a type of flat bread in most parts of Latin America. In some cases, a word is unique to a particular area, so understanding the meaning of that word may be challenging.

Based on their responses to the surveys, Trilingual VRS interpreters use a number of strategies to manage lexical variants. Several interpreters noted that they use context to help them decipher the meaning of an unfamiliar Spanish word or one that could be ambiguous, and asking the hearing caller for clarification or explanation of the word is also sometimes employed. One interpreter stated s/he fingerspells the word as it is pronounced by the Spanish speaker, hoping that the Deaf person may understand the word or may request clarification. Whereas interpreters are not allowed to keep notes pertaining to caller's identifications or the content of calls, it is commonly accepted for them to write down a word or gloss of a sign that was new to them during the call. This would then allow for further investigation, outside of the context of that particular call, regarding the best way to interpret that lexical item in the future. More than one interpreter noted how reference books and other resources, such as the Internet, prove to be extremely valuable after calls because they allow the interpreter to investigate a word's meaning in order to be prepared for the next time it surfaces in conversation. Google searches were noted as a good way to examine how words are used in Latin American texts and newspapers.

With regard to unfamiliar signs (for the interpreter) that are produced by the Deaf caller (e.g., signs from a Latin American signed language), one interpreter reported that s/he describes the unfamiliar sign—presumably by referring to the handshape, place of articulation, and/or movement of the sign—in hopes that the hearing caller might be able to assist with clarifying the meaning of that sign. An additional strategy mentioned in the responses involves requesting that a Deaf caller fingerspell the Spanish (or English) equivalent of an unfamiliar sign. Some interpreters mentioned that, in addition to fingerspelling, they rely on lipreading to help decipher the meanings of unfamiliar signs from other signed languages. Other interpreters, upon inferring the meaning of an unfamiliar lexical variant from context, paraphrase the meaning back to the Deaf caller in ASL or gesture for confirmation before sign-to-voice interpreting into Spanish. Interpreters also noted the importance of attending to the hearing caller's reaction to an interpreter's word choice in determining whether or not further explanation is necessary. Several interpreters pointed out that they avoid using regional variants in their sign-to-voice interpretations and instead prefer to employ vocabulary items that would likely be understood across various dialects unless they are certain of the hearing caller's nationality. In the latter case, use of regional variants seemed more acceptable.

NOMINAL, PRONOMINAL, AND VERBAL VARIANTS WITHIN THE GRAMMAR

Some Spanish nouns allow for phoneme alternations—not suffixes—to indicate the sex of the referent. However, the default forms are often those that refer to males, and a mixed group of males and females is normally referred to with only the male form—unless the speaker is making an effort to make reference to the females explicit. Some common examples of these nouns are: *amigo/a* ("male or female friend"), *profesor/a* ("male or female professor"), and *hermano/a* ("brother/sister"). Examples such as the first two provided here can be problematic for the Trilingual VRS interpreter because ASL and English nouns do not indicate sex of the referent in the same way, whereas references to siblings are likely easier to interpret because there are different lexical items for brother and sister in ASL, English, and Spanish. The only issue would be the plural form in Spanish which could either refer to a group of males or a mixed group of males and females. A group consisting entirely of females would be referred to using the form for females (e.g., *amigas*, *hermanas*, etc.). A related issue is that ASL pronouns do not contain information about the sex of the referent, whereas the same is not true in Spanish and English for third-person forms.

In their survey responses, interpreters mentioned various strategies for dealing with ambiguity of a referent's sex while having to decide which nominal variant to choose. One general strategy that was noted was to use non-gender-specific language whenever possible. For example, instead of deciding whether to utter *maestro* or *maestra* when the Deaf consumer produces the ASL sign TEACHER, an interpreter could consider saying "*persona que enseña la clase*" ("person who teaches the class"). Even with that type of strategy, interpreters mentioned that they relied on context to guide their decisions. In terms of pronouns, almost all interpreters who responded to the survey mentioned that they would seek clarification from the ASL user about the sex of the person being referred to when clues were not provided via context. As with other types of interpreting, there are no formal guidelines that must be followed for seeking clarification from either the Deaf or hearing callers, but some interpreters work under the assumption that minimal requests for clarification are ideal, and that when such a request is necessary it should be as unobtrusive as possible.

Spanish speakers must choose between formal and informal variants of pronouns and verb conjugations when addressing others, and there is some variability across dialects regarding the appropriate choice to make—from a cultural perspective. Examples of formal and informal pronominal variants, including some dialectal variants, are the following: second-person singular informal: *tú/vos* (variants based on regional dialect, as mentioned earlier) and second-person singular formal: *usted*. Verbs must be conjugated according to formal and informal suffixes as well with some common examples being the following present tense second-person singular formal and informal forms, respectively: *quiere/quieres* ("to want") and *habla/hablas* ("to talk"). As other examples of second-person singular variants, past tense forms have their own conjugations such as: *comió/comiste* ("to eat") and *lavó/lavaste* ("to wash").

This is one area of the grammar that interacts strongly with cultural conventions, since formal forms are often used with interlocutors who elicit a certain level of respect (e.g., older people, those higher on a social hierarchy, as in one's boss, an academic or professional mentor, or a government official), whereas informal forms are used in more intimate registers with family members, friends, and even acquaintances. However, there are variations in the cultural conventions such as: the formal forms are used with all elders in some dialects but not with family members in other dialects regardless of age, the formal is used extensively in some dialects (e.g., Colombian Spanish) even with peers, and speakers of some dialects use the informal forms when speaking to people who are perceived to be of lower socioeconomic status (e.g., some indigenous people)—even if they are strangers.

For many speakers of Spanish, the formal is used when meeting a stranger who appears to be a peer of some sort (e.g., with respect to age or social status), but over time a switch—either initiated by the interlocutor or not—is made to informal forms. The formal forms are often default forms when interacting with someone for the first time and in various settings. The challenge for Trilingual VRS interpreters arises for at least two reasons. First, the interpreters are not provided with visual information about their Spanish-speaking interlocutors, and cues such as age, environment, and appearance are not readily available to them—unless there are hints from voice quality or other audio cues. Secondly, as noted earlier, a significant amount of Trilingual VRS work occurs within intimate registers of Spanish—the type of language use that takes place within families and among friends. Because of the different cultural conventions for the use of formal versus informal forms across dialects, the interpreter may not be certain about which form may be best when addressing a particular hearing caller. All of this is, of course, also influenced by the Deaf caller's relationship with the hearing caller as well.

Based on the survey responses, one strategy for Trilingual VRS interpreters is to use *usted* as a default form, although that is not without its problems. For instance, one interpreter wrote the following: "One thing that sometimes is an issue is the Tú vs. Ud. [usted] I default to Ud. But, I wonder if I am causing the interaction between callers to be more formal than it should be." This point is very well taken—especially since a substantial number of Trilingual VRS calls occur between family and/or friends, and this normally elicits informal conjugations and other facets of intimate register. Additionally, the general trend that appeared from the

Deaf caller responses to the survey was that they do not normally inform the interpreter which pronominal and verbal forms—formal or informal— to use within a call. Yet, three of the Deaf callers noted that formal forms should be the default, which matches with what some of the interpreters seem to do.[3] However, this also conflicts with the idea that many of the Trilingual VRS calls occur within informal register. There could be a mismatch between the linguistic forms that are used and what might actually be most appropriate and comfortable for the hearing callers in these situations. There are likely other factors that affect which pronoun variant is chosen by the interpreter. Among some of the possible reasons might be: perceived dynamics of the two callers, the perceived nationalities of the two callers, the pronoun choice of the hearing caller, and even interpreter-influenced decisions based on his/her own upbringing (and cultural norms with regard to formal vs. informal variants) and/or the interpreters' own proficiency in conjugating verbs in formal or informal forms.

PRONUNCIATION VARIANTS:
SPANISH OR ENGLISH PHONOLOGY?

Trilingual interpreters in the United States also encounter a type of challenge that arises from pronunciation differences between English and Spanish. In particular, when presented with a name or word that has common pronunciation variants, a decision must be made by the interpreter about how to convey that item. For example, the name David can be pronounced with Spanish phonology as [davið], such as how the first author normally introduces himself to others, or as [deɪvɪd]—a common variant in English-speaking settings. Pronunciation variants for names also occur in many other names that are common in both English- and Spanish-speaking countries (e.g., Maria, Carmen, and Theresa). For instance, a trilingual interpreter interpreting an English call from a Deaf Latina VRS user "María" might pronounce the name using a Spanish pronunciation if he or she knows María is calling Alejandro. The same interpreter, however, might decide to use the English pronunciation if María is calling someone with a non-Spanish based surname. This approach, too, carries

---

3. Anecdotal accounts from two signed language interpreting colleagues who work in Latin American countries indicate that formal variants are often the default forms used in their sign-to-voice interpretations when they are unsure which variant would be most appropriate.

risks, as the interpreter must assume language preference and possibly even cultural identity based solely on a name. Issues of identity also surface when people describe their nationality (e.g., saying "I'm Mexican." versus "I'm *Mexicano*." as noted in Dowling, 2005). Of course, there are also names that are more common in one language or culture as opposed to the other with some having strong influence from naming patterns in Spanish-speaking countries (e.g., Juan, Dolores, or José) and others being influenced by common English-influenced name choices in the U.S. (Sarah, Nathan, and Kathleen). Whether or not a name is commonly used across borders, the interpreter must decide how to pronounce a name (or someone's nationality) that is fingerspelled by a Deaf consumer.

The question of name pronunciation was included in the interpreter survey. The majority of interpreters who responded to the survey indicated that they normally pronounce callers' Spanish-influenced names in Spanish by default, but this may be because the respondents are assuming that the Deaf caller is calling a Spanish-speaker. The survey question, however, did not specifically ask how trilingual interpreters pronounce names in English-ASL calls (with Deaf Latino callers). Four of the respondents did indicate, however, that they will adopt the hearing consumer's manner of pronunciation if that person mentions the name. One respondent added that he/she will use pronunciation based on the language of the person being called (i.e., if calling an English speaker, Spanish names will have an English pronunciation; if calling a Spanish speaker, English proper names will have a Spanish pronunciation). However, it is not always known from simply the name (as noted above) whether or not the person being called is a Spanish speaker, an English speaker, or both. The Deaf and hard of hearing callers who answered this similar question and who had Spanish names either said they hadn't thought about it before or preferred their name to be pronounced in Spanish.

WHAT IS BEING DONE TO MEET THE CHALLENGES AND WHAT CAN BE DONE FOR THE FUTURE?

In the previous section, we presented some of the challenges of interpreting Trilingual VRS calls. Clearly, what we describe are challenges that will continue to exist because of differences between languages, cultures, and identities of the callers. However, there are certainly ways to improve the success of interpretations in relation to these challenging areas.

Training and Support Challenges

There appears to be a lack of training opportunities that are specific to Trilingual VRS. For example, we examined the abstracts of 28 Video Relay Service–related workshops and meetings that have been held over the past three national conferences (2005, 2007, and 2009) of the Registry of Interpreters for the Deaf (RID), and none of them appeared to address interpreting in the multilingual, multicultural environment of Trilingual VRS. Additionally, from our interviews with TRS providers, it is unclear to what extent trilingual interpreters are receiving training specific to trilingual situations within their VRS work places. General training (e.g., related to the use of technology) is certainly offered to all interpreters who work at VRS agencies, but the degree to which trilingual learning opportunities are made available seems to differ from agency to agency. During our interviews, TRS providers did not provide us with information about specific types of cultural and linguistic training offered to their trilingual interpreters.

One particularly noteworthy challenge related to support of trilingual interpreters relates to the length of each call and abilities to depend on the assistance of a colleague—either through teaming or by transferring a call. For the majority of interpreters surveyed and TRS providers interviewed, the average length of Trilingual VRS calls was reported as nearly double that of English-ASL VRS calls. One of the interpreters noted, "The trilingual calls are more taxing mentally on me than ASL-English calls. It also causes me great stress when I am 'stuck' in a call that is too hard for me and there is no other TVI [trilingual video interpreter] available to take over." Another said, "VRS makes us interpreters deal with this kind of situation more often than we would working in the community and for prolonged periods of time. Also, I think, sitting while interpreting lengthy calls for this kind of caller makes it even worse on your body."

Some interpreters also noted that a Trilingual VRS caller will often make several consecutive calls, and this could also add to cognitive stress for an interpreter. For example, one interpreter commented, "I don't feel more fatigue with my hands and arms than regular ASL-English interpreting. I do, however, feel extremely exhausted mentally after a long string of Spanish calls."

While VRS providers report their interpreters have some degree of access to teaming with other Spanish-English-ASL interpreters, the vast majority of interpreters surveyed reported that they do not work with other trilingual video interpreters in teaming situations. One common reason given was that there are seldom two trilingual interpreters working in the same location at the same time. If these results are indicative of a wider trend (i.e., trilingual individuals interpreting longer calls than the average English-ASL VRS call but having less access to team interpreters), it is definitely an issue that will require attention as the demand presumably continues to increase. One interpreter articulated her/his concern using the following words: "The psychophysical demands of this kind of calls are grueling!"

It is evident from the survey data that are discussed in this section that Trilingual VRS interpreting presents some challenges that differ from those of bilingual (ASL-English) VRS interpreting. There is much to be learned by querying interpreters who do this type of work on a daily basis. However, we should also note that there are limitations to this research methodology. For example, as noted earlier, our data from callers (either Deaf or hearing) may be biased toward those who possess English literacy skills, and we may have neglected important information from those with only Spanish reading and writing skills or minimal literacy skills in general. Additionally, data from a survey are normally far from comprehensive—they only allow the researcher to take a snapshot of what people think about very specific questions.

Current Methods Used to Meet the Challenges

General training for trilingual interpreting has only recently begun. In recent years, several interpreter organizations (Florida Registry of Interpreters for the Deaf, Southern California Registry of Interpreters for the Deaf, Texas Society of Interpreters for the Deaf) have offered training for trilingual interpreters working with Deaf Latino clients, either at their annual conferences or as stand-alone workshops. The Southern California Registry of Interpreters for the Deaf created a committee to address the needs of trilingual interpreters. And, even individuals (who may or may not be affiliated with an interpreter organization) are responding to the need, as evidenced by the creation of blog called "*Intérpretes de ASL/Español—Donde intérpretes de ASL y español comparten noticias, ideas, conocimientos y cultura*" [ASL/Spanish Interpreters—Where Spanish-ASL interpreters share news, ideas, knowledge and culture]. In addition, to our knowledge two community colleges in the United States currently have trilingual components to their existing ASL/English interpreter preparation programs (Santa Fe Community College in New Mexico and San Antonio Community College in Texas). Some trilingual interpreters have also attended specialized training at formal institutions focused on interpreting between Spanish and English in either legal or medical settings, although there is currently not a signed language component to those training opportunities.

Perhaps the most focused training experience specific to trilingual interpreting has come from the Texas Department of Assistive and Rehabilitative Services, Office of Deaf and Hard of Hearing Services (DARS/DHHS). That organization has offered week-long training sessions for interpreters working between English, ASL, and Spanish every summer since 2007. Trilingual interpreters have traveled from areas throughout the country (e.g., California, Massachusetts, Idaho, Illinois, Arizona, Wyoming, Ohio, and Puerto Rico) to participate in the training.

In addition to providing training opportunities for trilingual interpreters (not specific to VRS interpreting, but certainly beneficial to such work), the Texas DARS has been intricately involved in the creation of a trilingual assessment instrument in order to certify trilingual interpreters at two levels of skill. This exam is discussed in Gatto et al. (this volume), and its development has influenced the training of trilingual interpreters throughout the country.

There are also two groups that provide opportunities for trilingual interpreters to interact professionally with their trilingual colleagues. One professional organization that came into existence to address the needs of trilingual interpreters is *Mano a Mano*. The organization, which has been in existence as a non-profit group since 2005 (but since the 1990s as sponsor and organizer of conferences for interpreters who work in Spanish-influenced settings), normally hosts a biennial conference offering skill-building workshops for interpreters working in the Deaf Latino community. Another group, the National Network of Trilingual Interpreters (NNTI), uses Yahoo! Group technology to connect interpreters throughout the United States and Puerto Rico (as well as Spain and various countries throughout Latin America). The bulk of the NNTI's activity takes place online via posts among members. Neither group is dedicated specifically to the field of Trilingual VRS, but both organizations offer some support to interpreters working in Trilingual VRS settings.[4]

---

4. All three authors of this work have been involved substantially in Mano a Mano and/or the NNTI.

It should also be mentioned that the assistance of Deaf colleagues who are versed in interpreting processes and who are multilingual would also serve as an invaluable resource to Trilingual VRS interpreters. It has been reported to us that occasionally Deaf communication specialists are employed by TRS providers in order to assist with linguistically challenging calls.[5] Such calls could include Deaf individuals from Latin American countries—the type that are represented in Figure 1 by the lighter oval encircling Spanish and portions of English, ASL, and one or more Latin American signed language. Some of our Deaf colleagues are multilingual in both signed and written/spoken languages, and they could provide important mentoring and assistance for our hearing Trilingual VRS interpreters.

Suggestions for the Future

Providing Trilingual VRS interpreters with training on various linguistic and cultural topics would be beneficial to the consumers. For example, learning about lexical differences across Spanish dialects and variations in cultural conventions for caller etiquette would be important. One current Internet resource is the material supported by the National Multicultural Interpreting Project, which contains a wealth of information about various cultural groups in the United States (including Latinos) and curricular modules that serve to instruct interpreter trainers and interpreters about cultural knowledge and sensitivity. With regard to lexical variants of Spanish or commonly used signs from Latin American signed languages, interpreters or interpreter organizations might consider developing online resources for trilingual interpreters. As one example, a database of commonly occurring terms in Trilingual VRS calls could be created and built upon over time with the assistance of one of the online groups such as the NNTI. Additionally, we suggest that interpreters can be trained on strategies to use when they are not provided with information about whether formal or informal variants of pronouns and verb conjugations would be best or what the sex of a referent in the discourse may be. Finally, becoming more aware of name pronunciations and the identities that they convey as well as appropriate ways for obtaining information

5. We thank Jeff Davis, one of the editors of this volume, for pointing this out to us.

from the Deaf caller about how to pronounce his/her name would be valuable in order to represent the caller appropriately to the hearing caller and be sensitive to issues of identity.

The training could come from various sources. Some opportunities for skill building could come from community and conference workshops, but the TRS providers, we suggest, could also provide opportunities for Trilingual VRS interpreters to improve their skills in these topic areas. We also suggest that Deaf callers and interpreters might want to work together in specific ways to support optimal interpretations during Trilingual VRS calls. In particular, the Deaf caller could provide information to the interpreter that would assist with decision making regarding informal versus formal addresses, the sex of a referent (only for some Spanish nouns), and the way to pronounce the Deaf caller's name or the names of others within the discourse of the call.

Another way for the interpreter and caller to work together would be to allow for some "pre-conferencing" (i.e., briefly describing the nature of the call and any other information that could be particularly useful for the interpreter) before all parties are on the call. The degree to which pre-conferencing commonly occurs depends on several factors. All interpreters should keep in mind that the FCC regulations currently discourage open-ended questions but allow for limited "yes" and "no" questions. The manner in which the regulations are interpreted may differ across the VRS service providers. For example, some VRS companies may encourage limited rapport-building between the interpreter and the Deaf caller while others may frown upon it. It is also likely that other factors (e.g., influences from training experiences and possibly the interpreter's own personality) will influence the degree of pre-conferencing that occurs between the Deaf caller and the interpreter. But, the Deaf caller (or hearing Spanish speaker in a voice-initiated call) certainly plays an important role. For instance, the caller may simply say/sign, "Call 555–123–4567. Whoever answers." or the caller may give an elaborate pre-conference ("Before you call, let me explain. I'm calling my cousin, who . . ."). Pre-conferencing may be a successful way for callers to assist the interpreters in building a foundational context for the call that will allow the interpreters to perform their task more efficiently, accurately, and in culturally appropriate ways. As such, Trilingual VRS interpreting could be the impetus for stronger working relationships between interpreters and the callers they serve. The signed language interpreting profession has believed for years that interpreters and clients—either Deaf, hard of hearing, or hearing—should work together in order to create an optimal interpreted event, and the case of Trilingual VRS interpreting provides more evidence that this truly needs to be the case.

Finally, it would be optimal to have more skilled trilingual interpreters who could provide support during Trilingual VRS calls as well as during those times that trilingual interpreters are working on their skills in order to improve their performance. The growing number of deaf children from Spanish-speaking homes has created a demand for Trilingual VRS that is requiring a greater supply of skilled trilingual interpreters. If there are more qualified interpreters for Trilingual VRS, perhaps TRS agencies could provide more support for the Trilingual VRS interpreter during a call.

In little over a decade, Trilingual VRS has created many new challenges for interpreters and TRS agencies. We suggest that providing resources for Trilingual VRS interpreters is vital, and that those resources include training and support along with identification of a growing group of colleagues who can assist with calls and professional development. In this world of increasingly globalized communications, we are seeing an interesting result in the field of sign language interpretation. It is our hope that we can meet the challenges presented by this new type of interpreting in order to provide all stakeholders with the highest quality of service.

ACKNOWLEDGMENTS

We would like to thank Anamae Freehauf for her assistance with the interviews that occurred for this project. Additionally, various other students from David Quinto-Pozos's research lab at the University of Illinois at Urbana-Champaign provided support with this project. We would like to acknowledge them as a group. Our editors, Rachel McKee and Jeff Davis, also offered insightful comments on an earlier version of our manuscript. Finally, we would like thank our trilingual interpreting colleagues and all those Deaf and hard of hearing individuals who completed the surveys for our data collection. We appreciate their willingness to share their experiences with us.

REFERENCES

Americans With Disabilities Act of 1990, Pub. L. No. 101-336, §2, 104 Stat. 328 (1991). Retrieved from http://www.ada.gov/pubs/ada.htm.

Callahan, L. (2003). The role of register in code-switching. *Bilingual Review*, 27, 12–25.

Davis, J. (1989). Distinguishing language contact phenomena in ASL interpretation. In C. Lucas (Ed.), *The sociolinguistics of the Deaf community* (pp. 85–102). San Diego: Academic Press.

Davis, J. (1990). *Interpreting in a language contact situation.* Unpublished doctoral dissertation, University of New Mexico, Albuquerque.

Dowling, J. (2005). 'I'm no Mexican . . . *Pero soy Mexicano*': Linguistic context of labeling among Mexican Americans in Texas. *Southwest Journal of Linguistics*, 24, 53–63.

Federal Communications Commission. (2008). *Video relay services: FCC consumer facts.* Retrieved from http://www.fcc.gov/cgb/consumerfacts/videorelay.html.

Federal Register. (2005). *Rules and regulations.* Retrieved on June 12, 2008, from http://edocket.access.gpo.gov/2005/05-17110.htm.

Gallaudet Research Institute. (November 2008). *Regional and national summary report of data from the 2007–2008 Annual Survey of Deaf and Hard of Hearing Children and Youth.* Washington, DC: GRI, Gallaudet University.

Inside Gallaudet. (2008). *Gallaudet announces honorary degree and professor emeritus awards.* Retrieved on June 16, 2008, from http://news.gallaudet .edu/?ID=12464.

Lane, H., Hoffmeister, R. & Bahan, B. (1996). *A Journey into the DEAF-WORLD.* San Diego: DawnSignPress.

Lucas, C., Bayley, R., Rose, M. & Wulf, A. (2002). The impact of variation research on Deaf communities. In M. A. Karchmer & J. V. Van Cleve (Eds.), *The study of sign languages: Essays in honor of William C. Stokoe* (pp. 137–60). Washington, DC: Gallaudet University Press.

Lucas, C., & Valli, C. (1992). *Language contact in the American Deaf Community.* San Diego: Academic Press.

National Multicultural Interpreter Project. (2008). *Online resource for information about interpreting for multicultural/multilinguistic groups.* Retrieved on November 7, 2008, from http://www.epcc.edu/nmip/Home/tabid/2729/language/en-US/Default.aspx.

Quinto-Pozos, D. (2008). Sign language contact & interference: ASL & LSM. *Language in Society*, 37, 161–89.

RID Video Interpreting Committee. (2008). Video relay service and video remote interpreting: What's the difference? *Views*, 25, 1–8.

Constructing a Valid and Reliable Trilingual Interpreting Testing Instrument

Roseann Dueñas González, Paul Gatto, and John Bichsel

In the United States, the provision of equal access to education and medical, legal, and social services for language minorities is often addressed at the federal and state levels by certification programs that ensure the availability of qualified interpreters. Among these language minority groups with a critical need for skilled interpreters are Hispanics who are Deaf and Hard of Hearing and their families. Although there is a well-established need to provide proficient trilingual interpreters who can bridge three differing cultures and languages—ASL, English, and Spanish—only recently has a trilingual interpreter certification process been successfully completed. To satisfy the demand for qualified trilingual interpreters, the University of Arizona National Center for Interpretation Testing, Research and Policy (UA NCITRP), and its partner, the Texas Department of Assistive and Rehabilitative Services—Deaf and Hard of Hearing Services (DARS-DHHS), began developing, piloting, and validating trilingual interpreting certification examinations in 2003, thanks to a grant from the National Institute for Disability and Rehabilitative Research, of the U.S. Department of Education.[1] These examinations will first be used to certify trilingual interpreters in the state of Texas and will then be made available to other state and federal agencies for wider use.

Throughout the creation of the trilingual interpreter certification program the test developers adhered to strict standards of the American Educational Research Association, American Psychological Association, and National Council on Measurement in Education (AERA, 1999). The process included three important components: (a) Reviewing existing empirical research, (b) conducting new research and analysis of the work done by trilingual interpreters, and (c) adapting UA NCITRP's widely accepted interpreter testing model to ensure validity and reliability.

1. Grant #H133G04115.

Locally and nationally, the Hispanic population has grown dramatically in recent years, which has had a profound impact on all aspects of American life. Much of this impact can be directly attributed directly to the unique bilingual attributes of U.S. Hispanics. The failure to address language barriers in legal, medical, and educational settings has resulted in inequality, unfairness, and a lack of opportunity for many Hispanics. For Hispanics who are Deaf or Hard of Hearing the language barriers and their detrimental consequences are even greater.

Within the large population of limited- or non-English proficient Hispanics is a large and growing population of Deaf or Hard of Hearing individuals for whom the primary language spoken by their families is Spanish, and who often require language services in ASL, Spanish, and English to participate fully in society. As Quinto-Pozos, Casanova de Canales, and Treviño point out (this volume), roughly 12% of deaf children in the United States are from Spanish-speaking families. Moreover, that number is increasing as a percentage of the overall Deaf and Hard of Hearing school age population (Mitchell & Karchmer, 2006).

The trilingual language barrier impacts the lives of a remarkable number of Americans, and these facts only begin to scratch the surface of the problem. While there are no official figures regarding the ethnicity of Deaf and Hard of Hearing Americans, particularly at the state and local levels, the size of this community can be estimated using 2006 Pew Hispanic Center data on the size of the Hispanic population (44,298,975) and 1994 data on the prevalence of hearing disabilities among Hispanics (4.2%) (Holt, Hotto, & Cole, 1994). Based on these sources, there are an estimated 1.9 million Deaf and Hard of Hearing Hispanic Americans, about one half of whom come from families in which Spanish is the primary language. This large population systematically confronts a trilingual language barrier, a problem that is compounded by the need to navigate cultural differences that are indivisible from three different languages.

Currently, the pressing need for trilingual interpretation is frequently unmet, or is marginally addressed by costly, time-consuming, and ineffective alternatives. Often, individual interpreters, who have not had their Spanish proficiency or trilingual interpreting skills evaluated, are compelled to engage in trilingual interpretation. These interpreters may not be adequately providing access to social and educational services, as is required by state and federal laws. This situation has created far too many instances where the Deaf and Hard of Hearing and their families are excluded from proceedings that directly and materially affect their lives. Early on, Texas DARS-DHHS formed the Hispanic Trilingual Task Force to begin seeking a solution, and in 2003 the DARS-DHHS and UA NCITRP received a grant from the Department of Education to create the first trilingual certification program.

THE CHALLENGE OF DEVELOPING AN INTERPRETER CERTIFICATION EXAMINATION

The central task in developing any valid and reliable criterion-referenced test of interpreter proficiency is to empirically establish the knowledge, skills, abilities, and tasks (KSATs) that are minimally required for a proficient interpreter to responsibly discharge her responsibilities and provide meaningful access to opportunities and services for her clients. Once these KSATs have been identified, the challenge is to ensure that the test reflects them in appropriate measure, and thus can be used to assess whether or not a candidate possesses the minimum required level of proficiency. Additionally, the test must make this determination reliably and consistently. The result is a valid and reliable assessment instrument. The importance of these goals of test development cannot be overstated:

> Validity is the most important consideration in test evaluation. The concept refers to the appropriateness, meaningfulness, and usefulness of the specific inferences from the test scores. Test validation is the process of accumulating evidence to support such inferences. (AERA, 1999, p. 9)

Producing a valid and reliable instrument requires test developers to balance three different criteria:

1. Authenticity—the test should, as closely as possible, concretely reflect the actual practice of proficient interpreters, which should be determined empirically.
2. Representativeness—the test should reflect a representative sample of the KSATs required of a proficient interpreter.
3. Testing Requirements—the test should be structured in such a way as to meet all standards of testing practice, such as practicality, fairness to candidates, and consistent administration and scoring.

Balancing these criteria is extraordinarily difficult, not least of all because these criteria are often in competition. For example, in conversation, people frequently ask elliptical questions (e.g., "So, you wanna?") and offer one- or two-word answers ("Sure."). The criterion of authenticity suggests that the test stimuli should reflect this kind of speech, as it is authentic speech that an interpreter will encounter. However, testing short, simple dialogue such as this is not practical because it does not contribute substantively to the assessment of a candidate's ability and is not representative of the KSATs required of a proficient interpreter. As a result, such questions and responses must be made more substantial and capable of eliciting valuable assessment information (e.g., "Sure" might become "I'd love to! I don't think I have anything scheduled then, but I'll need to double check my calendar. I'll let you know this afternoon. Will you be home around 4?").

Dialogues often heavily favor one language over the others; that is, one person does most of the talking. Again, while this is authentic, an interpreter certification test must assess a candidate's ability in all relevant languages, requiring that all languages are represented in suitable proportions.

Spoken/signed language is different from written language in many respects. Spoken/signed test stimuli must, therefore, be scripted to reflect the qualities of spoken/signed language to be authentic. In other words, authenticity demands that, to the extent possible, the scripts (and especially the video testing stimuli) present speakers/signers who look and sound natural rather than scripted.

The challenge to balance authenticity with representativeness while adhering to testing requirements demands that test developers make decisions that are essential to a practical, cost efficient, and valid and reliable instrument to assess interpreting proficiency.

From the beginning, test developers must document the construct and content validity of a performance test through a set of test specifications describing in detail the structure of the test and the type of test tasks that are involved (Bachman & Palmer, 1996; Douglas, 2000). In addition, issues of authenticity and representativeness of the testing tasks reflected in the content, settings, language, and interpreting modes must be submitted to expert judgments from various groups and their feedback and analyses should be solicited to convincingly document and substantiate the validity of the examination (Brown & Hudson, 2002).

Initiation of Trilingual Interpreter Certification

The trilingual certification project was initiated by David Myers, director of the Texas Department of Assistive and Rehabilitative Services—Deaf and Hard of Hearing Services (DARS-DHHS). Myers and his staff provided leadership, financial, philosophical, and technical support from inception through completion. In addition, the Texas Board for Evaluation of Interpreters (BEI) provided their expertise in the critical elements of ASL and research in parameters of the work performed by proficient interpreters for the Deaf and trilingual interpreters in the state of Texas.

The University of Arizona, with guidance from DARS-DHHS, also convened a panel of subject matter experts (the "Expert Panel") who contributed their extensive knowledge and experience to the project, from the initial design of the project through the final review of the resulting examinations. Throughout the development process, the Expert Panel served as an essential source of data. The Expert Panel included:

- Steven Boone, Ph.D., University of Arkansas; director of research, Rehabilitation Research and Training Center for Persons who are Deaf or Hard of Hearing.
- Yolanda Chavira, coordinator, Texas Hispanic Trilingual Interpreter Task Force, DARS-DHHS; trilingual interpreter.
- Linda Haughton, Ph.D., federal court certified interpreter–Spanish; staff interpreter, U.S. District Court (Texas districts), 1983–2004.
- David Quinto-Pozos, Ph.D., University of Texas at Austin; assistant professor, Department of Linguistics; former chair, Texas Hispanic Trilingual Interpreter Taskforce; trilingual interpreter.
- Douglas Watson, Ph.D., University of Arkansas; project director, Rehabilitation Research and Training Center for Persons who are Deaf or Hard of Hearing.

Additionally, a group of community members and stakeholders, Deaf and hearing, were convened to review aspects of the examinations and supplementary materials to help ensure that they met the real world needs of the community the examinations are intended to serve. The Participatory Action Research Group (PARG) members were recruited by DARS-DHHS and represented the leaders in the practice of trilingual interpreting in throughout Texas, including experienced trilingual interpreters, Deaf recipients of such services, and other stakeholders. The PARG included the following members: Edwin Cancel, Gerry Charles, Liza Enriquez, Gina González, Rogelio Hernandez, Linda Lugo Hill, Martha Macías, Mary Mooney, Julie Razuri, Eddie Reveles, Angela Roth, and Raquel Taylor.

As an essential step in validation, UA NCITRP held a Rater Training Conference for the trilingual interpreter performance pilot exams following their administration. The pilot rating team consisted of: Edwin Cancel, Yolanda Chavira, Gina Gonzalez, and Davíd Quinto-Pozos. Additionally, they were aided by Juan Radillo and Donna Whitman, both of whom are Spanish/English federally certified court interpreters. The recorded ASL test stimuli were reviewed for fidelity to ASL usage by Lauri Metcalf, Department chair of American Sign Language and Interpreter Training at San Antonio College and former chair of the Texas BEI, and Douglas Watson, a member of the Expert Panel who is also Deaf.

Finally, several incumbent licensed interpreters in the state of Texas (as well as nationally) provided UA NCITRP with invaluable empirical data about the nature of the trilingual interpretation they encounter in their work. Many incumbents also participated in the piloting of the exams and gave insightful feedback about the exams, providing evidence for the exams' validity and enabling the development team to revise and improve the final instruments.

All of these individuals devoted their time and talent throughout the development process to this worthy project, helping ensure that the resulting exams faithfully and reliably assess candidates' level of trilingual interpreting proficiency. What follows is a more detailed account of that development process and the resulting exams.

NATIONAL CENTER FOR INTERPRETATION TESTING MODEL

In developing the trilingual interpreter proficiency tests, the University of Arizona employed a test development model originally established by Roseann Dueñas González, director of the UA NCITRP. Roseann Dueñas González conducted the primary research, designed, and led the team who developed the *Federal Court Interpreter Certification Examination* (FCICE), which has set the standard for reliable and valid oral interpreter testing for the past 28 years and is the only interpreter test developed by a federal government agency to survive legal challenge (*Seltzer v. Foley*, 1980). The FCICE interpreter test model has been emulated by every state oral interpreting test that has been developed since 1980. It has also been employed by the state of Texas to redevelop its licensing exams for interpreters for the Deaf, which began in 2000. The hallmarks of this model are: (a) A rigorous, empirical foundation for test development; (b) a two-part testing design; and (c) an objective performance examination scoring system. Each of these aspects of the FCICE test development model is designed to maximize the authenticity, representativeness, and adherence to testing requirements of the exams that employ it.

Rigorous, Empirical Test Foundations

The aim of the test development process is to produce tests that authentically simulate the language and interpreting requirements of the settings at a complexity level that is commensurate with the need of the agency and the population to be served. Accomplishing this goal must begin with a sound investigation into the nature of the work actually encountered in the field and the determination of the KSATs required to responsibly discharge the duties of a proficient interpreter. All subsequent test development is then anchored to the findings of this investigation.

Rarely will a single source of data provide all the information required for test development. Moreover, using a multi-pronged approach to data collection allows for greater corroboration of data from disparate sources, as well as supplementation and expansion to ensure a robust, three-dimensional-view of the work being investigated. Toward this end, the FCICE model typically relies on at least four sources of empirical data: (a) review and analysis of extant research; (b) performance of a job analysis through the survey and interview of incumbents and other stakeholders, as well as through other data gathering techniques; (c) input from subject matter experts (the "Expert Panel") and other stakeholders; and (d) review and analysis of pilot administrations of the instruments, including feedback from pilot participants.

These sources of data are used to establish the essential parameters of the exams, including the settings in which interpreted encounters most often occur; the interpreting modes most often employed; the degree of register variation; the depth and breadth of general and specialized vocabulary required; the level of language proficiency required; grammatical and linguistic elements that are particularly challenging; and sources of potential cognitive stress (e.g., the length, complexity, and speed of discourse). Once established, these parameters (and others) are incorporated into the exams in proportion to their frequency and importance in the authentic discourse encountered by incumbent interpreters. They inform all aspects of the proficiency exams, including their format, structure, content, timing, and scoring.

Two-Part Testing Design

In developing the original FCICE, González examined various possible predictors of interpreting proficiency, including such factors as level of education, interpreting experience, language proficiency, and other demographic variables. Her research found that the only reliable predictor of interpreting proficiency was Spanish and English language proficiency. Though empirically based, this also stands to reason: a proficient interpreter must possess a minimum level of proficiency in each of the languages she interprets in order to be able to comprehend the source message, process its meaning, and render an equivalent message in the target language fast enough to allow for effective communication.

Language proficiency is a necessary condition for proficient interpretation, but it is not sufficient in itself. For this reason, the FCICE model employs a two-part testing cycle, consisting of a written test of language proficiency for the respective languages, followed by an interpreting performance exam. This not only allows for a more comprehensive assessment of essential KSATs, but also ensures a cost effective assessment of required KSATs by screening out candidates who do not yet possess the requisite language proficiency from the more costly and labor intensive performance test.

It may be argued that, given the spoken/signed nature of interpreting, a written language proficiency test might penalize candidates whose written language skills are not as strong. However, it must be noted that the minimum level of language proficiency required of proficient interpreters is very high, and that literacy is, prima facie, a necessary component. Moreover, comprehension of written texts is essential to the actual tasks performed by interpreters (for example, sight translation), making it important to assess.

However, in the case of interpreters for the Deaf, and interpreters who work with other languages that are not typically written, this approach needs to be amended. Straightforwardly, a standard written test of ASL proficiency would not yield valid and reliable results. While notation systems for ASL exist, they are not typically used in the Deaf community, but are used for specific purposes. Unlike English (and Spanish), ASL is not, in its everyday use, a written language. Alternative testing formats, such as video tests of ASL proficiency, would require great care to avoid imposing extraneous variables such as memory into the assessment, which would undermine its validity. For example, in a written English proficiency exam, a reading passage and subsequent questions are available to the candidate for reference throughout the exam. If a video ASL proficiency exam presented a passage and questions and then asked the candidate to respond, the candidate would have to both comprehend the passage and questions (which would be indicative of language proficiency) *and also* remember the content sufficiently to allow the selection of an appropriate answer. Alternately, if the candidate were able to view the ASL stimulus as often as she wished, obviating the requirements of memory, the ability to put time limits on the exam to help assess the candidate's ability to process ASL proficiently would be undermined. These problems are not insurmountable, but demonstrate the challenges of interpreter test development.

The University of Arizona had a similar experience in developing Navajo interpreter certification examinations for the federal courts and the states of New Mexico and Arizona. Written Navajo was developed relatively recently by academics interested in cataloging and studying the language. As such, most proficient Navajo speakers do not read Navajo and their Navajo proficiency cannot be validly and reliably tested with a written exam. Therefore, Navajo interpreter certification candidates are only required to pass a written test of English proficiency before taking the Navajo interpreter performance exam. In this case (as with ASL) it is essential that the performance exam contain a sufficiently broad and robust sample of Navajo (or ASL) to validly assess a candidate's ability to comprehend and produce the language in question.

PART 1: WRITTEN TEST OF SPANISH PROFICIENCY

The first examination developed as part of the trilingual interpreter proficiency battery was a written Test of Spanish Proficiency. In the recent redevelopment of its bilingual ASL/English interpreter certification, the Texas BEI has included a written exam of English proficiency as well. Because ASL/English interpreter certification is a prerequisite for trilingual candidates in Texas, no additional test of English proficiency was developed for this project (see "Meeting the Specific Challenges of Trilingual Interpreter Test Development" later in this paper).

The subject matter of the written Test of Spanish Proficiency was chosen in part based on the settings in which trilingual encounters most commonly occur. The test content was selected by Spanish-language educators and Spanish interpreters who considered readability, lexical density, and language complexity to ensure that the tests and items represented the 10–11th grade level. This level of complexity was based on the two factors of authenticity and testing requirements: (a) The level of language proficiency indicated by incumbents to be required by proficient interpreters (as determined by the job analysis conducted for the Texas BEI ASL/English interpreter certification); and (b) the testing consideration that, because the written test is only the first stage of the certification process, it should not falsely exclude good candidates by being too difficult. In addition, care was taken to ensure that Spanish regional variations that may be unfamiliar to candidates were not included in the exam.

The test of Spanish proficiency is 80 questions long, and 90 minutes are allowed for its completion. Here again, these specifications were determined empirically through the pilot process. The test consists of the following five subsections designed to assess candidates' Spanish proficiency at the lexical, syntactical, and discourse levels of languages:

1. **Reading Comprehension**, which tests the examinee's ability to read keenly and to analyze a written passage for explicit material, topics, assumptions, reasoning, rhetoric, and the interrelationship of words and ideas to whole passages.

2. **Synonyms**, which test direct knowledge of Spanish vocabulary and general as well as fine distinctions of the candidate's vocabulary.

3. **Usage/Idioms**, which test the candidate's understanding of the idiomatic expressions and syntactic and grammatical properties of the Spanish language.

4. **Sentence Completion**, which tests recognition of words or phrases that best complete the meaning of a partial sentence, with reference to both logic and style.

5. **Listening Comprehension**, which tests the aural ability of the candidate to comprehend spoken Spanish, attend to specific

detail, derive main ideas, make inferences, and understand vocabulary in context.

In many respects, these subsections are fairly standard and familiar to many people who have ever taken any language exams (such as the SAT). However, several special considerations were taken into account in developing this exam, based on the potential pool of candidates. In the United States, many potential trilingual interpreters are heritage speakers of Spanish. While "heritage speaker" is a complex, heterogeneous category, it is often the case that heritage speakers grow up in Spanish-speaking families and Spanish is their first language, but their formal education is carried out almost exclusively in English. One result of this is that, for many U.S. heritage Spanish speakers, the development of their Spanish heavily favors spoken Spanish as opposed to written. Moreover, their Spanish proficiency tends to reflect a greater familiarity with common usage as opposed to standard grammar and vocabulary (which is typically learned in school). These characteristics are by no means true of all heritage speakers, nor are all potential trilingual interpreters heritage speakers of Spanish. Nevertheless, in the interest of fairness to candidates and obtaining an accurate portrait of their language proficiency, two subsections of the exam were weighted to reflect these characteristics. First, the usage/idiom subsection focuses more on assessing idiomatic knowledge and knowledge of actual language usage, rather than on standard grammar (note, however, that grammar is tested in context in the sentence completion subsection). The content of the usage/idiom subsection is no less complex or systematic than standard grammar, but better reflects not only the way in which heritage speakers are likely to have acquired Spanish, but also the Spanish they are likely to encounter as interpreters. Similarly, the listening comprehension subsection is weighted more than the reading comprehension subsection to reflect the natural way that Spanish is acquired by the population of candidates.

The Test of Spanish Proficiency was pilot tested with 37 Texas incumbent interpreters. In addition, UA NCITRP and DARS-DHHS took advantage of the fact that the 2005 RID National Convention was held in Texas, and piloted the exam with an additional 14 interpreters from around the country. Interestingly, an analysis of the pilot candidate scores showed no significant difference in the performance of the Texas and the national samples, suggesting that the test may be readily adapted for use in other areas of the country. In addition, the analysis indicated that the final written examination accurately assesses the disparate language elements that contribute to the Spanish language proficiency of this population, including intersection correlations showing that all five subsections measure different, but related facets of language proficiency.

In addition to analyzing the performance of the pilot candidates on the examination, UA NCITRP and DARS-DHHS solicited their feedback regarding various aspects of the exam itself, which is paramount to both enable a more focused post-pilot revision of a test and to provide an additional measure of an examination's validity and appropriateness for its intended purpose (Downing & Haladyna, 1997). In addition to providing detailed comments, the pilot candidates were asked a series of questions using a Likert scale of 1–5, where 1 = "strongly disagree" and 5 = "strongly agree." Some of their responses related to the above discussion are reported in Table 1.

In all, these comments reflect the validity that ensues from a careful test development process and attest to the appropriateness of the instrument for the assessment of trilingual interpreter Spanish proficiency.

Part 2: Trilingual Performance Examination — Empirical Data and Its Relation to Testing

As noted, UA NCITRP gathered empirical data from a variety of sources in order to make sound determinations about the KSATs required of proficient trilingual interpreters. The first sources of data analyzed were the extensive job analysis carried out on behalf of the Texas BEI on the nature of the work conducted by BEI-certified interpreters in the state of Texas and the input provided by the BEI on critical elements of ASL during the development of the bilingual ASL/English interpreter proficiency exams (González, 2003). Additional data was available from the DARS-DHHS Texas Hispanic Trilingual Task Force, which was formed in 1994 to investigate Texas' need for trilingual interpreter services (two members of the Expert Panel, Davíd Quinto-Pozos and Yolanda Chavira, were involved in the Task Force). The Task Force surveyed Texas incumbent interpreters in 2000 (prior to the UA NCITRP's participation) to learn more about the extent and nature of trilingual encounters. In 2005, a follow-up survey was performed, which included an addendum from UA NCITRP to gather more specific data. Both of these surveys provided important empirical data for purposes of test development.

For example, in the original survey (with a sample of 247 interpreters), respondents indicated that roughly 45% of incumbent Texas interpreters

TABLE I. *Pilot Candidate Feedback on Test of Spanish Proficiency (TSP)*

Question	Response (Likert Scale)
"The emphasis on idioms over grammatical knowledge is appropriate."	89.1% Agree or Agree Strongly
The emphasis on Listening Comprehension over Reading Comprehension is appropriate."	91.8% Agree or Agree Strongly
"The variety of subsections is appropriate to assess the Spanish proficiency of candidates."	94.4% Agree or Agree Strongly
"The topics of the Reading and Listening sections reflected the sorts of language an interpreter would encounter in a trilingual situation."	86.6% Agree or Agree Strongly
"The level of difficulty of the TSP is appropriate and reflects the level of language required of a proficient interpreter during a trilingual encounter."	81.3% Agree or Agree Strongly
"Overall, the content of the TSP is comprehensive and should elicit results that are valuable in assessing trilingual interpreters."	86.6% Agree or Agree Strongly

Sample Comments

- "This test was very difficult for me, but I feel that had it been any easier it would not truly reflect the skills of an interpreter."
- "This pilot test really reflects the everyday language that takes place anywhere."
- "We need this kind of testing for a trilingual interpreter."
- "In this side of the state [El Paso], [idioms] are used every day."
- "This exam uses much cultural awareness and definitely gives real world examples."

encountered situations calling for trilingual interpretation. Table 2 shows the reported frequency of trilingual encounters.

These data clearly indicate that trilingual encounters are a regular occurrence for many Texas interpreters. In addition, the original survey asked incumbents to "Rank the following interpreting skills in terms of how important they are for being a successful interpreter where you

TABLE 2. *Frequency of Trilingual Encounters*

Frequency	% of Interpreters*
Daily	7
1–4 Per Week	13
1–4 Per Month	15
1–6 Per Year	55

*Please note that the percentages in this table do not equal 100 due to incomplete survey responses.

work." The responses indicated that throughout Texas, when Spanish or Mexican Sign Language (LSM) is involved, the most important interpreting modes are: **(a)** Spanish to ASL, **(b)** English to Spanish, **(c)** Spanish to English, and **(d)** ASL to Spanish (See Table 3). The findings of the 2005 survey addendum reflected a similar distribution.

These data contributed to the decision to exclude LSM from the performance examination. While they are no doubt important, trilingual encounters that include LSM are less frequent. Most importantly, the inclusion of a fourth language in testing would greatly increase the complexity of the test, reduce the number of potential candidates, add a great deal to the scoring burden, and likely undermine the validity and reliability of the test. Representativeness by itself would dictate the inclusion of LSM, as well as the inclusion of mime, home signs, and so on. The result would be extremely idiosyncratic testing stimuli that would not assess all candidates on a fair and equal basis. This, then, is another example of the criteria of authenticity and testing requirements competing with representativeness.

The 2005 addendum to the survey was distributed to a much smaller group of trilingual interpreters in Texas (a total of 9 responses), as well as a group in Florida (4 responses) for comparison. The addendum was used to help establish the settings in which trilingual encounters most frequently occur, as well as to gather more information about the exact nature of the encounters. The settings in which encounters occurred are presented in Table 4 (specific and detailed descriptions of encounters in these settings were also solicited through the survey).

Here again we see competing test development criteria. While authenticity would call for an emphasis on community interpreting scenarios, it is important to balance frequency with the relative importance of the settings. Some settings have significantly higher stakes than others, including

TABLE 3. *Most Important Modes When Spanish or LSM Is Involved (Weighted Rankings)*

Interpreting Mode	Ranking
1. Spanish to ASL	160
2. English to Spanish	153
3. Spanish to English	147
4. ASL to Spanish	147
5. English to LSM	141
6. LSM to English	129
7. Spanish to LSM	118
8. LSM to Spanish	105

TABLE 4. *Ranked Settings of Trilingual Encounters*

Texas (n=9)	Miami (n=4)
1. General/Community	1. General/Community
2. Medical	2. Medical
3. Educational	3. Educational
4. Social	4. Legal
5. Religious	5. Religious
6. Legal	6. Social

those where interpreting errors greatly impact the lives and well-being of the people involved. For example, misinterpretations in a community setting may have minor consequences, but misinterpretations in medical, educational or legal settings can have dire, material, and long-lasting consequences. For this reason, higher stakes settings were given more weight in determining the scenarios for the exams. This decision (as with all such decisions) was made in consultation with the Expert Panel and the PARG.

The addendum also asked about the nature of the trilingual encounters, and two areas are of particular interest. First, respondents reported what percentage of their interpreting encounters involved the following different combinations of ASL, Spanish, and English:

1. ASL and English—Two people, each using one of these languages.
2. ASL and Spanish—Two people, each using one of these languages.
3. ASL, English, and Spanish—Two people using a combination of these three languages (e.g., codeswitching, signing ASL with Spanish on the mouth, etc.).

4. ASL, English, and Spanish—Three people, each using one of these languages.

As Table 5 indicates, the three combinations involving Spanish occurred in roughly equal measure (the Florida interpreters had similar results). These data helped inform which language combinations should be included in the performance examinations, and suggested that all three of the combinations that include Spanish should be roughly equally represented. However, further inquiry with the Expert Panel and the PARG determined that testing the "ASL, English, and Spanish—Two people" combination in which codeswitching occurred largely duplicated the assessment of the ASL/English combination (on which all candidates would already be certified). This section was thus excised from the exam in an early draft in preference for more extensive testing of the other combinations.

The addendum also indicated that many trilingual interpreters regularly engage in sight translation (reading a written document and interpreting it into the target language). The BEI job analysis also found this to be true for ASL/English interpreters (González, 2003). This was the area with the starkest contrast between the Texas and the Florida interpreters. In Texas, 55% of interpreters reported sight translations occurring in about 10–20% of their interpreted encounters, whereas 100% of the Florida interpreters sight translated documents "very frequently."

Here again, this empirical data informed the structure of the exams, which include sight translations from Spanish to English, and from English to Spanish. These sections are weighted less than other sections, to properly reflect their relative frequency.

As mentioned above, these empirical data were reviewed, corroborated, and expanded upon by the Expert Panel and the PARG throughout the development process to ensure that the resulting test specifications reflected both the actual practice of trilingual interpreters and the needs of the community.

TABLE 5. *Frequency of Different Interpreted Encounters*

Language Combinations	Frequency
Two people/ASL & English	62%
Two people/ASL & Spanish	14%
Two people/ASL, English, & Spanish	10%
Three people/ASL, English, & Spanish	11%

Two different trilingual interpreter performance exams were developed, Advanced and Master, to reflect two levels of proficiency. In general, the approach used in their development was identical. They differ in terms of complexity, and their respective complexity was delineated in three specific ways: (a) The complexity of the language used in terms of vocabulary and sentence length and structure; (b) the complexity of the topics/settings included (and the resultant level of complex terminology); and (c) the speed of speaker/signer, which was controlled to keep it consistent throughout the exams. While the differences in complexity that result from the manipulation of these variables should not be underestimated, we will nonetheless present the remainder of our discussion of the challenges of developing these performance exams in a general way, discussing the similar issues that affected both of these examinations.

Some of these challenges were described earlier in our presentation of the empirical research that supported the development of the tests. For example, at the beginning the settings of the scenarios and the interpreting modes to be included were both open questions, to be answered empirically. Based on survey data, Expert Panel and PARG input, and other considerations, each of the exams consists of five sections:

A. Three-Person Interactive Interpreting: One ASL user, one Spanish speaker, and one English speaker.
B. Spanish to ASL Interpreting.
C. ASL to Spanish Interpreting.
D1. English to Spanish Sight Translation.
D2. Spanish to English Sight Translation.

The content of all sections of both exams consists of scenarios that reflect the topics, register, style, and level of complexity typically encountered in the settings identified in the survey and determined by the Expert Panel, with emphasis on education, healthcare, and social service scenarios. For example, the documents included in the sight translations are based on authentic documents of a kind that trilingual interpreters encounter in the field, such as a job application, which a trilingual interpreter in the United States would likely come across in English rather than in Spanish.

Steps to Ensure Validity and Reliability

The challenge to create a test that has high content and construct validity requires test developers to consider the essential linguistic and cultural complexity of interpreted encounters. For example, interpreted encounters frequently include specialized vocabulary, such as educational, medical, and legal terminology. In addition, a proficient interpreter must be able to navigate a variety of linguistic registers ranging from consultative and formal to colloquial and idiomatic speech (González, Vásquez, & Mikkelson, 1991). Similarly, there is tremendous cultural complexity embedded within the languages that an interpreter deals with. For example, when interpreting into Spanish, an interpreter must make culturally laden judgments in choosing an appropriate form of the second-person pronoun, "you" (Quinto-Pozos, Casanova de Canales, and Treviño, this volume). Terms of endearment also present an additional culturally specific linguistic feature; for example, the Spanish word "gordo" (literally "fat") is often used as a term of endearment, equivalent to "dear" in English. The difficulty inherent in this process of developing an interpreter proficiency test is multiplied substantially by the addition of a third language, as well as the inclusion of a language, such as ASL, that is not commonly used in a written form.

As noted previously, a set of test specifications are essential to document an examination's validity. The test specifications for the Trilingual Interpreter Certification Examination contain precise information about the number and sequence of tasks on the test. The length of each task, including any time limits that have been established, instructions for each test task, the topic and setting of each test task, the interpreting mode for each task, the scoring method, including the number of points for each task and overall, expected responses, and administration procedures. According to Standards for Educational and Psychological Testing (AERA, 1999), high-stakes examination developers should publish test information and sample tests to help candidates prepare for the exam and familiarize themselves with its structure and content; therefore, many of the test specifications are available in a candidate manual, along with an abbreviated sample test.

Another validation step meticulously followed by UA NCITRP and DARS-DHHS was to work with subject matter experts and stakeholders from the outset of the project. Each group contributed their particular expertise to the project, and their contributions have been enormous and indispensible to its success.

Objective Scoring System

The most important innovation in the FCICE model is the development of an objective scoring methodology that greatly eliminates rater bias and subjective and unreliable results (e.g., passing persons who should not pass, and failing persons who should pass). Formerly, interpreter evaluation was based solely on holistic multitrait scoring, which was overly complex with a high potential for subjective assessment and rater bias. The application of analytical scoring rubrics did little to ensure consistency of scoring across candidates and raters.

The FCICE objective scoring system introduced evaluation based on expert-judged, open-response scoring stimuli chosen specifically to reflect critical lexical, syntactical, and discourse elements of language derived from the testing parameters identified empirically through the job analysis, expert panel, and other sources—these include specialized terminology, register variation, rhetorical features, general vocabulary, grammatical structures, appropriate sociocultural discourse, the use of classifiers and non-manual markers, accuracy of fingerspelling, the use of sign space and grammatical space, and others. The FCICE objective scoring system requires that the testing parameters determined during the initial phase of development be scrupulously "loaded" into the testing stimuli during development, so that the scoring units and the text work together to create interpreting stimuli that are representative of the actual level of complexity found in the field.

Objective scoring units that reflect these parameters are identified throughout the examination by underlining and superscripted numbers and used as the basis for candidate evaluation. The objective assessment of a candidate's level of interpreting proficiency is determined by how many of these scoring units the candidate renders appropriately. For example, the following sentence has three objective scoring units that the candidate must render accurately:

> I don't think I have anything scheduled[1] then, but I'll need to double check[2] my calendar.[3]

The candidate's rendition of these scoring units is judged acceptable or unacceptable by the raters, according to the scoring criteria. The result is that every candidate is scored based on the same parameters, significantly improving the consistency of the scoring. At the same time, this system ensures that each candidate is rated across the full range of testing parameters in proportion to their relative importance, so that no parameters receive undue weight in the overall assessment of a candidate.

The function of this system is to assess an interpreter's ability to transform the full meaning from the source language and accurately convey *the equivalent meaning* in the target language, without omission, distortion, or addition. Consider this example from the Texas DARS-DHHS BEI Study Guide for Interpreter Certification Candidates (2006):

> [I]f the candidate sees the ASL gloss SKILL-TALENT-PROFICIENCY, it is important that the appropriate English word be chosen in the interpretation, so that the full meaning is conveyed. When interpreting for the Ms. Deaf Texas pageant, for instance, and the contestant signs, "For my talent this evening, I'll be performing a ballet," it is important that the interpretation conveys the English word "talent" rather than "proficiency" or "skill." (p. 45)

Use of the English words "proficiency" or "skill" would distort the meaning of the source message. Similarly, if a source message consisting of a doctor saying, "Be sure you give him ibuprofen to control his fever," were interpreted as, "Be sure you give him ibuprofen or aspirin to control his fever," meaningful information that was added to the source message would be inappropriately communicated, producing a non-equivalent target language rendition.

It is important to note here that the practice of expansion (e.g., noun listing) in ASL to communicate, for example, some English collective or mass nouns is not an error of addition. Rather, it is one of the methods used in that language to communicate some nouns of that sort (often combined with fingerspelling of the English word), and so can be an appropriate way to produce equivalent meaning in ASL.

The objective scoring process is strengthened by the creation of a list of acceptable and unacceptable items determined beforehand and expanded after each test administration. Experienced interpreter raters agree upon these items during the rater training sessions. This component of the rating process makes rating more efficient and ensures the consistent scoring of testing units by all rating teams.

Finally, the FCICE objective assessment model employs consensus scoring by a team of expert raters rather than composite scoring. In composite scoring, the scores of the different raters are averaged to produce the candidate's final score. Consensus scoring, on the other hand, requires that differences in raters' scores be analyzed until the rating team can come to a consensus on any disputed items. This method is far more sensitive to regional variations in language, changing usage, and other aspects of language, and takes into account the raters' disparate knowledge and expertise. The result is increased validity and improved fairness to the candidates.

Meeting the Specific Challenges of Trilingual Interpreter Test Development

As with any interpreter proficiency exam, applying the FCICE test development model to trilingual interpreter certification carried with it specific requirements and challenges unique to this particular combination of languages, and these will be discussed in this section.

First, however, it is important to briefly review the overall structure of the trilingual interpreter certification process.

1. **ASL/English Certification Prerequisite.** Early in the test development stage it was decided, in consultation with the Expert Panel, that the tests must assess whatever is uniquely relevant to trilingual interpretation and not to also test candidates' proficiency as ASL/English interpreters. While there is no doubt that proficient ASL/English interpreting is required in many trilingual encounters, full assessment of this skill in addition to all others required in trilingual settings would result in an extremely long test, and would thus interject extraneous variables such as candidate endurance and fatigue into the testing process, undermining the validity of the exam. Moreover, in Texas and nationally, valid exams already exist to assess ASL/English interpreter proficiency. It was thus decided that certification as an ASL/English interpreter would be a prerequisite for candidates for trilingual certification.
2. **Written Test of Spanish Proficiency Prerequisite.** Upon meeting the ASL/English Certification prerequisite, candidates are required to take and pass the written Test of Spanish Proficiency to become eligible for the trilingual interpreter performance examination. Two performance examinations were developed, Advanced level and Master level, to help ensure that trilingual interpreters have the requisite level of proficiency to work in even the most complex settings.

Numerous challenges had to be met to create a valid and reliable trilingual interpreting exam. For example, the unique nature of the objective FCICE scoring system developed by González, as described earlier, demands scrupulous attention to detail during the scripting process, to ensure that the resulting exams contain a representative sample of the relevant aspects of the languages being tested and language abilities required of interpreters, as established empirically. This process requires hundreds of hours and dozens of drafts to ensure that the relevant linguistic parameters are represented in the test stimuli.

This challenge is magnified by the inclusion of ASL in the testing stimulus. To the greatest extent possible, it is essential to maintain fidelity to the unique structures of ASL and prevent contamination from the scripting language. To this end, several steps were taken during development. First, during scripting notations were made to indicate specific ASL signs or approaches that should be used by the Deaf actors during the filming of the test stimuli. Second, Davíd Quinto-Pozos, Yolanda Chavira, both trilingual members of the Expert Panel, and John Bichsel of the UA NCITRP were present during pilot filming to consult with the Deaf actors who performed the scripts to help balance the needs of testing and the naturalness of their presentation of the stimuli. The resulting test stimuli renditions were then reviewed and the testing scripts were revised to ensure that they reflected the ASL stimulus. The panel of raters also reviewed and revised the scripts in light of both the testing stimuli and the pilot candidates' renditions. This was supplemented by an independent review of the scripts and their concordance with the ASL stimuli by Douglas Watson (a Deaf member of the Expert Panel) and Lauri Metcalf, then chair of the BEI and department chair of American Sign Language and Interpreter Training at San Antonio College. Finally, two sections that did not match the level of consistency of the other sections were filmed again to ensure clarity of the signing and the fidelity of the testing scripts with the contents of the stimuli. Similarly, the performances were scrutinized to ensure that the Spanish (and English) test stimuli reflected standard usage in terms of pronunciation and fluency, and to avoid the use of regional variations that might be unclear to candidates. Of course, in the field interpreters routinely encounter such regional variations (in Spanish, English, and ASL); but, unlike the testing environment, they also have the opportunity to seek clarification from their interlocutors.

These challenges are among those faced during the development of any interpreting proficiency test. In addition, two features particular to trilingual interpreting deserve special note. First is the issue of fingerspelling. In any proficiency exam involving ASL, fingerspelling is a special challenge for candidates, in terms of both comprehension and production, and is rightly an important focus for assessment. In trilingual situations, it is still more complex because there is an additional transformation required of the interpreter. For example, a trilingual interpreter must be able to both comprehend and produce words spelled in Spanish as well as words spelled in English. More important, however, consider a scenario in which an ASL user is communicating with a Spanish speaker. Unless she is using a Spanish term, the ASL user's fingerspelling will consist of English. The interpreter's task is to first process the fingerspelling into English, and *then* to render the English word in the target language, Spanish. This additional step adds to the cognitive load already inherent in the interpreting process. As a result, it was important to include an adequate sample of this special trilingual feature in the performance examinations.

Perhaps even more important, trilingual interpreters must employ a mode of interpreting not found in ASL/English interpretation, which we have called three-person interactive. This is the instance in which a scenario has three interlocutors: an ASL user, an English speaker, and a Spanish speaker. For example, a Deaf Hispanic child's pediatric appointment with an English speaking doctor may also involve the patient's Spanish speaking parents. Certainly, when such scenarios arise in the field, there may be more than one interpreter available to work in a relay. However, this is often not the case, as evidenced by our survey findings, and one trilingual interpreter must interpret for all parties.

This process requires the interpreter to interpret for each interlocutor twice, once into each target language. In the above example, the doctor's English questions need to be interpreted into ASL for the patient, and also into Spanish for the parent. Moreover, "SimCom," in which the interpreter would sign the doctor's question while speaking it in Spanish, is not the best practice, because the potential cross-contamination between languages may undermine the meaning of the source message. Instead, best practice dictates that the doctor's English question be interpreted first into one target language (e.g., ASL) *and then* into the second target language (e.g., Spanish) to ensure the conservation of meaning. This uniquely trilingual process places a premium on memory for the interpreter, in that the second rendition of the source message can only occur after both the source message *and* the first target rendition have been completed. The interpreter must be able to hold the source message in short-term memory long enough to allow this process to unfold.

In some respects, three-person interactive is similar to the consecutive interpretation mode frequently used in spoken language interpretation. In consecutive interpretation the interpreter begins her rendition of the source message only after the speaker has completed the message; for example, the interpreter renders the doctor's question into Spanish only after the question is complete. In this way it differs from oral simultaneous interpretation, which is interpreting into the target language with only a short lag time between the source speaker and the interpreted rendition. Simultaneous interpretation is in this way similar to the more typical practice of ASL/English interpreters.

However, there are at least two important differences between three-person interactive and spoken language consecutive interpretation. First, in consecutive interpretation the spoken language interpreter is interpreting into only one target language rather than two. Second, during consecutive interpretation, spoken language interpreters often take notes as an aid to memory, a technique that is often impractical for a trilingual interpreter who must use her hands to sign. Both of these issues add to the cognitive load in trilingual interpreting.

Moreover, the process can be more complicated when taking protocol issues into account. For example, depending on the interlocutors involved, it may be more appropriate to interpret into a specific language first; for example, if an English-speaking pediatrician is addressing the Spanish-speaking parent, it may be more appropriate to interpret into Spanish first and then into ASL for the patient's benefit. Other circumstances, based on the level of authority, the position in a family, to whom a message is directed, and other cultural issues may call for interpreting in a different language order. This has an impact on the difficulty of the interpretation because if the doctor's English is interpreted first into Spanish, the interpreter must hold the source message in memory longer before beginning her rendition into ASL. Otherwise, she would be speaking over and interrupting the doctor. Alternately, if she first interpreted into ASL, she could begin her rendition that much sooner.

For testing purposes, this point is important in two ways. First, in assessing a trilingual interpreter's three-person interactive ability, testing requires standardizing the order in which the candidate renders her interpretations to help ensure consistent scoring. The scoring process would be greatly complicated if the raters did not know which language to expect. To solve this, the directions on this section of the exam were standardized to require candidates to render their interpretation in a specific order regardless of what they would do in the field. In the above example, the interpreter would first render the doctor's question into ASL, and then into Spanish, even if the question were intended for the parent. The rationale for this order is both to improve consistency in scoring and to maximize fairness to the candidate because, by using this order, the candidate can begin her rendition as soon as possible. Similarly, the parent's Spanish reply to the doctor's question must be rendered first into ASL and then into English. Finally, the Deaf patient's ASL reply must be rendered first into English, and then into Spanish. During the pilot process, we worked hard to ensure that all candidates were aware of these testing requirements in advance, and that the directions during the exam were clear (protocols which will be followed during future general administrations of the exams as well). The pilot process allowed us to refine the directions and better prepare candidates for this section of the exam. Overall, pilot candidates reported that it was easy to amend their standard practice to conform to the testing requirements.

The second important consideration in testing three-person interactive is standardizing the length of the passages to be interpreted. In the field an interpreter can, if necessary, stop an interlocutor who has gone beyond the interpreter's ability to recall the message and even ask for repetitions. However, in a testing environment, the goal is to control as many variables as possible, so that the only variables that remain are those to be tested. This is one reason that the exams are recorded rather than presented live because doing so ensures that every candidate receives exactly the same stimuli. As a result, it was important to set a maximum length for each passage: on the Advanced examination the longest passage is approximately 30 words, and on the Master examination it is approximately 45 words.

Because of its centrality to trilingual interpretation, and the unique tasks involved, the three-person interactive is weighted to count for more than the other sections. Similarly, the sight translations, because they are less common, are shorter and weighted lower than the other sections.

All of these considerations were at the forefront during the scripting process, and were subject to review, expansion, and approval by the Expert Panel and PARG (as was every aspect of the development process). Further, the final versions of the tests were subject to review and approval by the Texas BEI. They were also tested during the pilot process by candidates who were selected based on passage of the written Test of Spanish Proficiency. A total of eight candidates took the Advanced exam, and seven took the Master exam. After the rating team was trained in the scoring methodology and protocol, they scored the pilot exams. This provided the opportunity to analyze the exams' performance by assessing candidates' reactions to and renditions of the exam stimuli. With respect to the validity of the exams, there were two findings of note. First, there were no candidates who the rater panel subjectively felt were sufficiently proficient but who still did not pass, nor were there any candidates who passed but were considered by the rater panel not to have an appropriate level of proficiency to responsibly discharge the responsibilities of a trilingual interpreter.

Second, a criterion validity study correlated candidates' scores on the Test of Spanish Proficiency with their scores on the performance exam. This provided an independent measure of the candidates' level of proficiency along a relevant dimension. Our assumption was that the candidates' scores on the Test of Spanish Proficiency would correlate strongly with their scores on the performance exam. Such a correlation would add to the body of evidence supporting the validity of the performance exams. Further, the candidates were grouped into high, medium and low proficiency groups based on their written scores (keep in mind that all the performance test candidates passed the Test of Spanish Proficiency). A total of six candidates passed the performance exam (three Advanced candidates and three Master candidates). Of these six, five scored in the high proficiency group on the Test of Spanish Proficiency. This suggests both that Spanish proficiency is an important component of trilingual interpreting proficiency, and that the performance exams successfully distinguish between levels of interpreting proficiency. Interestingly, the sixth passing score (of the candidate who passed the Test of Spanish Proficiency but whose score was not in the "high" proficiency group) was achieved by a candidate who is a child of Deaf parents, and whose first language is ASL rather than Spanish. Under these circumstances, it stands to reason that this candidate's Spanish proficiency score might be lower (though still, it must be noted, well within the passing range), but that her performance exam scores would indicate that she possesses the requisite level of proficiency.

In all, it is our hope that this snapshot of the test development process, and the resulting exams, illuminates not only the challenges inherent in interpreter testing, but also the challenges unique to trilingual interpreting and how they are represented in the exams. One performance exam candidate put it this way, "The test was very well organized and it focused on what I would encounter in interpreting situations. I feel it is a good tool for measuring our skills as trilingual interpreters."

FUTURE OF THE TRILINGUAL INTERPRETER PROFICIENCY TESTS

The development process of the trilingual interpreter proficiency exams is now complete. As of this writing (fall, 2009), the tests will soon be available for general administration in the state of Texas by DARS-DHHS, UA NCITRP's partner in the tests' development. DARS-DHHS will begin to certify successful candidates as trilingual interpreters, which will in turn greatly advance the professionalization of a field which was only recently recognized.

Moreover, the general administrations of the exams will afford opportunities for continued research and enable the adaptation of the trilingual exams for use in other states and organizations. The need for trilingual interpretation services is not limited to Texas, or even to border states, but is broad and growing. The pilot results of the written exam already provide evidence of the applicability of the exams to a wider population. However, testing requirements demand that the tests be reviewed for their applicability to new states or organizations prior to their use outside of Texas. Rather than simply administering the exams elsewhere, UA NCITRP must adapt them to ensure that they truly reflect the needs of the community that they are intended to serve in other states. For example, use by the state of Florida would require that the tests be reviewed to ensure an appropriate linguistic and cultural fit with the prevailing Cuban and Caribbean Spanish populations there. Similarly, the tests may require revision in order to be validly adapted for use in Puerto Rico, not only because of the variety of Spanish used there, but also because interpreters for Deaf people in Puerto Rico may encounter comparatively few trilingual scenarios and considerably more ASL/Spanish scenarios. Likewise, the settings of these scenarios may vary from those found in Texas and elsewhere.

Nonetheless, the work on trilingual interpreting pioneered in Texas by UA NCITRP and DARS-DHHS has the potential to make such essential services broadly available, providing access and new opportunities for this growing and underserved group.

REFERENCES

American Educational Research Association. (1999). *Standards for educational and psychological testing.* Washington, DC: American Psychological Association.

Bachman, L., & Palmer, A. (1996). *Language testing in practice.* Oxford: Oxford University Press.

Brown, J. D., & Hudson, T. (2002). *Criterion-referenced language testing.* Cambridge: Cambridge University Press.

DARS-DHHS/BEI. (2006): *Study guide for interpreter certification candidates.* Retrieved from http://www.dars.state.tx.us/dhhs/trngmat/bei_study_guide.pdf.

Douglas, D. (2000). *Assessing languages for special purposes.* Cambridge: Cambridge University Press.

Downing, S., & Haladyna, T. (1997). Test item development: Validity evidence from quality assurance procedures. *Applied Measurement in Education, 10*(1), 61–82.

González, R. D. (2003). *A job analysis of Texas interpreters for the Deaf and Hard of Hearing: Certification testing recommendations.* Tucson, AZ: University of Arizona National Center for Interpretation Testing, Research and Policy. Internal Report to Texas DARS-DHHS BEI.

González, Roseann Dueñas, John Bichsel, Paul Gatto, & Armando Valles. (2006). *Final report: DARS-DHHS BEI interpreter performance examinations.* Tucson, AZ: University of Arizona National Center for Interpretation Testing, Research and Policy. Internal Report to Texas DARS-DHHS BEI.

González, R. D., Vásquez, V., & Mikkelson, H. (1991). *Fundamentals of court interpretation: Theory, policy, and practice.* Durham, NC: Carolina Academic Press.

Holt, J., Hotto, S., & Cole, K. (1994). *Demographic aspects of hearing impairment: Questions and answers* (3rd ed.). Washington, DC: Center for Assessment and Demographic Studies Gallaudet University. Retrieved on November 10, 2008, from http://www.cihear.com/documents/ DEMOGRAPHICASPECTSOFHEARINGIMPAIRMENT.doc.

Mitchell, R., & Karchmer, M. (2006). Demographics of Deaf education: More students in more places. *American Annals of the Deaf, 151*(2), 95–104.

Pew Hispanic Center. (2006). *Statistical portrait of Hispanics in the United States, 2006.* Retrieved on November 10, 2008, from http://pewhispanic.org/ files/factsheets/hispanics2006/Table-1.pdf.

Seltzer v. Foley, 502 F.Supp. 600, 602 n.2 (S.D.N.Y.1980).

Part 2 Mediating Indigenous Voices

Constructing Roles in a Māori
Deaf Trilingual Context

Rachel Locker McKee and Stephanie Awheto

In everyday assignments interpreters notice the surface features of talk but not always the cultural "bones" of interaction that underlie the meaning of words and actions. Interpreting, though, always occurs within a set of cultural conditions created by the particular place and the identities and values of the participants, as well as by less obvious parameters such as discourse structure and concepts of time, space, and social relationships. In response to each combination of these conditions, an interpreter negotiates three important R's: her role, relationships, and responsibilities in the interaction. In the process, an interpreter also contributes to constructing the roles of other participants. This chapter explores a case of interpreting in a trilingual context in which the intersection of cultures accentuates the choices a Māori interpreter faces in negotiating her three R's. The role and responsibilities she adopts in this case include intercultural mediation and the co-construction of discourse; these roles are motivated by considerations of empowerment, maintaining cohesiveness of the collective, and the goal of constructing an event that upholds the integrity of traditions and the dignity of all participants.

The event discussed in this chapter is a Māori *tangi* (funeral/wake) for the deceased Pākehā Deaf wife of a Māori Deaf man.[1] The tangi, lasting several days, was an intercultural interaction, involving Māori Deaf and Māori hearing people, Pākehā Deaf and Pākehā hearing people, and two trilingual interpreters who were Māori. The Deaf people used New Zealand Sign Language (NZSL), the Pākehā hearing people used spoken English, and the hearing Māori people used English and Māori. The interpreters used all three languages.

1. *Māori* refers to an indigenous New Zealander. *Pākehā* refers to a non-Māori New Zealander, of European ancestry.

Contemporary interpreting theorists have critiqued the static notion of "professional role," arguing that it blurs understanding of what interpreters actually do when they mediate communication. Analysis of interpreted discourse in various contexts has revealed a finer-grained understanding of situated interpreting practice that acknowledges the agency of interpreters in coordinating the flow of interaction, making strategic decisions about message construction and responding to the sociopragmatic demands of situations (Angelelli, 2003; Berk-Seligson, 1990; Bot, 2003; Leeson & Foley-Cave, 2007; Metzger, 1999; Napier, 2001; Roy, 2000; Wadensjö, 2001). To account for the different kinds of turns produced by interpreters in medical dialogues, Metzger (1999) applies Goffman's notion of "footing shifts" between participant roles as animator (transmitter) and author (originator) of utterances, finding that interpreters alternate between these footings as they manage bilingual interaction. This more contextualized view of the interpreting process emerges from the paradigm of interactional sociolinguistics, which analyses situated language use in order to explain the organization of interaction, especially how language is used to negotiate relationships and participant positions in relation to the wider sociocultural context (Gumperz, 1982; Schiffrin, 1994).

Acknowledgement of interpreters' visibility in the discourse they mediate highlights the tension between a narrowly defined ideal of professional practice (based on the conduit model) and the spectrum of ways in which interpreters really enact their role in response to the human dynamics of situations (e.g., Cokely, 2000; Dean & Pollard, 2001, 2005; Llewellyn-Jones & Lee, 2009; Tate & Turner, 2001). Exponents of the interpreting-as-interaction paradigm (notably, Wadensjö, 1998; Metzger, 1999; Roy, 2000) have shown that interpreters' awareness of discourse norms and social outcomes of interaction motivate their decisions and actions more powerfully than a prescribed definition of "role." Moody (2007) summarizes a contemporary view of the interpreter's task, highlighting contextual and interpersonal dimensions:

> Interpreters . . . are working with the participants to accomplish their goals in the interaction; helping them project the image of themselves which they think will further their intentions in the situation given the social roles of the participants; relaying the information that will help each assess the

other's intentions; orchestrating their turn-taking (in addition to dealing with utterances directed to the interpreter or even turns initiated by the interpreter); and even deleting utterances which may violate social roles or expectations. (p. 196)

In this chapter we aim to show how the interpreter, from her own cultural position as a trilingual Māori woman, responds to the sociocultural dimensions of the event in negotiating her role. Her macro-level awareness of peoples' intentions, identities, and varying cultural schemas for the event determine the way in which she mediates interaction, often motivating her to take participant positions that depart from the "normative" interpreter role. For instance, she responds to a need to co-construct ("orchestrate") the delivery of ritualized, formal speeches with Deaf participants, and at another moment, accepts an invitation to contribute a personal anecdote of her connection with the deceased as culturally demanded at one point in the proceedings. Some recent research has explored the theme of the sign language interpreter as a "contributing" participant, especially in interactions that extend or repeat through time (e.g., Leeson & Foley-Cave, 2007; Hauser, Finch, & Hauser, 2008). But few have considered this issue in an indigenous context, where the ethnic orientation of participants toward social relationships is a salient element in the production of interaction. Our analysis highlights how professional precepts about the interpreter's role are culturally embedded, and as such, do not capture practice realities for interpreters in and of diverse cultures, working in multicultural situations.

APPROACH AND AUTHORS' POSITIONS

The basis for this article is self-reported practitioner reflection on an interpreted event. It is a collaboration between an interpreting practitioner/researcher who is non-Māori (McKee) and a practitioner who is Māori and trilingual (Awheto). Awheto's retrospection on interpreting a tangi was tape-recorded in a 90-minute interview/discussion between the authors soon after the event. In writing this chapter, we treat the tape transcript as data that is analyzed to reveal how Awheto contributed to producing the event from her various positions as a participant. Extracts of the transcript give a closer description of the event and a direct sense of the interpreter's reflective voice.

We acknowledge that an interpreter's perspective is only one of multiple views of an event, and that retrospection affords different insights to those arising from live data captured on film. These are real limitations in our treatment of this topic. Nevertheless, we take Turner's (2005) call for critical practitioner reflection as a relevant starting point:

> It is vital that the interpreter has the self-awareness to consider with integrity the identity that she is presenting, the objectives that she has for the interaction, the language resources at her command, and her own conception of the interactional patterning at play. (p. 35)

MĀORI DEAF PEOPLE

Māori make up approximately 15% of the total New Zealand population of four million (Statistics New Zealand, 2001), although the number of Māori children diagnosed with hearing impairment is more than double this proportion (National Audiology Centre, 2002, p. 16).[2] The two deaf schools in New Zealand, which generally enroll students with severe to profound hearing loss, identify approximately 22% of their students as Māori, and a higher proportion are in mainstream schools (DEANZ, 2003). Ethnicity data on the adult Deaf community are not available, but Māori are visible participants in the NZSL (New Zealand Sign Language) community and users of Deaf services (Dugdale, 2001, p. 208). NZSL is the common sign language of Māori and Pākehā Deaf people, who historically attended the same schools and generally socialize in similar social networks and organizations of the Deaf community. In New Zealand, over half of those who identify as ethnically Māori have mixed biological heritage and have non-Māori partners (Callister, 2004); contemporary Māori ethnicity is thus socially and contextually, as well as biologically, defined (O'Regan, 2001).

2. *Māori* as a collective noun to refer to "Māori people" is contemporary usage in New Zealand and is preferred by Māori speakers. The word *Māori* has intrinsically animate reference, making the addition of "people" in every case redundant. *Māori* is also commonly used to refer to the language itself (formally, Te Reo Māori).

The colonized history of Māori in New Zealand is reflected in the disparity in socioeconomic, educational, health, and well-being indicators relative to the Pākehā majority (Chapple, 2000; Robson & Harris, 2007). For Māori Deaf people (MD), the linguistic, educational, and social impacts of childhood deafness often compound these inequalities. Until the 1990s when sign language interpreters became available to NZSL users generally, MD had only superficial access to their heritage culture and to the politics of Māori empowerment. A 1995 report concluded that "deaf Māori, because of their deafness, face not only the problems common to all who are deaf, but also face isolation from their cultural heritage." (AKO Ltd, 1995, p. 39). In a study of MD people's life experiences and perception of identity, Smiler (2004) found that their strongest cultural-linguistic affiliation tended to be with the Deaf-world, and summarized their position in relation to Māori culture as follows:

Socialization experiences within *Te Ao Māori* (the Māori world) were consistent with the universal experiences of Deaf people, namely isolation through lack of communication, negative attitudes towards Deaf people, the expectation that Deaf people should assimilate into hearing society, and the lack of acknowledgement of sign languages as a necessary alternative to spoken language. Within *whānau* (family) settings, *whānau* members were not equipped with the insight and experience to raise a Deaf child, which placed strain on the resulting affiliation participants had with their *whānau*. These barriers . . . made it very difficult for Māori Deaf to naturally acquire the cultural knowledge and relationships which underpin a clear sense of Māori identity. (p. 139)

This resonates with the position of Deaf people from minority culture backgrounds in other countries (Aramburo, 1989; Gerner de Garcia, 1995; James & Woll, 2004). As also observed for Black Deaf people in the United Kingdom (James & Woll, 2004), the absence of same-ethnicity role models in the education system exacerbates the distancing of MD from their family's culture and impedes a positive sense of ethnic identity.

Since the 1970s, hearing Māori people have been engaged in a process of cultural revitalization and political empowerment. At institutional level, this has prompted government return of significant assets and resources to Māori control, a proliferation of Māori-led initiatives in language revitalization, education, and health, and increased representation of Māori in institutional processes of power. A focal point of the grassroots movement has been the revitalization of Māori language as a marker of ethnic identity and pride. While the decline of Māori language has now been arrested, its health remains fragile: It is spoken with native fluency by only 9% of Māori (mostly over the age of 50), and in varying degrees of proficiency by 25% of the Māori population and by 1% of non-Māori (Te Puni Kokiri, 2003, p. 15).

Access to NZSL interpreters and confidence gained from a Deaf pride consciousness since the early 1990s have encouraged MD to seek participation in the Māori hearing world and also to assert a Māori voice within the Deaf community (McKee et al., 2007; Smiler & Mckee, 2007). Smiler (2004) reports:

> Although [MD] participants had limited socialization experiences within *Te Ao Māori* [the Māori world] they still felt an intrinsic identity as Māori. This was expressed through positive acknowledgment of Māori identity and ways of behaving characteristic to Māori culture. Maintaining this identity within the Deaf community however, was difficult to achieve because they felt the Deaf community was a homogenous group framed within Pākehā culture and values. (p. 140)

MD participants in Smiler's study aspired to construct a cultural space for themselves as MD, on Deaf terms, rather than assimilating into hearing Māori communities (McKee et al., 2007). Ironically, the raised status of Māori language as a symbol of ethnic identity presents new challenges for MD: Interaction in Māori contexts is increasingly likely to involve spoken Māori as well as English (requiring trilingual interpreters), and creating positive pressure for Deaf individuals to display knowledge of a second spoken/written language to signal their Māori identity. MD have, to a degree, paralleled the use of indigenous language as an ethnicity marker in their recent efforts to coin "Māori signs" to express Māori concepts in NZSL and to signal Māori identity (see McKee et al., 2007 for detailed discussion of this phenomenon).

TRILINGUAL MĀORI INTERPRETERS

Interpreters who can work between Māori and NZSL have been available in very small numbers since the mid-1990s; they are regarded by MD as a vital resource for connecting with Māori culture, and as natural allies in advancing MD ethnic identity goals (McKee et al., 2007). Māori interpreters, whether trilingual or not, may be preferred by MD, particularly in Māori contexts (i.e., situations in which Māori custom or social norms prevail, regardless of whether the communication is in English or Māori), although we have no data on this question (see also Jones, 1990 re: Black interpreters and Black Deaf people). Anecdotally, we know that MD frequently look to trilingual interpreters to directly impart their knowledge of Māori language and culture, as an extension of their interpreting function. Trilingual interpreters thus respond to multiple role expectations—as mediators of language and culture by interpreting, as cultural advisors (engaging in briefing and dialogue with hearing and Deaf parties), and implicitly, as collaborators in strengthening a MD voice in the Māori world. Consequently, trilingual interpreters may experience a heightened sense of the role tension and shifting positionality that Moody (2007) observes within the profession generally:

> Community interpreters . . . may feel torn between a perceived duty to the minority community and the demands of the profession . . . (they) may be more willing to forego faithful renditions of linguistic utterances in order to enable the participants to achieve their aims as efficiently as possible—they may even come to the assignment with an expectation of fairness and equality. (p. 206)

Currently, there are three trained NZSL interpreters considered fluent enough in both Māori and NZSL to interpret in this language combination. This scarcity is not surprising, given that most of the highly fluent Māori speakers in the wider community are reportedly over 50 years of age. Adult children of MD parents are rarely trilingual since Māori is not a home language for Deaf parents, unless there is extensive contact with hearing extended family members (e.g., grandparents) who speak the language. Author Stephanie Awheto was exposed to Māori spoken by grandparents and relatives, although her parents spoke little Māori to their children, due to being raised in an English-medium education system. Awheto began to learn NZSL through contact with the Māori Deaf partner of one of her siblings; she went on to study NZSL, and decided to extend her Māori language skills through academic study, after qualifying and working as an NZSL interpreter. There is no formal training or accreditation in Māori/NZSL interpretation available in New Zealand. Awheto is the senior (by experience and qualification) of the trilingual interpreters, and this chapter draws on her experience over the past decade.

CULTURAL CONSTRUCTS OF POLITENESS
AND THE INTERPRETING ROLE

In mediating interpersonal relations between parties, interpreters tend to use linguistic moves to minimize threats to the "face" of each party, according to their understanding of normative politeness practices in each culture and the status of the individuals involved (Mason & Stewart, 2001). Brown and Levinson's influential politeness theory (1987) posits two complementary dimensions of polite communication behavior: negative politeness moves, which maintain distance and avoid imposition between parties, and positive politeness moves, which promote affiliation or solidarity between parties. Applying this traditional model to intercultural interaction, Scollon and Scollon (2001) argue that "distancing" and "involvement" strategies are delicately counterpoised, and may conflict, in cross-cultural exchanges. While contemporary discussions of linguistic politeness have moved beyond the Brown and Levinson model, the key concepts remain relevant to describing the Western interpreter's role as shaped by negative politeness norms; that is, behaving in ways that minimize the interpreter's imposition on, and connection to, other participants.

In a Māori context, this professional imperative runs up against different norms for polite behavior as an "outsider." Māori researchers have critiqued Western research methodologies that position a researcher as a neutral bystander, pointing out that trying to remain unobtrusive is likely to be perceived as disrespectful or odd. Because Māori social norms emphasize interconnectedness of the collective, all interlocutors are obliged to observe customary forms of interaction—such as personal introductions—regardless of their purpose in being there (Metge & Kinloch, 1978; Smith, 1999). Respect and rapport is achieved in a Māori context not through distance, but through building solidarity and acceptance within the group. In practice, this entails a guest (such as a researcher or interpreter) developing a relationship over time, being visible and available, being involved, accepting and reciprocating hospitality (Marra, 2008). Moreover, Western notions of privacy, which motivate the ethics of confidentiality and professional distance, are not prioritized in the same way in Māori society (Metge & Kinloch, 1978). For an interpreter working in a collectively oriented hearing culture, these considerations must shape professional behavior.

Balancing dimensions of involvement and distance in interaction is an ever-present concern for all interpreters. In considering "responsibility" as an element of an ethical practice model, Dean and Pollard (2005) conclude that evidence from situated practice is needed. They argue that if researchers, professional bodies, and trainers do not address a "gap between de facto (actual) practice and the prevailing rhetoric or belief system regarding how that profession conducts its work," they risk promoting unexamined interpreter practices that lead to potentially harmful impacts for consumers and stress for practitioners (p. 264). There is growing consensus that interpreters' responses to ethically or interactionally problematic situations should be guided by considering impacts on the dignity, humanity, and communicative needs of consumers, rather than a universally "hands off" principle (Cokely, 2000; Dean & Pollard, 2005; Stewart & Witter-Merrithew, 2004; Tate & Turner, 2001).

CONSTRUCTING A TANGI IN NZSL, MĀORI, AND ENGLISH

A constructionist view of interaction posits that communicative events and the identities, roles, and relationships of participants within them are discursively constituted through the ways that people talk (Holmes, 2003). This section looks at the communicative work done by an interpreter in the process of co-constructing the "expected" discourse of a tangi and participant roles of Deaf people within it.

The term *tangi* or *tangihanga* refers to a Māori process of mourning someone who has died. Traditionally, tangi are held on a *marae* (a sacred meeting place) to which the deceased has family links, although today they are also held at urban (pan-tribal) marae, as in this situation, or in private homes. A tangi lasts for several days, from the time of death until the rituals and ceremonies of grieving are complete after the burial. In Māori custom, the deceased person is never left alone after death, and family members, especially older female relatives, stay close to the casket throughout the tangi. Before burial, the coffin is usually left open so that mourners can see, touch, and cry over the *tūpāpaku* (corpse) to express their grief. Relatives and friends often travel long distances to pay their respects and to offer support to the family. If the tangi is at a marae, visitors arriving day or night are formally welcomed in groups with a *pōwhiri* (traditional welcome ceremony), during which speeches are exchanged between hosts and visitors. Speeches usually contain both formulaic and spontaneous elements.[3]

Constructing this tangi was complicated by the diverse cultural and linguistic backgrounds of the main participants. The deceased Deaf woman was Pākehā, married to a MD man, both of hearing parents. Because the bereaved husband's main social network was with MD peers, and his family were Māori, he chose to hold a tangi rather than a European-style funeral. The Pākehā family of the deceased woman agreed to this, and the MD group and their hearing Māori supporters were thus accorded the role of chief mourners and hosts for the event. Aspects of the Pākehā family's own religious and cultural traditions also needed to be incorporated into the plans, but they approached the event with little knowledge of the protocols for a tangi. Some of the Māori family of the bereaved husband also had superficial customary knowledge, having migrated to urban areas, away from traditional practices; nor were they conversant in NZSL. The Pākehā hearing parents, who had two Deaf daughters, were familiar with Deaf people but not conversant in NZSL. Through both their daughters' intercultural marriages, they had some prior exposure to Māori social situations, but were not well versed in that culture. Thus, for all participants except the interpreters, two interacting layers of unfamiliarity with respect to Māori culture/language and to Deaf culture/language created considerable potential for "talking past each other" (see Metge & Kinloch, 1978). A profile of the cultural competencies of each category of participants is summarized in Table 1.

Table 1 shows that there are no matching profiles between the five main categories of participants. Only the interpreters are competent in all three cultures and languages: NZSL, Māori, English. Accordingly, this increased the need for intercultural bridging in mediating the communication. Moreover, it was not always clear which group of participants was in charge of decision-making, and the shifting balance of language use and leadership taken by Deaf/Hearing/Māori/Pākehā throughout the tangi meant that the interpreters had a difficult task monitoring all parties' sense of inclusion and agency in discussions. Awheto, the lead interpreter at the tangi, is the narrator:

3. Information in this section draws on the source: http://www.korero.maori .nz/forlearners/protocols/tangi.html (retrieved June 2008).

TABLE I.

Category of Participants	Level of cultural and linguistic competence		
	Māori culture/lang	Pākehā culture/lang	Deaf culture/NZSL
Māori Deaf	Minimal–partial	partial	strong
Pākehā Deaf	minimal	partial	strong
Pākehā hearing	minimal	strong	minimal
Māori hearing	partial–strong	strong–partial	minimal
Māori interpreters (H)	strong	strong	strong

At times the tangi became a Deaf-to-Deaf *hui* [gathering], and I felt as though I didn't want to keep interpreting at those times. At other times it was more of a hybrid. It only became a hearing event at the family meeting to discuss the arrangements—and then, the father expressed the feeling of having been left out of some Deaf communication situations. There was quite a clear communication gap between Deaf and hearing.

One element of the context is Awheto's relationship to the bereaved man. She had known him (and his friends helping with the tangi) for approximately 13 years, as an interpreter and participant in MD community activities. She had interpreted at many community and personal events (such as the birth of this couple's child), and was regarded by them as a community member, as well as an interpreter. She was also known in her interpreting capacity to the deceased woman's family, and to the hearing Māori members of the marae committee who were helping to host the tangi. In other words, she was not an outsider in this situation.

Negotiating a Plan for the Event

Awheto entered this situation as an interpreter two days after the death, when family and supporters were working out a plan of action for the forthcoming days. Their goal at this point was to agree on details of place, time, procedure, and responsibilities for the tangi, so that relatives and visitors could be informed of the plans. Negotiating a plan across languages was complicated by differing Māori and Pākehā ideas about funeral rituals. Hearing Māori family members were unsure of tangi protocol, and uncertain about their role in relation to the Deaf participants whose bonds with each other were clearly stronger than their family ties, thus disrupting normative expectations for who should assume the roles of supporting the bereaved husband and welcoming guests onto the marae. Initial discussions were, in effect, determining whether this was to become a Deaf event, a Māori event, a Pākehā event, or a hybrid.

Pseudonyms are used in all of the following extracts. We refer to the deceased as Susan, the bereaved husband as John, and his close MD male friends as Manu and Rangi.

> She died on the Tuesday and I came back Thursday around one in the afternoon and got told that we were going to the marae. There was a whole lot of stuff though, that culturally, I was really uncomfortable with when I got to the house. Because what traditionally happens is—if my partner dies, I am not involved in the details of organizing of the tangi . . . I'm left to go and grieve, and so are my children, and close family. Somebody will naturally appoint themselves into the role of spokesperson for us. And that's what normally happens in Māori settings. But John's (hearing) family lacked that mana (authority/confidence) to be able to direct that. Perhaps that's because they hadn't grown up with *tikanga* (custom), or because they had been over in Australia so far apart from each other. Or it may have been as well that John was deaf and his deaf *whanau* (community/"family") were much more supportive of him during this process, so his immediate family weren't quite sure where their role was. And of course there were the communication issues as well. His immediate whanau couldn't sign so they didn't know whether John wanted them to do it. So I got there and John was doing things that I thought he shouldn't have been doing, culturally: They had him outside, talking about the service and all those types of details and Susan was inside on her own and he hadn't had a chance to go in there by her. So I ended up saying, when they had a break—"You know, you don't really need to worry about this. Your role is to be in there with your wife. Maybe you could find somebody else who could take this over." And he just burst out crying when I said that. He says, "Oh, I didn't wanna do it, but they wanted me to." So, we took him back inside by Susan. He just laid down and went to sleep. But before he did that he said to Manu, "Can you please go out there and talk for me, and tell them what I want. You know what I want." So Manu came in and did that for John.

The interpreter's response at this point is driven primarily by her enculturation as Māori—knowing "what normally happens" in this situation—and by a relationship of support to the bereaved. She responds from a human "ethic of care," (Karlin, 2005, as elaborated later in this chapter), but also from a sense of professional responsibility to address the mismatches in cultural knowledge (between Deaf and hearing Māori participants), by advising Deaf participants about cultural norms for their respective roles in this new situation. To withhold this information would not have seemed ethically responsible, given that the interpreter was the only accessible source of guidance on performing their role. Once Manu assumed the spokesperson role, the interpreter could step back and resume interpreting the ensuing discussions with family members.

The manner and nature of some decisions made by non-Māori family members created further discord between the interpreter's cultural and professional instincts. As described below, she chose to respond to, rather just relay, threatened breaches of protocol:

> So there were still some more cultural clashes because Manu wasn't sure of the process of what we do at tangihanga. And some really bizarre decisions had been made . . . . Thursday afternoon at five they were moving her from the house to the marae. And what Susan's family and what a couple of John's cousins had decided was that they would put the lid on the coffin on Friday at 11 a.m., leave her there till Monday morning, take her to [Susan's] family church . . . have a service, and then bury her. And I was like—"No! We don't do *that*! What do you mean—put the lid on her, and lock up the marae and leave and come back Monday?!" I was like, "Oh, no, no." I just couldn't believe it. And Deaf Māori didn't like it. I got there, and they moaned the minute I walked in the door . . . It didn't feel right to them but they didn't feel like they had the right to say anything because they weren't directly in charge. Hearing Māori family members were there too and they just kind of all nodded with it. But when I had a talk to everybody about how it didn't seem to sit right with tikanga [custom], nobody liked the idea but nobody would say anything either, so . . . I did end up speaking up about it. I asked John how he felt. And I didn't want to press too much on him either, because he just needed to grieve, he didn't need all this added pressure. So this was on the Thursday, and they had already sent the plan out to family and friends in both John's and Susan's families, and of course I came in and said, "Well, you really can't do that, you can't leave her there over the weekend. It's just not the thing we do."

The interpreter's expression of disagreement in her recount ("No! We don't do *that*!") appears on the face of it to be a self-authored opinion. But it can also be understood as expressing her knowledge that the MD participants (and apparently the hearing Māori participants) did not have access to enough customary knowledge to autonomously challenge decisions that were being made, even though they were patently uncomfortable with them. In this instance her own Māori voice merges with her role as "animator" of the MD response (Goffman, 1974). In her comment, "It's just not the thing we do," the interpreter includes MD in her collective and personal Māori "we." Awheto understood their "moaning" to her, as really intended for an audience other than herself—a form of indirection that is common in interaction (Hymes, 1972). Her decision to "intervene" by re-articulating their concerns was in consultation with the Deaf participants, and took into account the emotional stress of the situation, as well as the difficulty for them, in terms of their weaker status as MD, to voice dissent to people who were both hearing and Pākehā. When it became clear that unexpressed Pākehā-Māori and Deaf-hearing differences of perspective were impeding understanding, the interpreter adopted a more visible role as mediator:

> So, after talking to John and he said he actually wanted her buried on the Saturday—this is where you have the Pākehā culture and the Māori culture clash—the family pastor who wanted to do the service wasn't available on the Saturday or Sunday, he had a conference to attend. So the family wanted to put it off till he was available, which was the Monday. And yet from a Māori perspective, we know that three days is "it." And as much as possible, family and loved ones come, but if they can't, we don't hold up the tupāpaku [deceased's body] . . . So trying to get those two talking and understanding where they're coming from—nobody actually *tried*. When I said "This isn't going to work from a Māori perspective," Susan's family said "Oh, we could just have a memorial service on the Monday instead." I was thinking, if you guys had just actually talked, you would have sorted it out. But nobody would say anything.
>
> **Q: So you ended up actually, being a Māori-Pākehā mediator, not so much a sign language interpreter?**
> A: Yeah, just trying to get things back on track from a Māori cultural point of view.

The actions taken in this scenario go beyond strict definitions of an interpreter. The motive for the interpreter's actions here lies in her comment, *"if you guys had just actually talked, you would have sorted it out . . ."* The interpreter adopts the role of intercultural facilitator at this point, not simply because the decisions being made violate at least one set of cultural norms, but because it is apparent that none of the participants in this three-culture exchange can access the unspoken thoughts of the other parties, nor initiate a dialogue that might reach a mutually acceptable outcome. She chooses to express a Māori perspective on behalf of the MD participants, who cannot, in this situation, articulate that perspective with the same timing or authority that she can, as a hearing, enculturated Māori person. This is a judgement on her part to take a broad view of her responsibility to support both Deaf and Māori elements of the MD people's position, by intervening in a manner that steers the interaction back towards the larger goals of the collective.

Co-constructing Speaking Roles

In most cultures, rituals concerning death invoke certain protocols, including who should do and say what; at tangi, practices may vary but generally conform to a traditional "situational grammar" (Salmond, 1977). The experience of interpreting at this tangi demonstrated how interpretation may afford a semblance of linguistic access to situations in which Deaf people cannot participate on an equal footing because they do not have access to the cultural script and pragmatic cues that organize interaction (as shown in various settings by Brennan, 1999; Metzger, 1999; Van Herreweghe, 2002; Winston, 2004). Schematic knowledge of discourse in different contexts enables people to enact social roles by talking in expected ways:

> Our socialization into a cultural group's ways of communicating is partly a matter of learning institutional genres—learning how to "read" them and sometimes learning how to enact them . . . participants have some significant awareness, as part of their cultural and communicative competence, of how the event-types they are engaging with are socially constituted as ways of speaking. (Coupland, 2007, p. 15)

A trilingual Māori interpreter works within an "ethnicized community of practice" (Schnurr, Marra, & Holmes, 1977); that is, in contexts where interaction is organized by Māori values and discourse norms. In such situations, the interpreter's challenge is to include MD within that "community of practice,"[4] but starting from the point of non-shared linguistic and conceptual repertoires. The shared cultural schemas of an ethnic community of practice are acquired through social interaction across generations; unfamiliarity with these templates can lead to discomfort and misunderstanding in interaction (Bowe & Martin, 2007, p. 42). Acquiring genre-specific competence

4. For a definition of the concept of "Community of Practice," see Wenger, 1998, 2008.

in a spoken linguaculture is challenging for sign language users.[5] For example, a Māori Deaf person recounts:

> During my childhood my parents always went to the marae for hui [Māori gatherings], whānau [family] reunions, etc., and at the hui they talked about lots of things that I was expected to learn from . . . there was no interpreting—I had no idea what they were saying . . . I'd just sit there and watch and not know what was happening. (Smiler, 2004, p. 110)

Smiler's study reported that MD adults felt unable to competently assume normative roles in Māori contexts, especially those constituted through language, such as oratory and song, and that they had sketchy understanding of rules for behavior at hui.

Central to the interpreter's and Deaf people's participation in a tangi is knowledge about the "rituals of encounter" and the "situational grammar" that structure hui (Salmond, 1977, p. 193)—in particular, the *pōwhiri* (formal welcome) that opens any event on a marae, and is repeated as each successive group of visitors arrive. The pōwhiri comprises a conventional exchange of speeches between host and visiting elders. In the speeches, genealogical relationships are acknowledged before greeting the other party and addressing the purpose of the gathering. This oratory often contains metaphorical language, frozen and archaic texts, and historical reference points. To perform a speech thus requires a set of cultural knowledge about the expected content (what to say), form (how to organize and deliver it), and sequence (when to say it). Similarly, an interpreter must know the situational grammar well enough to predict the discourse and to mediate Deaf people's participation within those constraints. At this tangi, the interpreter had the competence to relay meaning between Māori and NZSL, but Deaf participants in key speaking roles lacked the genre knowledge to approximate the "situational grammar" in the medium of NZSL.

> The marae had offered for deaf to sit on the *paepae* [host speaker benches], because they expected a lot of deaf coming through. So we had Manu and Rangi who have kind of done that role, but never—not really. They know you're meant to stand up and say something, but they don't really know the

5. *Linguaculture* refers to the idea that language is embedded in culture, including its visible manifestations (artifacts, practices) and shared understandings of these (Agar, 1994).

process, the structure of *whaikorero* [formal speech]. There is an expectation that you'll follow a set process . . . it normally flows through from first acknowledging those who've passed on, and at a tangi you then go to acknowledging the *whanau pani* (bereaved family), and the *tupaapaku* (deceased). Then you'd acknowledge the people at the marae, and then you'd wrap it all up. So there's a process you go through. And our Māori Deaf men had never had to do that before, so they didn't know how to do that role, and they didn't realize how serious it was, either . . . So, I just interpreted what they said, and I tried my best to make it sound as if it wasn't just, "Hey, guys, how are ya? Welcome. Nice to see ya here!" I tried to put a bit more formal language to it. The process for whaikorero is so prescribed that there's not much room for flexibility . . . and so when Māori Deaf don't follow that same process, there's nothing I can do with it other than interpret it. It's not like I can try and fit it into any of these boxes. It just doesn't fit. So I just end up having to interpret what they've said. It feels awful.

Producing a target language interpretation that deviates so far from discourse norms conflicts with the interpreter's cultural script for the event. The interpreter feels discomfort about how the unexpected utterances reflect on herself, since the distinction between her voice (as animator) and theirs (as author; Goffman, 1974) may not be understood by all audiences. The departure from a culturally prescribed script also creates interpreter anxiety about the potential for Deaf speakers to cause offense and even derailment of the event, by appearing to flout protocol. In cultural mediator mode, she feels responsible to address the problem, trying two strategies: first, "smoothing" the target language message into a more formal register. Cultural or register adjustment is a pragmatic strategy often used by interpreters to avoid an unintended impression of impoliteness or disrespect, particularly where this would carry high stakes, such as in legal settings (Berk-Seligson, 1990; Brennan, 1999). But when both content and style of utterances depart from norms, linguistic repackaging cannot disguise the breach.

Aware that register adjustment would not resolve this problem and that the Deaf speakers were oblivious to the potentially adverse consequences of their faux pas, the interpreter secondly adopted a cultural informant role, to directly advise them on how to organize a speech in the expected manner. Because the welcome process was repeated for each group of visitors arriving, there were opportunities to talk with the Deaf speakers about it.

After the first couple of times I ended up saying to them, "This is really how it should be going. So maybe you should try saying this first, and then this, and then this." And they were cool with it. The guys were, "Oh okay, we'll try that!" Because you see—there's a whole different way you make a speech when you're just welcoming a group of people to your marae, as opposed to when they come to a tangi. And they didn't know that. All Manu was told was, "When you stand up, you need to let them know the day that she'll be buried, the time of the service is, and so on." So other than that, he didn't know what he had to do. So he told them about John's 50th birthday coming up, and, "Hope you guys had a good journey, and you're all safe, got plenty of food back there, and if you wanna stay you're welcome!" And I'm like, "Oh no, don't—just drop the birthday thing!" From a Māori point of view, our tikanga [custom] was thrown right out the window. And for some—like our elders—they just weren't going to sit with it.

Making Problems Visible to Interlocutors

Although her advice had some effect, it did not resolve the difficulty. Predicting that relations between Deaf and hearing groups would deteriorate without further intervention, the interpreter moved to a third, more intrusive, strategy of transferring "role coaching" responsibility to the hearing elders. In so doing, she chose to reveal rather than disguise the extent of the linguistic and cultural gap, in order to start a process of direct learning between Deaf and hearing parties.

> So I ended up talking to the *tangata whenua* [host committee] because they were just happy to let it go, and I was of the mind that if Māori or any Deaf people are going to do something they have the right to have enough information to be able to do it right. Sometimes the hearing people just go "It's okay, they're deaf, let them do it." So if they screw it up, everyone just laughs it off and says "Oh well." But Māori Deaf were quite keen to take up the role. They have right to know how to do it properly, so I ended up asking the chairperson, "Can you support these guys to be able to do their role properly, because it's gonna reflect badly on John, it's gonna reflect badly on all of them. Not just within the Māori community but the Deaf community as well. If anything goes wrong, and Māori come in here and they get offended, it's not going to be *you* that's gonna get baled up, it's gonna be these guys." And it did happen. They ended up having a hui (meeting) on the Friday, and Manu and John got growled at by both sides of the family. At one point during the evening, this *kuia* [woman elder] got so fed up with it, she stood up and said, "This is not a playground!" And she just told them off. John and Rangi were like, "What?!" And that's when I felt, "Oh, you can't just chuck them in there." Because our kuia's thinking, "This isn't right!" Because she's looking at it from her experience of what should be happening on the marae and she doesn't care if they're deaf . . . She wasn't going to compromise. It was good in a sense that Māori Deaf got a wakeup

call—"Oh, this isn't something we can muck around with." So I felt more responsibility should have been laid on the feet of the tangata whenua, the committee, to get it right, to get them ready.

In this description of the tension between the parties' motives and perspectives, the interpreter alternates her viewpoint from one side to another: Māori to Deaf. Using the inclusive possessive pronoun "our" to refer to each of the parties in turn, she reveals her allegiance with both the Deaf group (*"our MD"*) and the hearing Māori parties (*"our tikanga was thrown out the window . . . our kuia . . ."*). The interpreter's bilateral stance reflects her awareness of the motives and intentions of each group, and the inherent potential for cross-cultural misunderstanding. At a meta-level, the interpreter recognizes and is concerned that MD are being constructed as incompetent in this situation, and chooses to act in a way that promotes access to the information they need in order to participate more competently. Her actions are also motivated by considering the consequences if MD breach social etiquette and are judged as representatives of the entire Deaf community in doing so. Conscious that social evaluations are occurring (especially hearing-to-Deaf), Awheto feels that she has some responsibility as an interpreter to "manage" those perceptions, which are, in essence, generated by underlying differences in language backgrounds.

To facilitate the overall goal of accomplishing a tangi, and to harmonize relations between the parties so that this can proceed, the interpreter initiates direct dialogue between herself and other parties to make visible the problems in the interaction, and hands over responsibility for rectifying them. This resonates with Moody's (2007) reference to an "open process model," which calls for the kind of exchange with consumers that seeks to share control of communication processes. In deciding to act upon consumers' larger goals for the event rather than sticking with rendering their talk, the interpreter is not only addressing the immediate problem of getting the discourse back on track; she is also challenging a cultural set of paternalism towards Deaf people and strategically guiding hearing participants to recognize and support MD participants' desire to assume new roles and statuses. By handing the task of guidance over to the elders, the interpreter reclaims her primary function as an interpreter, and also responds to the cultural need to maintain the *mana* (prestige) of each party (Deaf, elders, visitors) and the cohesiveness of the collective.

The rather proactive moves described above risk crossing the line between facilitating and controlling. In an earlier study relating to MD language use, one informant commented that he sometimes resented the expectation that he conform to hearing discourse norms, saying, "from the perspective of Māori protocol, I could be displaying inappropriate cultural conduct when I'm actually communicating effectively in my language" (McKee et al., 2007, p. 67). The risk of an interpreter contributing to this could only be evaluated directly by the MD participants in a situation. However, ethically effective actions may justifiably shift to the more "intrusive" end of the spectrum when interpreters are guided by their assessment of participants' overall intentions and the risk of adverse outcomes of the interaction (Dean and Pollard, 2005).

VISIBILITY OF THE INTERPRETER'S IDENTITY

Linguistic interaction is never neutral in terms of interlocutors' identity. As well as physical characteristics, people project features of their identity and respond to the identities of others through their nuanced use of language (Coupland, 2007). Since they are visible and using language, an interpreter's personal identity is therefore manifestly apparent in any interpreted interaction. As noted in other intercultural contexts (e.g., Cooke, 2002; Davis & McKay-Cody, this volume; Quinto-Pozos et al., this volume), the personal identity of an interpreter is foregrounded when they must work around cultural constraints on speaking rights and linguistics forms that are based on gender, seniority, and conventional participant roles.

At an event where people of more than one ethnic identity are present, the interpreter's ethnicity and biography (particularly their enculturation) do not blend into the background, they are visible elements that shape the interpreter's interaction with participants. A tangi is a Māori event, which immediately foregrounds the identity and interactional repertoires of the interpreter and the other interlocutors. For example, by choosing to have their NZSL interpreted into Māori rather than English, Deaf participants deliberately construct themselves as ethnically Māori. Accordingly, there is no possibility, nor advantage, of a neutral identity position for the interpreter because being culturally and linguistically Māori is precisely what enables the trilingual interpreter to mediate the participation of MD as people juggling insider/outsider statuses.

In an ethnicized context, "interpreter," as a role, is likely to be seen as secondary to the primary personal identities that entitle participation in the context:

> In these situations, I have to respond to people as a Māori person because that's how hearing participants identify me; they don't see me in a separate category of "interpreter." But when I work in a situation where the hearing Māori people understand what an interpreter does, then I can interact just as an interpreter.

In the Māori world, personal identity and connection is established by disclosing *iwi* (tribal) connections. Remaining anonymous by abstaining from personal introductions, (the "professional" stance for interpreters), is not an acceptable option. While Māori interpreters can and do work in settings outside their own iwi (tribe), they may need to be socially located by others as a preliminary to performing their work:

> whenever Piripi [MD] has introduced us [interpreters] in a situation, he has always stated our iwi affiliation. Part of the *whakawhanaungatanga* [becoming related] process is to work out how we all connect, and because we [interpreters] have no neutral identity [to Māori consumers] there is the expectation that we will share in that process of making connections.

An interpreter's tribal identity may also affect their ability to understand and interpret oratory that references local knowledge; for example, an outsider may not know if a proper noun used in an historical context refers to a tree, a mountain, a bird, or a human ancestor. When the interpreter does not recognize local referents, they employ coping strategies (Napier, 2001) such as paraphrasing what is being talked about and omitting specific referents, or literally conveying the referents without making contextualized sense.

LINGUISTIC CHALLENGES

Interpretation and its outcomes are shaped by the linguistic forms and schemas available to participants; that is, what the various participants understand, the ways in which they can express it, and how readily these transfer across the languages being used (Turner, 2005). In a trilingual or multicultural context, the complexity of achieving understanding between parties exceeds the bilingual scenario, particularly when one party has a history of limited exposure to one of the other lingua-cultures involved, as is true for MD in relation to spoken Māori.

How effectively can an interpreter construct a bridge across thought-worlds when certain conceptual domains in one language do not exist in the other? Creating equivalence between spoken and signed thought-worlds is a real challenge to trilingual interpreters working in indigenous contexts that invoke knowledge that is highly dependent on oral traditions. A large proportion of the Māori spoken at Māori events occurs in formal and ceremonial discourse, which presents interpreters with "culturally rich" texts (Taylor, 2002). These may be highly metaphorical, poetic, political, and historical in reference—the meaning of which can be opaque and extremely difficult to render for NZSL users. One response has been for interpreters and MD to coin signs to express core Māori concepts that do not have equivalents in NZSL (see McKee et al., 2007). Another strategy interpreters employ is to provide commentary on the function and character of utterances rather than translate the form: for example, "The speaker is introducing himself by saying an ancient chant that names important ancestors of his tribe and their journeys." Awheto notes that spoken Māori-English interpreters also adopt this strategy in similar circumstances where either a literal or free rendition would not adequately transfer sense into the target language. Interpreters' support of cultural learning events organized with MD is another way of addressing this issue in the longer term.

Choice of language code is another decision to be made at any given moment in a trilingual situation. Language revitalization has increased the expectation that Māori will be spoken exclusively during formalities on a marae, but not necessarily throughout the entire event. When voicing from NZSL into a spoken language in this setting, the interpreter must select Māori or English, or a mixed code (English with some Māori words), as their target language. Empirical data would better reveal how this actually works (cf. Martinez, 2007), but we observe that the choice seems to be determined by several interacting factors. The balance of participant ethnicity (more Māori or Pākehā), their language status (predominantly monolingual or bilingual), the location, explicit direction by the Deaf speaker ("switch to Māori/English now"), but most strongly, by the form of the discourse itself:

> I interpret into Māori for the openings and closings which follow a conventional pattern, and into English when they bring up the main topic or

agenda of the day. This follows usual non-native speaker behavior, where they will usually do the traditional greeting, welcome, and closing in Māori, but switch to English to discuss other business.

Trilingual interpreters may switch between Māori and English within an interpretation of a single Deaf speaker, depending on how closely the signer's stream of thought resembles the type of expression that is characteristically Māori (as opposed to Deaf, or non-Māori)—such as, using metaphor, or naming Māori referents. Equivalence in Māori is more achievable for the interpreter when the Deaf speaker approximates a Māori discourse structure in terms of content and sequence. When the NZSL user's content and structure do not reflect a recognizably Māori discourse function or topic, the interpreter tends to switch to English or a mixed code. This appears to mirror the code-switching behavior of Māori-English bilinguals interacting in a marae context.

SAVING FACE

Not violating social expectations requires talking appropriately to others according to who they are. Mason and Stewart (2001) discuss the "face work" that interpreters do, using politeness and message modification to achieve equivalence of pragmatic impacts across cultures. This effort is often triggered by the interpreter's ability to decipher the social statuses and relationships of participants. A Māori interpreter may be managing this on two levels: She is conscious of performing her own identity as a culturally competent participant (in order to maintain the respect of hearing participants and the freedom to operate), while also endeavoring to construct Deaf participants as culturally competent by navigating them away from breaches of protocol.

At the tangi, the interpreter's knowledge of the identity and status of participants in their respective communities is brought to bear on her decision to actively co-construct the discourse. For example, when a very high-ranking Māori person arrived with a visiting party at the tangi, Awheto, but not the MD participants, recognized him. Knowing that he had important political links with this marae, she judged that it was important that protocol be observed carefully by the Deaf speakers when welcoming his group. The need to display appropriate deference to the visitor's status created tension for the interpreter between the boundaries of interpreting and her instinct to save face for all parties, by facilitating an acceptable interaction.

I was very protective of them [MD] . . . My heart was racing when I'd see them stand up. I'd think, "Oh please don't say anything silly." Because at one point an elder who was the spokesperson for Kingi Tuheitia came on with the group.[6] And I thought "Oh my god, he's gonna rip you fullas to shreds!" And I looked over to Manu and I signed, "Be careful, he's the top guy for the king," and I started feeding him [what to say]. Oh, he got nervous, he got anxious, which I think is good. I pointed out that this guy is a bigwig in Tainui [tribe]. . . . I recognized him because I live down in Hamilton and I see him at a lot of the hui there. . . . I don't think he would have been so accommodating. I think he would have taken real offense if protocol was broken, because at the end of the day that marae sits under Tainui rule. So even though it's pan-tribal, it sits on Tainui land and Tainui take quite a bit of responsibility for any marae that's within their area. So Manu was like "Oh, oh, okay," and was quite careful about it, kept looking to me. I was just going, "Carry on, you're doing good."

This co-constructed performance of a speech by the interpreter and Deaf participant is outside a conventional model of interpreting, but resonates with Moody's (2007, p. 199) observation that interpreters sometimes need to "help navigate awkward moments" and orchestrate turns. The interpreter's decision to cue Deaf participants here is motivated by a Māori imperative to acknowledge the status of an important guest, which in turn maintains the mana of the hosts and the integrity of the whole event. By acting on her background knowledge about sociopolitical relationships of people in this encounter, the interpreter demonstrates awareness of the "link between the local organization of talk, and macrolevel social structure" (Coupland, 2007, p. 16).

THE THREE R'S IN CULTURAL CONTEXT:
ROLE, RESPONSIBILITY, AND RELATIONSHIPS

At the end of the taped discussion in which we explored Awheto's position(s) as an interpreter in the tangi and in other trilingual situations, she asks rhetorically:

6. A paramount chief of the Tainui iwi (tribe), recognized as having king-like status in the Māori world. This guest, his envoy, carries associated prestige.

Am I an interpreter or something else? How should boundaries be defined in a Māori context? What is my responsibility? Is it just being faithful to the message? There are other cultural responsibilities: If the Deaf participants don't have the cultural framework for participating, then we should help to build that framework, to give them something to hang the content and the communication on. That sometimes means providing extra information around the edges—and not just in Māori settings.

Understanding the position of MD in relation to hearing and non-Māori society through a personal lens of Māori identity can make it difficult for an interpreter to reconcile a "straight" interpreting function with the motive to support MD to participate in meaningful ways in Māori contexts. This tension is acute, but not necessarily unique, for indigenous trilingual interpreters; Moody (2007) observes more generally, that:

> Community interpreters . . . may feel torn between a perceived duty to the minority community and the demands of the profession . . . [they] may be more willing to forego faithful renditions of linguistic utterances in order to enable the participants to achieve their aims as efficiently as possible— they may even come to the assignment with an expectation of fairness and equality. (p. 206)

Awheto notes the transformative power of the new participant roles that MD experienced, in collaboration with the trilingual interpreters, during the tangi:

> I tell you, as sad as the occasion was, it almost became the catalyst for Māori Deaf to take the next step up. You know a lot happened that challenged Māori Deaf and where they've always been sitting in Māoridom. They were pushed into this role of being on the paepae. And they were pushed to be out there in *karanga* [the calling of visitors onto a marae]. And even though they didn't know what they were doing—they always thought they were doing okay—they suddenly realized that there's a whole lot more expectations put on you when you're on the marae. Afterwards, we were sitting around talking about it, and they [MD men] were going, "We need to wananga [workshop], we need to learn about this process." . . . So the tangi started a whole lot of really good discussion, and Māori Deaf started saying, "We need to get more training on this, this, this."

In the dialogue described above, Awheto positions herself as a contributor to, and observer of, a collective process of cultural advancement. By sharing the frame of identity recognition politics, trilingual Māori interpreters can perhaps more openly acknowledge this aspect of their relationship with the Deaf community than interpreters who work with the "mainstream" Deaf community. Acceptable forms of interpreter engagement with the Deaf agenda change with time and place (see Cokely, 2001). In the pioneering days of the interpreting profession and the emergence of Deaf consciousness, it was more expected that interpreters show commitment to advancement of the community in ways that sometimes went beyond interpreting. While a need for advocacy still exists in many areas, the state of empowerment politics within a particular Deaf community or sub-group determines the way that interpreters as a "technology of voice" are seen to relate to this bigger picture (see Padden & Humphries, 2005). In the Māori situation, trilingual interpreters have a prominent role and are cognizant of the responsibility that confers.

Responsibility, Autonomy, and Caring

Karlin (2005, 2009), among others, deconstructs the cultural basis of the "detached interpreter" role. He argues that the interpreter's code of impartiality and non-intervention stems from a justice-based professional ethic that elevates objectivity and the autonomy of consumers over actual consequences. This model, he argues, problematically assumes that parties in an interpreted encounter have equal degrees of autonomy, which is not the case, given the disparity in power between Deaf and hearing people:

> The dilemma facing interpreters is how to treat all parties as autonomous equals when one interlocutor is clearly disadvantaged? Must they intervene to ensure equality between the signed- and spoken-language users, the minority and majority culture members? Or does respecting autonomy require treating both parties equally, even if it means being complicit in disadvantaging the Deaf client? (Karlin, 2005, p. 2)

Karlin contends that the emphasis on professional distance and neutrality reflects a Western, masculine, individualistic orientation to social relations, which values independence. Feminist paradigms and collectivist (non-Western) cultures, by contrast, adhere more to the "relational" ethic of care, which values empowerment, connection, satisfaction, and respect above personal autonomy (Karlin, 2009, p. 3). In applying this as an alternative ethical framework, Karlin (2005) emphasizes that a relationship of caring is reflexively negotiated (rather than actions directed from one party to the other), and aims to promote the agency of the less powerful party:

Application of an ethic of care requires interpreters to act in ways that empower Deaf people to lead their own fight against audism. This means that interpreters cede leadership to Deaf people, giving support to individuals and organizations that will, in their own time, challenge the disadvantage imposed on them. (p. 7)

This orientation manifests itself in Māori trilingual interpreters' expressed sense of alignment with, and responsibility towards MD people's cultural and social aspirations.

Social Values: Connectedness, Solidarity, and Deference

In the situation discussed in this chapter, the interpreter's perception and enactment of her role and responsibilities are conditioned by Māori social values, overlaid on professional skills. Especially influential are the Māori concepts of *kotahitanga* [collective unity], *whanaungatanga* [relatedness] and *tautoko* [support, solidarity], which define preferred ways of relating to others. These concepts promote the inter-relatedness of people, as opposed to "compartmentalization and over-strict differentiation of roles" (Metge, 1976, p.72). Hearing Māori participants thus tend to regard the interpreter as a participant with a supportive, rather than just relaying, function. Māori interpreters recognize this in the way that they represent their role to consumers as a collaborative one that supports the collective process:

> When I go into a Māori situation, I'll always say "I'm here to *tautoko*" [support]—but I wouldn't say "*awhi*" [help]. People see me as a support person, not just for the Deaf but for the whole whānau [family/collective]. So your role is presented slightly differently than in a Pākehā setting. You have to put it in a way that's understandable for them. The interpreter, whether they are Pākehā or Māori, can say, "I'm here to support the process, and my part in supporting this process is to translate everything that's spoken in the room." (Awheto 2004, quoted in Napier et al., 2006, p. 165)

The approach to negotiating a role in this context is more deferential than directive, in keeping with Māori norms for interpersonal relations.

> With *kaumātua* [elders], I would do a *mihi* [greeting and personal introduction] and return their acknowledgement. And I take on a passive role: I don't go in there telling them, "This is how it's going to work, and this is what I do. It's more like asking them if it's okay—taking a subservient role, saying "*Mātua* [male elder], is it okay for me to be standing here so I can do this?" rather than saying, "I'm going to be standing here, and this is how I'm

going to do my role." I have to maintain a culturally appropriate relationship. Being a woman too, I take the role of being quieter—I let them take the lead as to where I stand. If their suggestion isn't going to work, I'll drop a hint like "Maybe that will be a bit difficult Mātua, because they won't be able to see me—it might be good if we could do it there, for example." In a Pākehā setting, I'd go in, introduce myself, and say exactly where I need to be—or say "Where will you be sitting? I'll sit next to you." So with Māori generally, I'm less directive. I will say, "This is how it would best work," and wait and see how they can still manage to follow tikanga [custom] and accommodate for the Deaf and my needs as well. So we get there in the end but it takes a little bit longer.

In the extract above, Awheto indicates much "face work" being done before interpreting even begins, using culturally situated strategies to minimize her imposition on others and on the conventional sequence of events. In essence, this is simply effective professional practice that is sensitive to the context. Beyond mediating messages, interpreters must also respond to the sociopragmatic demands of the whole situation—trying to operate within cultural norms for how talk should proceed and how participant roles may be enacted. Much unconscious effort may go into this task; in this situation, these dimensions were at the forefront of the interpreter's mind.

In a double minority community (or any small social network), relationships and responsibilities in the interpreted situation are affected by wider and longer networks of contact with participants. Trilingual interpreters generally have extended interaction with Deaf and hearing Māori interlocutors beyond interpreting situations, sometimes including kinship connection. This not only alters perceptions of role boundaries and obligations, but may bring different considerations to the way that interaction is facilitated; for example, basing decisions on longer-term histories and ongoing relationships among participants, and also knowing that there will be time later to debrief with consumers about how the interpreted interaction played out.

Awheto's frame for defining her responsibility as an interpreter is therefore larger than a sense of professional role with a given situation. It extends to "including MD in our culture" by enabling connection with their cultural heritage via NZSL. As a trilingual Māori person at this time in the history of Deaf and Māori communities, Awheto feels responsible, both through and beyond her interpreting function, to "share my basket of knowledge"— a metaphor taken from a proverb about collective responsibility and reciprocity: *Nā tō rourou, nā taku rourou ka ora ai te iwi* [With your food basket and my food basket the people will thrive].

Sharing resources, (or cultural capital, in Bordieu's terms), and displaying ethnic solidarity are culturally motivated values that underpin Awheto's ethic to empower Māori Deaf. Karlin (2005, p. 6) might characterize this orientation as the kind of "feminist caring" that encourages autonomy and recognizes relational reciprocity. In view of MD people's sociocultural position, Awheto chooses at times to adopt a position that evokes the ally model of interpreting that emerged in the late 1980s from critical consciousness of Deaf people's disadvantaged position in society. This model recognized that interpreters potentially contribute consciously to the empowerment of Deaf people through their role in facilitating access to communication (Baker-Shenk, 1986).

CONCLUSION

We have examined how an indigenous interpreter negotiated a position as an interpreter in a trilingual situation involving hearing, Deaf, Māori, and Pākehā participants with disparate cultural schemas and discourse repertoires. In working with three languages, a prime challenge was to approximate pragmatic and discourse equivalence across wide linguaculture gaps. Our analysis highlights how the goal of constructing accessible interaction can motivate actions driven by cultural as well as professional imperatives. As an illustration of situated practice that departs from the canonical professional model, the interpreter's facilitating contributions here positioned her in a highly visible and multi-footed role, with the outcome of enabling a culturally hybrid event to transpire.

The actions of this interpreter reveal a conscious concern to protect the integrity of the cultural norms of all parties; at times, this meant adopting a position as mediator, encouraging each party to make their perspectives more explicit to the other, in order to mitigate potential social damage within and beyond the event.

Our case study reinforces that it is impossible to neutralize the impact of an interpreter's cultural orientation and identity on the way in which she negotiates her role and contributes to constructing the roles of others in a given interaction. The interpreter's decisions in mediating communication in this situation were clearly shaped by her own enculturation, her ethnic alliance with, and social network knowledge of, other participants, and were promoted by her tricultural perception of the gap between parties in knowing how to construct this particular event together. Studying interpreting experiences outside the more familiar majority culture contexts highlights that evaluating the impacts of interpreter practices must explicitly take into account the sociocultural factors shaping expectations and behavior in an interaction. The low-profile interpreter, grounded in Western modes of professionalism and social relations, does not capture the spectrum of situated practice realities in diverse cultural contexts; in many such contexts, the display of collaboration and connectedness is necessary to being trusted and getting things done.

REFERENCES

AKO Ltd. (1995). *Tautoko Tangata Turi. (Support Deaf Māori): A report for The Deaf Association of New Zealand.* Auckland, New Zealand: Te Puni Kokiri and the Auckland Deaf Association.
Angelelli, C. (2003). The visible co-participant: The interpreter's role in doctor-patient encounters. In M. Metzger, S. Collins, V. Dively, & R. Shaw (Eds.), *From topic boundaries to omission: New research on interpretation,* (pp. 3–26). Washington, DC: Gallaudet University Press.
Aramburo, A. (1989). Sociolinguistic aspects of the Black Deaf community. In C. Lucas (Ed.), *The sociolinguistics of the Deaf community.* New York: Academic Press.
Baker-Shenk, C. (1986). Characteristics of oppressed and oppressor peoples. In M. McIntire (Ed.), *Interpreting: The art of cross-cultural mediation* (pp. 43–53). Silver Spring, MD: RID Publications.
Berk-Seligson, S. (1990). *The bilingual courtroom: Court interpreters in the judicial process.* Chicago: University of Chicago Press.
Bot, H. (2003). The myth of the uninvolved interpreter interpreting in mental health and the development of a three-person psychology. In L. Brunette, G. Bastin, I. Hemlin, & H. Clarke (Eds.), *The critical link 3: Interpreters in the community* (pp. 27–36). Amsterdam: John Benjamins.
Bowe, H., & Martin, K. (2007). *Communication across cultures: Mutual understanding in a global world.* New York: Cambridge University Press.
Brennan, M. (1999). Signs of injustice. *The Translator, 5,* 221–46.
Brown, P., & Levinson, S. (1987). *Politeness: Some universals in language usage.* Cambridgeshire: Cambridge University Press.

Callister, P. (2004). Māori/non-Māori ethnic intermarriage. *New Zealand Population Review*, 29, 89–105.

Chapple, S. (2000). Māori socioeconomic disparity. *Political Science*, 52, 101–15.

Cokely, D. (2001). Exploring ethics: A case for revising the code of ethics. *Journal of Interpretation, Registry of Interpreters for the Deaf*. Silver Spring, MD: RID Publications.

Cooke, M. (2002). Indigenous interpreting issues for courts. *The Australasian Institute of Judicial Administration*, 64.

Coupland, N. (2007). *Style: Language variation and identity*. Cambridge: Cambridge University Press.

Davis, J., & Supalla, S. (1995). Language use in a Navajo family. In C. Lucas (Ed.), *The sociolinguistics of the Deaf community* (pp. 77–108). Washington DC: Gallaudet University Press.

Dean, R., & Pollard, R. (2001). The application of demand-control theory to sign language interpreting: Implications for stress and interpreter training. *Journal of Deaf Studies and Deaf Education*, 6, 1–14.

Dean, R., & Pollard, R. (2005). Consumers and service effectiveness in interpreting work: A practice profession perspective. In M. Marschark, R. Peterson & E. A. Winston (Eds.), *Interpreting and interpreter education: Directions for research and practice*. New York: Oxford University Press.

Dugdale, P. (2001). *Talking hands, listening eyes: The history of the Deaf Association of New Zealand*. Auckland: Deaf Association of New Zealand.

Gerner de Garcia, B. (1995). Communication and language use in Spanish speaking families with Deaf children. In C. Lucas (Ed.), *The sociolinguistics of the Deaf community* (pp. 221–44). Washington DC: Gallaudet University Press.

Goffman, E. (1974). *Frame analysis*. Cambridge, MA: Harvard University Press.

Gumperz, J. (1982). *Discourse strategies*. Cambridge: Cambridge University Press.

Hauser, P., Finch, K., & Hauser, A. (Eds.). (2008). *Deaf professionals and designated interpreters: A new paradigm*. Washington DC: Gallaudet University Press.

Holmes, J., & Marra, M. (2007, July). *Relativity rules: Politic talk in ethnicised workplaces*. Paper presented at The Third International Symposium on Politeness at the University of Leeds.

Holmes, J. (2003). Social constructionism. In W. J. Frawley (Ed.), *International encyclopedia of linguistics* (2nd ed.) (pp. 88–91). New York: Oxford University Press.

Hymes, D. (1972). Models of the interaction of language and social life. In J. Gumperz & D. Hymes (Eds.), *Directions in sociolinguistics* (pp. 35–71). New York: Holt, Rinehart & Winston.

James, M., & Woll, B. (2004). Black Deaf or Deaf Black? In A. Pavlenko & A. Blackledge (Eds.), *Negotiation of identities in multilingual contexts* (pp. 125–60). Bristol, UK: Multilingual Matters.

Jones, P. (1986). Issues involving Black interpreters and Black Deaf. In M. McIntire (Ed.), *Interpreting: The art of cross-cultural mediation* (pp. 61–68). Silver Spring, MD: RID Publications.

Karlin, B. (2005, March). *Should interpreters care?* Paper presented at Supporting Deaf People Online Conference.

Karlin. B. (2009, January). *Fair enough? In support of care ethics.* Paper presented at Supporting Deaf People Online Conference.

Leeson, L., & Foley-Cave, S. (2007). Deep and meaningful conversation: Challenging interpreter impartiality in the semantics and pragmatics classroom. In M. Metzger & E. Fleetwood (Eds.), *Translation, sociolinguistic, and consumer issues in interpreting: Studies in Interpretation Series, Volume 3* (pp. 45–70). Washington, DC: Gallaudet University Press.

Llewellyn-Jones, P., & Lee, R. (2009, January). *The 'role' of the community/ public service interpreter.* Paper presented at Supporting Deaf People Online Conference.

Marra, M. (2008). Recording and analyzing talk across cultures. In H. Spencer-Oatey (Ed.), *Culturally speaking: Culture, communication and politeness* (2nd ed.) (pp. 304–32). London: Continuum.

Martinez, L. (2007). Initial observations on code-switching in the voice interpretations of two Filipino Interpreters. In M. Metzger and E. Fleetwood (Ed.), *Translation, sociolinguistic, and consumer issues in interpreting* (pp. 71–102). Washington DC: Gallaudet University Press.

Mason, I., & Stewart, M. (2001). Interactional pragmatics, face, and the dialogue interpreter. In I. Mason (Ed.), *Triadic exchanges* (pp. 51–70). Manchester: St. Jerome Publishing.

McKee, R., McKee, D., Smiler, K., & Pointon, K. (2007). 'Māori Signs': The construction of indigenous Deaf identity in New Zealand Sign Language. In D. Quinto-Pozos (Ed.), *Signed languages in contact* (pp. 31–84). Washington, DC: Gallaudet University Press.

Metge, J. (1976). *The Māoris of New Zealand, Rautahi* (Rev. ed.). London: Routledge & Kegan Paul.

Metge, J., & Kinloch, P. (1978). *Talking past each other: Problems of cross-cultural communication.* Wellington: Victoria University Press.

Metzger, M. (1999). *Sign language interpreting: Deconstructing the myth of neutrality.* Washington, DC: Gallaudet University Press.

Mindess, A. (1999). *Reading between the signs: Intercultural communication for sign language interpreters.* Yarmouth, ME: Intercultural Press.

Moody, B. (2007). Literal vs. liberal: What is a faithful interpretation? *The Sign Language Translator and Interpreter, 1*, 179–220.

Morgan, E. (2008). Interpreters, conversational style, and gender at work. In P. Hauser, K. Finch & A. Hauser (Eds.), *Deaf professionals and designated interpreters: A new paradigm* (pp. 66–80). Washington, DC: Gallaudet University Press.

Napier, J., & Rohan, M. (2007). An invitation to dance: Deaf consumers' perceptions of sign language interpreters and interpreting. In M. Metzger & E. Fleetwood (Eds.), *Translation, sociolinguistic, and consumer issues in interpreting* (pp. 159–203). Washington DC: Gallaudet University Press.

Napier, J., McKee, R. & Goswell, D. (2006). *Sign language interpreting: Theory and practice in Australia and New Zealand.* Sydney: Federation Press.

Napier, J. (2001). *Linguistic coping strategies of sign language interpreters.* Doctoral thesis, Macquarie University, Australia.

O'Regan, H. (2001). *Ko Tahu, ko au: Kai Tahu tribal identity.* Christchurch: Horomaka.

Padden, C., & Humphries, T. (2005). *Inside Deaf culture.* Cambridge, MA: Harvard University Press.

Robson, B., & Harris, R. (2007). *Hauora, Māori standards of health. IV. A study of the years, 2000–2005.* Wellington: Te Ropu Rangahau Hauora a Eru Pomare.

Roy, C. (2000). *Interpreting as a discourse process.* Oxford: Oxford University Press.

Salmond, A. (1977). *Hui: A study of Māori ceremonial gatherings.* Auckland: Reed.

Schiffrin, D. (1994). *Approaches to discourse.* Cambridge, MA: Blackwell.

Schnurr, S., Marra, M. & Holmes, J. (2007). Being (im)polite in New Zealand workplaces: Māori and Pākehā leaders. *Journal of Pragmatics, 39,* 712–29.

Smiler, K., & McKee, R. (2007). Perceptions of Māori Deaf identity in New Zealand. *Journal of Deaf Studies and Deaf Education, 12*(1), 93–111.

Smiler, K. (2004). *Māori Deaf: Perceptions of cultural and linguistic identity of Māori members of the New Zealand Deaf community.* Master's thesis, Victoria University of Wellington.

Smith, L. T. (1999). *Decolonising methodologies: Research and indigenous people.* Dunedin, NZ: University of Otago Press.

Statistics New Zealand. (2001). National Māori population projections (2001–2021). Statistics New Zealand.

Stewart, K., & Witter-Merrithew, A. (2004, February). *Teaching ethical standards and practice within pre-service and in-service interpreter education programs.* Paper presented at Supporting Deaf People Online Conference.

Tate, G., & Turner, G. H. (2001). The code and the culture: sign language interpreting—in search of the new breed's ethics. In F. Harrington and G. H. Turner (Eds.), *Interpreting: Studies and reflections on sign language interpreting* (pp. 53–66). Coleford, UK: Douglas McLean.

Te Puni Kokiri & Te Taura Whiri i te Reo Māori. (2003). *Te Rautaki Reo Māori: The Māori language strategy.* Wellington: Ministry of Māori Development.

Turner, G. H. (2005). Toward real interpreting. In M. Marschark, R. Peterson, & E. Winston (Eds.), *Sign language interpreting and interpreter education: Directions for research and practice* (pp. 29–56). New York: Oxford University Press.

Wadensjö, C. (1998). *Interpreting as interaction.* London: Longman.

Wadensjö, C. (2001). Interpreting in crisis: The interpreter's position in therapeutic encounters. In I. Mason (Ed.), *Triadic exchanges: Studies in dialogue interpreting* (pp. 71–86). Manchester: St. Jerome.

Wenger, E. (1998). *Communities of practice.* Cambridge: Cambridge University Press.

Wenger, E. (2008). Communities of practice: A brief introduction. Retrieved June 29, 2008, from http://www.ewenger.com/theory/index.htm.

Winston, E. (2004). Interpretability and accessibility of mainstream classrooms. In E. Winston (Ed.), *Educational interpreting: How it can succeed* (pp. 132–68). Washington DC: Gallaudet University Press.

Signed Languages of American Indian Communities: Considerations for Interpreting Work and Research

Jeffrey E. Davis and Melanie McKay-Cody

This chapter explores the roles of signed language interpreters working in American Indian and Alaskan Native (AI/AN) settings.[1] The findings reported here are based on the authors' ethnographic fieldwork and observations from over two decades of combined experiences—collaborating, interpreting, and participating in North American Indian communities. The central focus of our collaborative research (1990–present) has been the study of traditional and contemporary varieties of indigenous sign language used among North American Indian communities. From 1995 to 2000 we also served as consultants for the National Multicultural Interpreting Project (NMIP). This chapter features the combined results of our research studies and reexamines the major objectives and outcomes of the NMIP, in order to suggest strategies, best practices, and links to resources for signed language interpreters working in these contexts.

Sign language interpreters are called to work in a variety of AI/AN (Native) settings and there is great linguistic and cultural diversity among Native individuals and groups. Though approximately 200 American Indian languages are spoken in the United States and Canada today, the majority of these are endangered, with about one-third of these languages

1. *American Indian and Alaskan Native* is the convention recommended by the National Congress of American Indians (http://www.ncai.org/). *Native* is the more commonly used shorter term. Depending on the reference cited and context, the terms AI/AN and Native are used alternately. While labeling conventions are sometimes necessary in written language, *it is extremely important to recognize that Native individuals and communities, both Deaf and hearing, are heterogeneous populations with diverse languages and cultures.*

being nearly extinct (cf. Mithun, 1999). Currently, there is an extreme urgency to maintain and revitalize Native languages.[2]

The rapid decline of Native languages in past years has been due to many historical, social, cultural, and educational factors, which are being called to attention in this chapter. One of the main outcomes of intensive language and cultural contact has been a shift towards English as the dominant or primary language of most Native individuals. These matters are tightly intertwined, and rendered more complex considering the variety of signed and spoken languages used among American cultural groups (e.g., Deaf, American Indian, and Deaf Native).

DEAF NATIVE VOICES

In the literature (Dively, 2001; Goff-Paris & Wood, 2002; McKay-Cody, 1997, 1998, 1999; Miller, 2004; NMIP, 2000) the shorter term *Deaf Native* is generally used instead longer official designations such as *Deaf American Indian/Alaska Native* or *Deaf First Nations of Canada*. The label *Deaf Native* reflects that cultural identities are predicated on a complex array of factors and choices—for example, degree of assimilation or membership and multiple cultural backgrounds. Deaf Natives often walk in *three worlds* and three distinct cultural experiences—Deaf American, American Indian, and Deaf Native. The notion of interpreting between multiple thought worlds and cultural identities is a unifying theme of the chapters in this section of the volume.

As mentioned above, a major consequence of intensive language and cultural contact has been a shift towards English as the dominant or primary language of most individuals from AI/AN backgrounds. Likewise, Deaf Natives of the United States and Canada generally attend schools for the deaf and are predominately learning American Sign Language

2. *Language revitalization* involves Native individuals and communities in language *documentation* (e.g., storytelling narratives and the oral histories of elders) and linguistic *description* (e.g., the lexicon and grammar); and uses modern technologies to develop sustainable resources for the language to be studied.

(ASL) instead of the traditional varieties of North American Indian Sign Language (NAISL).[3]

American Sign Language is the predominant sign language of most Deaf Natives in the United States and Canada. At the same time, sign language interpreters working in Native contexts may come into contact with NAISL varieties. Depending on language group, cultural affiliation, and geographic location, interpreters may also encounter one or more of the spoken American Indian languages. Interpreters cannot generally be expected to be proficient in the multiple signed and spoken indigenous languages they might potentially encounter in AI/AN contexts. However, later in this chapter, we will be considering certain interpretation/translation techniques and multicultural interpreting approaches designed to enhance comprehension and increase awareness about interpreting in Native settings.

This chapter is the first to bring together our linguistic research about North American Indian Sign Language (NAISL) and ethnographic fieldwork about the experiences of Deaf Natives in the United States and Canada. We have struggled to do justice to topics as vast and multifaceted as Native languages and cultures. Signed language interpreters are called to work in a broad range of settings involving Native individuals from diverse backgrounds. With this in mind, we have referenced other major works containing a cornucopia of information about Native histories, languages, and cultures as well as web-based resources for interpreters and others interested in studying these subjects. Again, it is important to recognize that Native individuals and communities, either Deaf or hearing, are heterogeneous populations representing diverse languages and cultural backgrounds. The purpose of the categorizations and macro-descriptions of multicultural groups and multiple languages presented here are to broadly frame the places, participants, and practices common between Deaf Native (AI/AN) contexts.

3. The varieties of indigenous signed language used among North America Indian groups are collectively referred to as *North American Indian Sign Language* (Davis, 2007; Wurtzburg & Campbell, 1995; McKay-Cody, 1997, 1998, 1999)

REVIEW OF PREVIOUS RESEARCH

The co-authors' (Davis and McKay-Cody) linguistic research and ethnographic fieldwork have focused on the indigenous signed language varieties of North American Indians.[4] Historically, the extreme linguistic and cultural diversity of North America led to frequent contact between Native groups speaking mutually unintelligible languages. It has been well documented in the research literature that a highly conventionalized and linguistically enriched signed language emerged as a means of communication between various American Indian language groups—a signed *lingua franca* of sorts (Campbell, 2000; Davis, 2005, 2006, 2007; McKay-Cody, 1997, 1998; Mithun, 1999; Taylor, 1978, 1997). The focus of our linguistic research has been cases of indigenous sign language being used and transmitted across generations among North American Indians.

Indigenous Sign Language Studies

Though the use of sign language is generally associated with individuals who are Deaf, several types of indigenous signing communities have also emerged globally. Both historically and contemporarily, conventionalized signed languages have developed among some hearing indigenous communities *as an alternative to spoken languages*, in addition to being the primary languages of Deaf communities.

Our previous studies compared the use of indigenous sign language between Deaf communities and predominately hearing communities. Two broad categories of signed language have been suggested, each containing several other types of sign language (ibid.). Though further elaboration about each of these types is beyond the present focus, these broad categories help frame our references to signed language being used in Native settings. At the same time, these categories are not mutually exclusive—there is interaction between primary and

4. Different varieties of indigenous sign language have been identified among American Indian groups (e.g., Inuit-Inupiaq, Keresan Pueblo, Navajo/Diné, among others). Plains Indian Sign Language (PISL) has been the most well documented and described variety of American Indian signed language (cf. Davis, 2007; McKay-Cody, 1997; Taylor, 1978, 1997; West, 1960). These varieties of American Indian signed language are broadly categorized as NAISL.

alternate types of signed language and historical language contact among these signing communities.

Primary signed languages have evolved within specific historical, social, and cultural contexts and have been transmitted and acquired natively from one generation to the next—such as ASL, Mexican Sign Language (LSM), or New Zealand Sign Language (NZSL). Signed language has also emerged within some communities that were predominately hearing, but with a high incidence of genetic deafness—such as the historical case of Martha's Vineyard, Massachusetts (Groce, 1985), or the present-day occurrence of Al-Sayyid Bedouin Sign Language (Sandler, Meir, Padden & Aronoff, 2005).

Alternate signed languages have been developed and used by individuals who are already competent in spoken language. Well documented with some indigenous communities around the world: South America (Umiker-Sebeok & Sebeok, 1978) and Central Australia (Kendon, 1988).

McKay-Cody (1997) went further than earlier studies and described what happened when the alternate signed language of North American Indian cultural groups was acquired as a primary sign language by members of the group who are deaf. The deaf members of these Native groups demonstrated a higher level of sign language proficiency when compared to hearing members of these groups. These findings suggested that the alternate sign language becomes linguistically enriched when learned as a primary language by members of these Native communities who are deaf.

In short, the sociolinguistic evidence suggests that alternate signs are used to varying degrees of proficiency, ranging from signs that accompany speech, to signing without speech, to signing that functions similarly to a primary sign language. In other words, these forms of signing are best considered along a communication continuum (Davis, 2007).

As mentioned earlier, due to sociocultural and historical factors, fewer AI/AN individuals are learning Native languages—signed or spoken. Few Deaf Natives have been learning traditional Native ways of signing for two main reasons. First, Deaf Natives are predominately using ASL and no longer learning NAISL. Second, signed language has been replaced by English as the lingua franca among North American Indian nations. The fact that NAISL has survived and continues to be used is remarkable, especially considering the pressures for linguistic and cultural assimilation historically imposed on indigenous peoples.

Although NAISL is considered endangered, and the extant number of varieties and users is unknown, it has not vanished. It is still used within some Native groups in traditional storytelling, rituals, legends, prayers, conversational narratives, and is still being learned by a few Deaf Natives. Thus, in some AI/AN contexts, interpreters may encounter varieties of indigenous signed language, as in formal ceremonies, making introductions, showing name signs for tribes, or signing traditional cultural narratives.

Revitalization of NAISL

Today, most indigenous languages around the world are endangered (Crystal, 2000). Language documentation and description for the purpose of revitalizing an endangered language are enormous undertakings. Native leaders and other community members have generally recognized and even embraced the need to record and preserve their languages, traditions, and cultural practices for this and future generations—as long as the documentary materials are treated with respect when made available outside of American Indian communities. As interpreters and researchers we must be aware and sensitive about storytelling traditions—e.g., some signed or spoken narratives are intended for sacred purposes, and some stories should be shared only in the winter season or at night. For the work of language revitalization to be successful it is essential to involve native users of the endangered language. Interpreters/translators, ethnographers, and linguistic researchers are potentially Native community allies in these efforts.

For nearly two decades, we have been developing a corpus of NAISL documentary materials in the form of written texts, lexical descriptions, illustrations, and films critical to language preservation, scholarship, and revitalization. This includes descriptions, illustrations, and films showing Indian lexical signs spanning more than two hundred years (1800–present). To allow readers to view examples of NAISL, we have established a research website featuring a language corpus of historical documentary materials from written, illustrated, and filmed sources (http://sunsite.utk .edu/plainssignlanguage/).[5]

5. We have also collected films of North American Indians signing from the 1930s up until the present time. Though these are central to our studies (reported below) the website presently features only the historical NAISL data. Our documentation and description of these signed language varieties is ongoing.

Looking to the Horizon

The authors have been encouraged by American Indian individuals, groups, and communities to continue our research of sign language in Native communities. During our fieldwork we have frequently encountered Deaf Natives who are keenly interested in participating in their Native communities and learning as much as possible about their cultural heritage. We are strongly committed to working with Native communities where indigenous signed language continues to be learned today. While the study of indigenous signed language is a major focus of our collaborative research, this work has also been informed by our years of experience in the field of sign language interpretation and education.

In sum, interpreters working in Native communities are likely to encounter a variety of signed *and* spoken indigenous languages. We now shift our attention to the array of AI/AN multicultural domains, in which interpreters are called to work. The chief aim is to examine ways that interpreters can work more effectively in Native contexts through increasing awareness, developing alliances, and forming interpreting in teams with individuals from Native backgrounds. While the following principles and practices are particularly critical to interpreting in AI/AN multicultural and multilingual contexts, they are also broadly applicable and inform many areas of general interpretation/translation work.

THE NATIONAL MULTICULTURAL INTERPRETING PROJECT (NMIP)

One decade has passed since the results of the NMIP were published (2000), and we reexamine the major objectives and recommendations most relevant to interpreting in AI/AN communities. The NMIP (1996–2000) was funded by the U.S. Department of Education to assist interpreter preparation programs with curriculum reform to address the interpreting needs of individuals who are D/deaf and Deaf-blind from diverse cultures. The project implemented a national multicultural interpreter consortium, published the results of the project's collaborative research findings, provided assistance to federally supported regional interpreter training projects, developed and disseminated four curriculum packages (*American Indian/Alaskan Native, African American, Asian American,* and *Hispanic American*), and provided training that focused on increasing awareness of cultural and linguistic diversity among practitioners, educators, students, and consumers of interpretation (see Mooney, 2006).

The following sections highlight some of the main tenets of the NMIP's (2000) *American Indian/Alaskan Native Curriculum Modules* (*AI/AN Curriculum*, for short).[6]

AI/AN Interpreting Objectives

The NMIP involved extensive collaboration among numerous AI/AN community members, consultants, and interpreter practitioners (including the author's of this chapter). These collective efforts spanned the five-year period of the project (1996–2000) and resulted in the development of the *AI/AN Curriculum* comprised of several modules, position papers, and films. These modules contain an abundance of cultural information and numerous activities designed to enhance interpreter preparation and practice in AI/AN contexts.

One of the overarching themes of the *AI/AN Curriculum* is the importance of interpreters recognizing the diversity of American Indians/ Alaskan Natives. The senior editor of the *AI/AN Curriculum* (2000), Howard Busby (Mississippi Choctaw/Eastern Cherokee), described that the chief defining objective was: "*Inclusion*—the experience of full participation in this project was the driving force, yet there was an urgent need to capture these words, thoughts, concepts, or descriptions that could convey a sense of the culture we were attempting to describe without falling into stereotype" (p. 1). Busby also writes that:

> Our aim is not to get the student [of interpretation] to understand everything Indian, but simply to help them become aware that there are perhaps more differences among tribes than they had previously thought. As the student starts to become more comfortable with the various signs, concepts, and cultural positions of interpreting with and for American Indians and Alaskan Natives, it is hoped that further study and awareness of particular groups or tribes would ensue.

This reflects *an* overarching principle of multicultural interpreting work. That is, interpreters can cultivate greater awareness of racial, ethnic,

---

6. The NMIP curriculum is available online through The National Consortium of Interpreter Education Centers (NCIEC) http://www.asl.neu.edu/ TIEM.online/curriculum_nmip.html.

cultural, and linguistic diversity through the formation of intercultural alliances and participation in multicultural activities—e.g., community-based learning, interpreting teams, and mentorship. Simply stated, the chief objective is that interpreters become more aware of their own cultural heritages and increase their knowledge about other cultures.

Respect for Native Nomenclature

Recognizing that AI/AN communities are highly diverse linguistically and culturally; the first learning objective highlighted in the *AI/AN Curriculum* (p. 2) is to "*identify and explore the diversity of labels and cultural communities encompassed by the term American Indian/Alaskan Native.*" Awareness of various naming practices, preferences, and meanings of some common cultural terms are especially critical to interpretation and translation. Fundamentally, there are multiple ways of describing self and others—such as, terms used within the cultural group and with outsiders, to describe animate and inanimate entities, traditional and contemporary usage, and so forth.

Evan Pritchard (descendent of the Micmac people of the Algonquin Nations) and author of *Native New Yorkers: The Legacy of the Algonquin People of New York*, has written: "By naming something, we take possession of it; by losing that name, we lose possession of it" (2002, p. 15). It is essential to keep in mind that naming is the province of the native groups themselves. At the same time, individuals from various Native communities do have different naming practices and preferences. If this were not complicated enough, we find different terminology and labeling conventions, often specific to each group, professional/academic discipline, or government.

Some terms (e.g., *Aboriginal* or *Native American*) have been coined by Europeans or Euro-Americans and/or for governmental purposes (e.g., in the United States, Canada, or Australia). Although the term *Native American* has been widely used and considered "politically correct," it is also a non-specific term.[7] Generally, members of these cultural groups refer to themselves as *Indians* (Karttunen, 1994). However, the term *American Indian* is sometimes needed to distinguish individuals from the country of

---

7. The term *Native American* was coined by the Department of the Interior to classify together all of the Indigenous Peoples of the United States, and its trust territories—including native Hawaiians, American Samoans, Alaskan Natives, and the Indigenous People of Puerto Rico.

India, and *North American Indian* distinguishes the indigenous peoples of North America from those of Central and South America.

Ideally, specific tribal affiliation or cultural-linguistic groups are acknowledged whenever possible, for example, Assiniboine, Blackfoot, Eastern Cherokee, Inuit, Lakota, Northern Cheyenne. Whenever possible, we have used the newer self-designations of AI/AN groups; though these terms are used interchangeably depending on the historical contexts and individual sources being cited. Interpreters can expect to encounter a great deal of diversity in terms of naming preferences and practices and it is generally best to ask the individuals themselves of their naming preferences, and to respect the traditional practices of native groups. For example, Melanie McKay-Cody (co-author of this chapter) identifies herself as Cherokee-Choctaw; and she also has been adopted by the Okemsis Band of the Willow Cree First Nation.

Recognizing Indian Nations and Tribes

Waldman (2000, p. vii) writes that "many contemporary Native Americans prefer the term *nation* rather than *tribe*, because it implies the concept of political sovereignty, indicating that their people have goals and rights like other nations." According to the *AI/AN Curriculum* (2000, p. 2), "Nations are divided into tribes, bands, and clans. In Alaska, a nation may be composed of many villages and corporations." A clan is defined as "a family-based infrastructure, including extended family members, and adopted members, who share common ancestors." Thus, nations may be comprised of several tribes, which may encompass several clans.

Culturally specific terms and references to tribal affiliations are also commonly used in Native contexts. For example, Busby (2000) writes:

> *Mi takuye oyasin!* These Lakota words perhaps capture the essence and the spirit of the American Indians and Alaskan Natives. The closest English translation of these words would be; "all my relations." To the Lakota and most other tribes or nations in North America, the concept behind these words goes beyond human description, beyond human relations, and indeed beyond the ability of any language to do them justice. When these words are uttered by American Indians, there is no conscious effort at description or explanation. It is just simply a thought process that includes every animate and inanimate object on earth, in the sky, and below the ground. It involves a consciousness carried through seven generations and to be passed on to the next seven generations. It encompasses the four sacred directions, mother earth, grandfather sky,

and the ground upon which one stands. It is part of their belief system, yet is more than simple spiritual experience. (p. 1)

This passage exemplifies that in AI/AN contexts even the cardinal directions have multiple meanings based upon cultural and spiritual nuances.

THE PEOPLE

In the preface of the *AI/AN Curriculum* (2000), Howard Busby writes:

All tribes view themselves as "the people," as can be seen in their names for themselves, but this does not mean that they see other tribes as different, alien or less than themselves. The names they have for themselves: Lakota, Cheyenne, Muskogee, Cherokee, Choctaw, Mohawk, and numerous others are really identities of pride to which the tribal member can point as his or her source of being. In other words, American Indians do not identify themselves in isolation from their tribe or nation. (p. 1)

Traditionally, some native groups have called themselves "The Principle People," or "Keepers of the Fire." For example, Melanie sometimes identifies herself as being from "The Thunderbolt People." Signs from NAISL are typically used to convey these affiliations depending on individual nomenclature.

SOVEREIGN RIGHTS

The terms *nation* and *culture* are generally preferred over *tribe*, which more accurately refers to a non-state group of genetically related people. The justification for sovereign American Indian groups to be considered nations has been maintained into the twenty-first century by leaders and members of these communities. Stuart (1987, p. 3) has described that "American Indian communities have a unique political relationship to the United States, enjoying what has come to be called a 'government to government' relationship." As sovereign entities (i.e., distinct culturally, politically, and nationally), the First Nations/American Indians of the United States and Canada could be considered *nations within nations*. The Canadian government uses the term *First Nations* to respect the rights of indigenous people to describe themselves.[8]

8. *First Nation* is not an official designation in the United States, and the term is also not without controversy. Collectively, First Nations, Inuit, and Métis peoples constitute Canada's indigenous peoples; suggesting that these people are the sole original occupiers of the land that is now Canada. However, the Inuit are also ancient inhabitants, but not included in the term *First Nations*.

Demographic and Geographic Considerations

Knowledge about the histories, politics, traditions, and languages of the community are essential elements of interpreting work. In addition to stressing the importance of naming practices, the *AI/AN Curriculum* (2000) aims to help interpreters better understand "the implications and impacts of demographics and geographic locations of American Indian and Alaskan Natives in general and what is known regarding the percentage of D/deaf, Hard of Hearing, and Deaf-Blind in those communities" (p. 1). This goal addresses the varying demand for interpreting services in AI/AN communities depending on geographic locations ranging from reservation to urban.

The 2000 Census reported that the U.S. population was 281.4 million (304 million and growing based on 2008 estimates).[9] The Census counted individuals who reported "American Indian and Alaska Native" as their principal or enrolled tribe—that is, people having origins in any of the original peoples of North and South America (including Central America), and who maintain tribal affiliation or community attachment.[10] In the 2000 Census, 4.1 million (1.5%) individuals identified themselves as AI/AN. This number included 2.5 million people who reported only American Indian and Alaska Native in addition to 1.6 million people who reported American Indian and Alaska Native as well as one or more other races.

Number of AI/AN Individuals Who Are Deaf

The exact number of AI/AN individuals who are deaf, deaf-blind, or hard of hearing is indeterminate, as the U.S. Census does not collect population data about individual disabilities. This makes it necessary to estimate the number of individuals with a hearing loss based on other criteria. Miller (2004, p. 4) draws from prevailing statistical estimates that 9% of the U.S. population have some degree of hearing loss, including 2% who are generally identified as deaf and hard of hearing. Based on several prevalence studies indicating that hearing loss among American Indians

9. Retrieved June 11, 2008 from http://www.census.gov/population/www/popclockus.html.

10. The U.S. Census requires only that ethnic or racial identity be self-proclaimed, and no documentary proof is required.

and Alaska Natives to be higher than that of the general population, Miller (ibid.) estimated that 4% of the AI/AN population are deaf or hard of hearing (i.e., individuals with a significant to profound hearing loss). Applying Miller's 4% estimate to the 2000 U.S. Census's roughly 4.5 million AI/AN residents gives us 180,000 AI/AN individuals who are deaf or hard of hearing in the United States. These figures are only estimates, and do not suggest that all of the American Indians/Alaska Natives who have a severe to profound hearing loss are culturally Deaf, or that they would be exposed to sign language or the services of a sign language interpreter.

DEAF NATIVES

Deaf Native is commonly used instead of the longer designations of "Deaf American Indian/Alaska Native" and "Deaf First Nations of Canada" (Dively, 2001; Goff-Paris & Wood, 2002; McKay-Cody, 1997, 1998, 1999; Miller, 2004). Nevertheless, it is important to keep in mind that the term *Native* is not exclusive to any one indigenous language or cultural group and is somewhat comparable to other generic reference terms for multicultural/multinational groups (e.g., African, Asian, Australian, European, etc.) or multiethnic groups (e.g., Anglo, Black, Hispanic, etc.). Cultural identities are predicated on a complex array of factors and choices like degree of assimilation and multiple cultural backgrounds. To help illustrate this, Christensen (2000, p. 267) uses this example: "a Deaf man, born and raised in the Navajo nation, might choose to identify himself as Deaf Navajo, Navajo Deaf, Deaf Native American Indian, American Indian Deaf, or one of another set of descriptors which he feels best communicate the way in which he chooses to identify himself." Again, finding a common reference term for populations as diverse as American Indians proves challenging.

Based on our years of fieldwork in these communities (1990–present), we have preliminarily identified approximately one thousand Deaf Native individuals. Thus far our studies have focused mainly on American Indian groups in the United States. These findings suggest that the Navajo and Cherokee are two American Indian groups with the largest number of deaf members, which is not surprising given that these are the largest nations today. At the same time, many Deaf Natives have been identified within most of the other AI/AN groups of the United States and Canada. Further research surveys and fieldwork are currently underway (McKay-Cody, Davis, and collaborators).

Tribes and Nations

The NMIP's theme of diversity among AI/AN groups is borne out by the large number of extant tribes. According to the Bureau of Indian Affairs (BIA) there are 561 federal recognized tribal governments in the United States. The 2001 Canada Census recognizes 123 First Nations communities (i.e., reserves); 53 Inuit Communities in Arctic regions; and 38 communities with high concentrations of Métis people, or a large number of Indigenous people. In the United States there are approximately 245 "federally non-recognized" tribes. However, many of these are in the process of making proposals to become federally recognized. Most of the federally non-recognized tribes are already recognized by the states in which they are located, but not yet at the federal level. For example, the Lumbee Tribe of North Carolina is the largest non-federally recognized American Indian Tribe in the United States. California also has a large number of federally non-recognized tribes.[11]

To outsiders, these determinations may at first glance seem trivial. However, they are often high-stakes, potentially impacting land rights, entitlements, and tribal membership. Signed language interpretation is critical to Deaf Natives' inclusion and participation.

FULL-BLOODED INDIAN (FBI) OR MIXED-BLOOD INDIAN (MBI)

AI/AN population descriptions are elusive because of the reliance on self-identification, blood quantum, varying terms and definitions. Miller (2004) writes that:

> This is due in part to the difference between the official federal definition of blood quantum and tribal definitions based on membership and birth. An additional factor is the perception of the individual regarding his or her heritage. For example, one may be self-identified as American Indian or Alaskan Native, yet not officially listed on tribal rolls or federal registers such as the Bureau of Indian Affairs (BIA). Even public and tribal schools have differing identity criteria that may not be based in the same demographic descriptors. (p. 3)

To identify the degree of one's Indian ancestry or genetic background (e.g., blood quantum), members of AI/AN communities sometimes use

---

11. An extensive proposal process is required to be recognized at the federal level, which is also administered through the BIA.

the terms *Full-blooded Indian* (FBI) and *Mixed-blood Indian* (MBI). These acronyms are commonly used among Deaf Natives—especially among the members and participants of the Intertribal Deaf Council (IDC). Within most AI/AN groups there are often serious discussions regarding the imposition of blood quantum to determine membership, levels of participation, and benefits that may accrue from being recognized as an Indian.

For example, Phil Fontaine, National Chief of the Assembly of First Nations (see footnote 1), and others have argued that a citizenship-based membership for each First Nation is needed, instead of memberships based predominately on bloodlines, race theories, and records of ancestry. In addition to blood quantum, membership could be based on other factors, such as loyalty to one's community and familial ties and knowledge about the histories, politics, traditions, and languages of one's community.

URBANIZATION
Further complicating cultural membership is the trend towards urbanization, the movement of American Indians and Alaskan Natives to cities and towns from reservations, ancestral Indian lands, Indian towns, or Indian country, and the cultural shift that accompanies this geographic shift. Today, the majority of Native Americans/Alaskan Natives (more than 60%) live outside the reservations (AI/AN 2000, p. 11). Also, the 2000 U.S. Census reported that 43.3% of the AI/AN population were living in 15 major U.S. cities. They attended public schools or in some cases attended Indian Schools located in or near some cities. Almost one half (49%) of the Canadian AI/AN population lived in urban areas.[12]

RESERVATIONS
The reservation is commonly called the "rez" and often fingerspelled R-E-Z in ASL (by Deaf Natives), even for land that has been divided into allotments and has lost reservation status (AI/AN 2000, p. 3). Individuals who grew up on the reservation (U.S.) or reserve (Canada) generally have very different cultural experiences and views from those who grew up in urban areas. Moving away from the reservation can lead to individuals

12. Information retrieved June 12, 2008, from http://www12.statcan.ca/ english/census06/data/topics/.

being isolated from tribal affiliations and extended family. Today there are 304 reservations and trust lands in the United States and 123 reserves in Canada. In the United States, the largest reservation and trust land populations are Navajo, Pine Ridge (Oglala Sioux), Fort Apache, Gila River, Papago (Tohono O'odham), Rosebud (Rosebud Sioux a.k.a. Sicangu Oyate), Hopi, San Carlos (Apache), Zuni Pueblo, and Blackfeet.[13]

In the United States, Indian reservations are mainly spread across the Southwestern and Northwestern states, and mostly in remote locations from which one must drive many hours to reach a major urban center. For example, the Navajo reservation, the nation's largest, straddles four states (hence the "Four Corners") but lies several hours' drive from any city. Likewise, many Deaf Natives live in remote areas—in an "invisible country" of sorts. Melanie McKay-Cody (1999, p. 49) reports that many Deaf Americans have often asked: "Where are the Deaf Indians?" McKay-Cody has studied, written, and presented extensively about the "well-hidden people," (i.e., Deaf Natives) who often straddle multiple cultures—that is "a group within the Deaf and Native Communities."

EDUCATIONAL EXPERIENCES OF DEAF NATIVES

One of the major contemporary issues identified in the *AI/AN Curriculum* (2000) concerned "raising Indian children and maintaining the traditional cultural linkages with family and community" (p. 37). Many common experiences were reported among Deaf Native participants. In most cases, Deaf Natives attended residential schools for the deaf instead of living and attending school on the reservation. This often leads to very different cultural views and preferences compared with individuals who grew up on the reservation. Many Deaf Natives who attended state residential schools for the deaf acquired ASL and Deaf culture. They usually did not have the same access or opportunities as their hearing family members did to acquire Indian cultural ways and languages.

In the past, many Deaf Natives were stripped of their native culture. While attending residential schools for the deaf, they were often told not to follow Native cultural traits or ways of the tribe, clan, or family.

13. Information retrieved June 12, 2008, from http://www.nps.gov/history/nagpra/DOCUMENTS/ResMapIndex.htm.

Consequently, this has led to artificial and stereotypical labels and misconceptions of what American Indians should look like in the eyes of the dominant or majority culture. For example, Deaf Native individuals who have attended IDC conferences (1994 to present) "often have shared experiences of having a lack of cultural support during their school years; having a lack of Indian Deaf role models or staff; remembering the curriculum as Euro-centric [e.g., Columbus discovered America]; remembering prejudicial treatment such as being 'deloused' or having one's hair cut without parental permission" (AI/AN 2000, p. 37).

While the experiences of Deaf Natives have been highlighted in the *AI/AN Curriculum* and described in the literature (Dively, 2001; Goff-Paris & Wood, 2002; McKay-Cody, 1997, 1998, 1999; Miller, 2004) additional ethnographic studies about the unique enculturation experiences of AI/AN children who are deaf are needed. In short, geographical, historical, social, cultural, and educational threads are tightly interwoven in Native contexts. These form the fabric of the Deaf Native experience.

Between Worlds

Deaf Native identity is predicated on a complex array of social, cultural, and educational factors and choices, which impacts individual cultural affiliation and degree of assimilation. The *AI/AN Curriculum* (p. 37) reported a variety of individual Deaf Native experiences—ranging from limited or no cultural assimilation to greater acculturation; for example, "individuals who due to the early influences of Indian Sign Language had direct access to the cultural knowledge and teachings of their nations." Though some educational and enculturation experiences "resulted in a disconnection or dissonance from community life and language; and a lack of recognition of cultural values and languages that the individual possessed," the AI/AN curriculum also reminds us that "each individual experience is unique based on all of the factors of deafness such as age of onset, degree of loss and in addition the cultural acculturation and assimilation influences experienced by other Indian peoples. Deaf Natives often walk in three worlds and three distinct cultural experiences." Likewise, the notion of interpreting between multiple *thought worlds* and cultures is a unifying theme across the chapters of this volume.

In the course of our fieldwork, we have met hundreds of Deaf Native adults who managed to learn about their tribal culture in adulthood in the face of the complexities and challenges described above. Often times their experience would be shared and acquired through inter-tribal learning, rather than learned directly from their own tribes or clans. Moreover, during gatherings where sign language interpreters are available or provided, some Deaf Natives are exposed to and learn about tribal and cultural traditions. While sign language interpretation serves a major function in these and other contexts, this does not suggest it replaces the vital role of direct linguistic and cultural transmission.[14] Furthermore, we have observed that Deaf Natives who are exposed to and have access to a tribe's cultural teaching and learning often serve as mentors to the Deaf Natives who have little or no experience in their tribal traditions.

In summary, the *AI/AN Curriculum Modules* (NMIP 2000) identified a range of assimilation and enculturation factors common among the reported experiences of Deaf Natives—such as "reservation versus urban up-bringing, distance or closeness to extended family"; "educational experiences including state school and mainstream experiences"; and "religious affiliations—traditional spirituality versus other religious influences" (p. 24). Deaf members of other minority or ethnic groups—such as Hispanic, Asian, or African American—reported similar enculturation challenges. And according to the NMIP (2000), Deaf individuals from minority or ethnic backgrounds can easily encounter "double discrimination." As members of hearing cultural groups, deaf people generally do not have the same access to spoken language, which is a major vehicle for cultural transmission. Thus, deaf people often share different experiences (e.g., educational placements and Deaf culture) than the hearing members of the same ethnic group. See Christensen (2000), McKee and Awheto (this volume), and Ramsey and Peña (this volume) for additional descriptions about the enculturation experiences of deaf individuals from minority and ethnic backgrounds.

SPOKEN LANGUAGE INTERPRETATION IN AI/AN COMMUNITIES

The NMIP (2000) made historical reference to native peoples' distrust of interpreters, who were sometimes seen as being aligned with dominant European-American cultural forces. In reviewing the literature, we

14. This is also borne out in other studies of sign language interpretation in educational settings (Marschark, Peterson, & Winston, 2005).

find a dearth of research about signed or spoken language interpretation in AI/AN communities. In the United States, the only American Indian language that has a formal interpretation certification process is Navajo. Navajo interpreters are used mainly in Arizona and New Mexico in legal and medical settings, generally involving Navajo speakers with limited English proficiency.[15]

Recent studies conducted by a cohort of medical doctors and practitioners (McCabe, Morgan, Curley, Begay, & Gohdes, 2005) described some of the problems that Navajo interpreters encounter in medical settings, especially translating medical terminology and disease pathologies to Navajo patients. The researchers collaborated with Navajo interpreters and conducted comparative assessments of the initial translations, with back translations and final translations of medical terms, forms, and interviews. Although translation and interpretation operate under different time constraints (consecutive vs. simultaneous), these findings are significant nonetheless. The researchers found that back translation of key medical concepts was the best way to determine accuracy and consistency of the translations among Navajo interpreters, and that bringing the interpreters together to discuss translation choices greatly enhanced their ability to interpret key concepts accurately.

McCabe et al. (2005) identified issues that are similar to those encountered by interpreters of other minority languages. For example, they found that the translations of body organs or diseases ranged from literal word for word renditions to translations deemed more culturally and linguistically enriched. The case studies of Navajo interpreters working in medical contexts also demonstrated that fluency in Navajo alone is not adequate to ensure accurate and acceptable interpretation or translation. McCabe et al. (p. 304) concluded "that attention not only to language translation but also to cultural and geographic factors is vital to obtain an accurate and meaningful translation and will be widely applicable in many situations." Additional comparative case studies such as these would further illuminate the complexities of multicultural interpreting.

15. The Navajo Interpreter Project/Certification Examination is administered through the National Center for Interpretation Testing, Research and Policy at The University of Arizona (http://nci.arizona.edu/) and is designed to identify competent Navajo/English interpreters to work mainly in New Mexico and Arizona State Courts.

Sociolinguistic Studies of Navajo Interpretation

The only major sociolinguistic study that we are aware of about interpreters in AI/AN contexts is Alice Neundorf's (1987) unpublished doctoral dissertation, *Bilingualism: A Bridge to Power for Interpreters and Leaders in the Navajo Tribal Council*. In her ethnographic study, Neundorf (a Navajo native) focused on interpretation in the domains of the Navajo Council. She reported that most participants in the Council gatherings could comprehend English (Navajo monolinguals being rare). Nevertheless, for a variety of social, political, and cultural reasons the Council meetings were conducted mainly in Navajo, so interpreting occurred predominately from Navajo into English, and much less so from English into Navajo.

Neundorf's findings emphasized the importance of interpreting being "carried out at the level of ideas and concepts, rather than at the level of word-for-word or 'literal' interpreting" (p. vi). Her ethnography showed that "the Navajo Tribal Council is created in an ongoing way by bilingual Navajo leaders, and constitutes a Navajo and Anglo-American cultural hybrid with its own language, values, behavior patterns, and ethics" (p. vii). Historically, the Navajo nation has been multilingual, widely using Navajo, Spanish, English, and other Indian languages. Throughout the documented history of the Navajo, "interpreters performed functions essential to the leaders with whom they worked, and . . . they often assumed leadership roles themselves" (p. 182).

Neundorf (1987) concluded that among the Navajo, interpreters have shared several commonalities:

> First, they were all at least bilingual; second, they were more thoroughly bicultural than their contemporaries; third, they were men; fourth, they were highly intelligent; fifth, they were mobile, because they had to travel where they were most needed; sixth, they were drawn close to power by the nature of the work; seventh, with few exceptions, they became powerful themselves, and took on leadership roles; and last, some of the interpreters became wealthy by the standards of the periods in which they lived. (p. 183)

Neundorf posits that in today's Navajo society, "the power belongs to those who are fully coordinate [balanced] bilingually and biculturally." She also writes that: "Speaking in Navajo is based on not only how well one speaks but one's powers of persuasion. Naat'aanii means one who is a leader by virtue of being an orator, not by forcing people to follow [and] this is probably the biggest difference in leadership qualities between the Navajo and Anglo cultures" (p. 183)

OVERARCHING THEMES

The central finding of the studies reported above is that quality interpretation and translation requires considerations of cultural contexts in addition to linguistic fluency. We can also recognize several recurring themes, which are common to other multicultural interpreting context, for example, cultural alignment, assimilation, and nativization.

The multicultural and multilingual issues identified thus far—ranging from educational placements to enculturation patterns—remained beyond the scope of the NMIP. Nevertheless, the project raised awareness in the field and issued an urgent call to the interpreting profession (e.g., Registry of Interpreters for the Deaf and Conference of Interpreter Trainers) to provide American Indian and Alaska Native (as well as African American, Asian American, and Hispanic American), hearing and Deaf individuals opportunities to become professional interpreters.

The NMIP called attention to the issue that the majority of sign language interpreters are not from ethnically diverse backgrounds, and few interpreters from AI/AN cultural backgrounds were identified. Thus, the centrality of involving members of AI/AN communities in the process of recruiting, training, and mentoring prospective interpreters from native backgrounds.[16]

A major hallmark of the NMIP was to encourage authentic team building among interpreter practitioners, educators, and various stakeholders with a range of multicultural backgrounds. Mindful of the diversity of AI/AN individuals and communities, its overarching principle was that interpreters develop stronger AI/AN backgrounds through ongoing exposure, specialized training, mentorship, and participation in multicultural interpreting teams—involving hearing and Deaf AI/AN community members as well as hearing and Deaf interpreters from AI/AN and non-AI/AN backgrounds.[17]

16. Based on RID/NMIP data collected in 2000 (reported in Mooney, 2006); 52 members selected AI/AN as their ethnic background (0.7 percent of the total RID membership of 7,063).

17. See Roth, Mooney, Nishimura, Aramburo, Davis, Dunbar, Hopkins, Bruce, & Zavala, (2000) for additional best practices along these lines and more extensive descriptions about developing interpreting teams to work in multicultural contexts.

Developing Interpreting Teams With Deaf Natives

Hearing and Deaf team interpretation and translation are central to the co-authors' work.[18] Based on our interpreting and ethnographic field experiences, we see the need to explore and expand the professional roles of Deaf Natives as interpreters, translators, cultural mediators, and indigenous signed language specialists (e.g., as members of language revitalization teams). The centrality of Deaf Natives as collaborators and members of interpreting teams is highlighted here. Based on our participation as members of interpreting teams in AI/AN contexts, we have observed the interpretation work and cultural mediation of Deaf Native in several ways ranging from interpreting for Native Deaf-blind participants to relay interpreting between ASL and Indian Sign Language varieties.

For example, Intertribal Deaf Council (IDC) gatherings are generally held on AI/AN ancestral lands or reservations and hearing family members of Deaf Natives are among the participants. There are usually several Native Deaf-blind participants, and Native Deaf interpreters have served a major role providing tactile, close-vision, tracking, and visual support interpreting. The central role of Deaf Natives also extends to other types of interpreting and translation work (e.g., linguistic descriptions and revitalization work). In short, AI/AN activities span different environments and encompass a broad spectrum of Native educational, cultural, and spiritual events.

Code-switching typically occurs between varieties of ASL, NAISL, English, and one or more AI/AN spoken language—that is, these types of gatherings generally involve at least three languages, and oftentimes four. Collaborations that involve Deaf Natives and qualified Deaf interpreters who have knowledge of NAISL varieties and backgrounds in AI/AN settings potentially contributes to more culturally and linguistically accurate interpretations and translations. Thus, establishing qualified interpreting teams comprised of hearing and Deaf members with strong linguistic and

18. Historically and contemporarily, Deaf individuals have commonly served as interpreters in their own communities. Internationally, there is a trend for Deaf interpreters (previously known as intermediary or relay interpreters) to be involved in more interpreting work. See Boudreault (2007) for an extensive review of Deaf interpreter roles, models, approaches, and ethical considerations; and Fayd'herbe & Teuma (this volume) for descriptions of the critical role of Deaf interpreters in other contexts.

cultural backgrounds, and prior experience and/or training to work in AI/AN contexts is essential.

INTERPRETERS IN AI/AN CONTEXTS

AI/AN cultural background and knowledge varies among signed language interpreters, and these distinctions inform best practices for interpreter placement, preparation, team development, and mentorship. Table 1 illustrates the range of AI/AN cultural knowledge among hearing and Deaf sign language interpreters from diverse backgrounds.

Description of Categories

Table 1 includes categories of interpreters along a continuum ranging from minimal to strong AI/AN cultural background and knowledge. These categories are not definitive; rather, they are intended to highlight the importance of AI/AN cultural background and knowledge in interpreter preparation, placement, and the formation of interpreting teams in AI/AN settings, and to serve as a jumping-off point for forming inclusive, heterogeneous, authentic interpreting teams.

INTERPRETERS OF AI/AN DESCENT

Category 1: Interpreters of AI/AN descent with a strong cultural background, knowledge, and involvement with Native communities. They are experienced and skilled at interpreting culturally and linguistically appropriate information.

Category 2: Interpreters of AI/AN descent, but with minimal or partial knowledge about their own or other Native cultures, languages, or traditions. They have not been acculturated in their own Native culture or language, nor have they received adequate exposure or preparation to interpret in Native settings.

Category 3: Native interpreters who are Deaf and have been acculturated into both AI/AN culture and American Deaf culture (i.e., dual-exposure to Native and Deaf cultures). These interpreters have AI/AN knowledge comparable to the Native interpreters in category one; however, dual-exposure to Native and Deaf cultures gives them a unique position among the other categories of interpreters described here. In other

TABLE 1. *AI/AN Background and Knowledge Among Sign Language Interpreters*

Ethnicity	Native				Non-Native			
Auditory Status	hearing		Deaf		hearing		Deaf	
AI/AN Knowledge	strong	minimal	strong	minimal	strong	minimal	strong	minimal
Category	1	2	3	4	5	6	7	8

words, Deaf Native interpreters in this category are important members of teams comprised of interpreters from the other groups described here.

Category 4: Deaf Native interpreters with minimal AI/AN cultural knowledge. That is they have not been acculturated to their own Native cultural group, nor have they received special training to work in AI/AN contexts (comparable to interpreters in category 2).

Interpreters of Non-AI/AN Descent

Category 5: Interpreters representing a variety of ethnic backgrounds other than American Indian (e.g., African American, Asian American, and European American). However, they have been involved in AI/AN communities: participation in AI/AN cultural gatherings, NMIP specialized training, or similar cultural enrichment programs. In other words, these interpreters have been involved with Native cultural groups and received specialized training to work with individuals from culturally and linguistic diverse backgrounds.

Category 6: Hearing interpreters with minimal AI/AN cultural knowledge and no specialized training to work in AI/AN contexts.

Category 7: Deaf interpreters with strong AI/AN knowledge, exposure, and training comparable to category 5.

Category 8: Deaf interpreters with minimal AI/AN knowledge or specialized training, comparable to category 6.

SUMMARY

Both hearing and Deaf interpreters may be called upon to work in AI/AN contexts. Some interpreters of AI/AN ancestry may or may not be acculturated in both American Indian culture and American Deaf culture, and some non-AI/AN interpreters may develop strong backgrounds in AI/AN languages and cultures. Essentially, interpreters working in these and other multicultural settings need to develop a high level of familiarity and comfort with racial, ethnic, and cultural diversity to provide high-quality interpretation. Such qualities may be acquired natively and/or enhanced through practices and principles of multicultural interpreting: specialized training, team building, and mentoring.

Another major tenet of multicultural interpreting work is that quality interpretation and translation requires careful consideration of cultural context in addition to linguistic fluency. With this in mind, the following suggestions for interpreting in specific AI/AN settings are intended to raise awareness and lay the groundwork for better interpreter preparation and placement.

Use of Space

The interpreter should be well aware of special linguistic and cultural considerations, as well as the logistics specific to American Indian settings—that is, not making uninformed assumptions or simply following interpreter practices as usual. This is particularly true of ceremonial gatherings. In these contexts, it is best practice to first seek the advice of Indian leaders or elders about where the interpreter could be positioned. However, one cannot assume that all Deaf Natives have this information. The Indian leaders or elders (hearing or Deaf) are the best sources to give the interpreter permission and guidance about where to stand or sit.

During some events, it may be appropriate to sit or stand near the stage or platform (such as when using a microphone for voice interpreting), but not within the sacred space or circle (that is generally forbidden for outsiders to enter). During a pow-wow (gathering), for example, rather than standing in the middle of the circle, it is generally advisable that the interpreter stands or sits near the Deaf individual(s) outside the sacred circle or place where they are allowed to interpret.

Gender-Related Issues

Traditionally, in AI/AN communities, women and men have or hold certain stories, which typically do not cross gender lines. In respect to Indian cultural traditions, there are times when women or men may or may not be allowed to interpret the stories of the opposite gender. Likewise, some ceremonies or practices may be gender segregated. For example, at one Intertribal Deaf Council gathering, we observed a female who was very eager to interpret at a sweat lodge; however, the male Indian leader insisted that the female interpreter not enter the sweat lodge. Without the proper cultural background and preparation, such incidents could be taken badly. Furthermore, during "Moon Time" (when women are menstruating) they are prohibited to go into the circle, sweat lodges, and other sacred spaces.

Clothing

There are times when the interpreter should not wear black, but there are times that it is permissible. At a pow-wow, blue jeans are generally recommended. Formal attire is best suited for conferences—such as the National Indian Education Conference or National Congress of American Indians. Casual attire is appropriate for most gatherings; however, in some instances there may be other considerations. In general, it is always best to consult with AI/AN community leaders, organizers, or Deaf Natives before each assignment.

Use of Native Cultural Terms

Many Native gatherings involve singing, chanting, storytelling, culturally laden terms, and metaphorical language (e.g., *Medicine, The Circle, Four Directions, etc.*). As well described in the *AI/AN Curriculum* (2000, p. 27), "medicine is an array of spiritual practices, ideas, and concepts rather than only remedies and treatments as in *western medicine*" (emphasis in the original). Furthermore, "medicine men and women are viewed as the spiritual healers and leaders of the community. They have the role not only as a *doctor*, but they can be the diviner, rain-maker, prophet, priest, or chief" (p. 27, emphasis in the original). *Medicine* in Native terms is anything that brings one closer to the Great Spirit, to the Divine. In this tradition, all space is sacred space. Every place on the planet holds a specific energy connection to some living creature and is to be honored for that reason.

In short, based on traditional Native values and beliefs, interpreting for Indian elders would be equivalent to interpreting for someone with a Ph.D., and the interpreter must be aware of the status and roles of Native participants. Likewise, interpreting for an Indian healer, spiritual leader, or medicine woman/man is equivalent to interpreting for a medical doctor, minister, or priest. Great awareness, respectfulness, and community engagement are needed to be well prepared to interpret in these settings.

Discussion

The strong AI/AN background knowledge and specialized skills described above sometimes make it difficult to find the best-suited interpreter. This in turn has consequences for Deaf Natives' level of participation in AI/AN cultural activities. If an interpreter does not have the training, knowledge, and exposure to Native cultures, or if they are not comfortable accommodating certain cultural practices, then it is recommended that they not accept such assignments. It is also suggested that interpreters and interpreter coordinators become more aware of the multicultural factors and protocols for each assignment. As is true for most interpreting work, being flexible and open-minded to the dynamics and diversity of settings is essential. Again, the AI/AN curriculum modules contain excellent recommendations for interpreters to become more knowledgeable and better prepared to interpret in Native contexts.

Though well established in the AI/AN curriculum, there continues to be a need to develop special training opportunities and to encourage the formation of alliances between interpreter practitioners and members of AI/AN communities, thus enhancing the skills of interpreters and broadening the participation of Deaf Natives these settings.

INDIGENOUS SIGN LANGUAGE STUDIES

Thus far, the focus of this chapter has been multicultural considerations for sign language interpreters working in AI/AN settings. However, as stated in the introduction, some AI/AN contexts involve participants who know more than one spoken and/or signed language. Similar to other bilingual or multilingual communities, more than one language is used depending on numerous factors—such as the background of participants, types of settings, topics being covered, discourse purposes and functions. While describing more fully the outcomes of multilingualism or the linguistic features of the multiple languages involved is beyond the scope of this chapter, here are some highlights of our research findings about Plains Indian Sign Language (PISL).[19]

19. As described earlier, PISL functioned as a signed lingua franca among American Indian nations of the Great Plains cultural area and between native groups in contact with the Plains Indians. While its role as a lingua franca has

Today, PISL is still being learned and used to varying degrees by some American Indians in the United States and Canada among the following cultural and linguistic groups: Algonquin (Blackfoot, Piegan, Chippewa, Northern Cheyenne, Plains Cree); Sahaptian (Nez Perce); Salishan (Spokane, Kalispel); Siouan (Assiniboine, Crow, Hidasta, Gros Ventre, Sioux, Lak(h)ota, Dakota, Nakota); and Uto-Aztecan (Bannock, Shoshoni, Ute).

Distinct varieties of indigenous sign language have also been identified among other AI/AN cultural groups, such as the Inuit-Inupiaq, Keresan Pueblo, and Navajo. We are still investigating and documenting these and other cases. As stated earlier, North American Indian signed language varieties are broadly categorized as NAISL (see footnote 4).

SUMMARY OF RESEARCH FINDINGS

Previously (Davis, 2007), we compared the descriptions and illustrations of American Indian signs gathered during several historical time periods (the early 1800s, late 1800s, 1930s, and 2002). Taking into account language change and variation, we have found that 80–90% of the signs from the early 1800 descriptions were identical or similar (i.e., differing in only a single parameter—handshape, movement, location, orientation) to the signs used by subsequent generations of American Indian signers. While our research is ongoing, these preliminary findings suggest that PISL varieties have existed for many generations.

Davis (2007) also conducted research to determine if there was historical language contact between early ASL and PISL. In these studies (ibid.) a range of 50% lexical similarity was identified between historical varieties of ASL and PISL. These findings suggest that ASL and PISL are separate languages—that is, they are unlikely to be genetically related, or to have a common language ancestor. Nonetheless, this is a relatively high range of lexical similarity and indicates possible lexical borrowing between the languages. In short, we have identified a significant number of cognates between PISL and ASL. Based on these findings (ibid.), lexical borrowing likely occurred as a consequence of language contact between

---

diminished from previous times, it is still used today within some native groups in traditional storytelling, rituals, legends, prayers, conversational narratives, and by Deaf Natives (Davis 2007, 2009; McKay-Cody 1997, 1998, 1999).

American Indians and individuals who were deaf. Our studies of other sociolinguistic and historical linguistic evidence related to American Indian sign language varieties are ongoing.

QUESTIONS OF HISTORICAL SIGN LANGUAGE CONTACT

What types of sign language contact occurred between American Indian groups and early Deaf communities? Were Indian signs ever used to teach deaf students attending schools for the deaf? When did Indian children who were deaf begin attending deaf schools? Although these long-standing questions warrant further research, our preliminary findings are summarized here:

- There has been historical contact between American Indians and Deaf Americans from 17th-century colonization until today.

American Indians inhabited the areas being colonized by the first European immigrants—including Martha's Vineyard. Contact between Deaf Americans and Indians, as early as the 17th century, likely occurred. Historical records indicate that frequent contact took place between American Indians who signed and students and faculty at schools for the deaf (Mallery, 1881).

- The establishment of the first American Schools for the Deaf and dissemination of the published descriptions of American Indian signs to educators at these schools (1850–1890)

The historical evidence suggests that sign language contact could have occurred in several ways, for example, the historical proximity of the first American deaf schools having been established in the early 1800s and American Indians having commonly used sign language. Furthermore, between 1847 and 1890, early publications prominently featured lexical descriptions of Indian Sign Language, and these publications were widely distributed to educators and deaf schools through the periodical *American Annals for the Deaf and Dumb* (Gallaudet 1848, 1852). Thus, it is plausible that during this historical period American Indian signs were introduced to deaf students.[20]

20. Thomas H. Gallaudet, cofounder of the first school for deaf students in the United States in 1817, used the Dunbar (1801) and Long (1823)

- Deaf children from American Indian backgrounds attended educational programs and schools for the deaf.

Additional contact between the American Indians and deaf people was also likely to have occurred. For example, the New Mexico School for the Deaf and the School for Indians were constructed next to each other in Santa Fe in the late 19th century. Indian children who were deaf also began attending some state residential schools for the deaf around the United States during the historical period that sign language was commonly used among Indian groups. Furthermore, it has been documented and reported that some deaf children from Indian families *first acquired the alternate signed language as a primary language* before attending schools for the deaf and learning ASL as a second language (see Davis & Supalla, 1995; McKay-Cody 1997, 1998).

TRADITIONAL INDIAN SIGN LANGUAGE

Although greatly diminished from its widespread use in previous times, we have found that NAISL varieties are still being used today within some American Indian groups in storytelling, rituals, legends, and prayers. As discussed above, sign language has been used among Native groups as an alternative to spoken language, and some deaf members of Native communities learned NAISL as a first language. Previously, our research (Davis, 2005, 2006; McKay-Cody 1997, 1998) identified the following ways that North American Indian Sign Language was used traditionally.

Intertribal Communication

There were many different spoken languages and sign language was used to make communication possible between different Indian nations. It was often considered the language reserved for diplomatic relations, especially among chiefs, elders, and medicine women/men.

---

descriptions, which were titled the "Indian Language of Signs," to strengthen the case that "the natural language of signs" was essential to teaching and communicating with the deaf (see Davis, 2007).

Storytelling

Traditionally, storytelling was practiced from the first to last frost/snow of the year, but not all year round. During other times of the year other activities were more common—planting in the spring, hunting in the summer, harvesting in the fall. In other words, activities were seasonal, and during the winter months stories helped pass the time. Stories remained the same over time, similar to frozen texts. The tradition of storytelling from first to last snow is still practiced by some tribal groups today. This is comparable to the tradition of Christmas stories that are very specific to the December holidays in some Western cultures. Similarly there are cultural norms and rules related to traditional Indian stories.

Rituals

During certain rituals speech was not permitted and silence observed. However, signing was permitted in some rituals. In Native spiritual practices, there are certain signs that are considered restricted, or the domain of spiritual communication—that is, not to be used in everyday conversation.

Distance Communication

Sign language was also a useful way to communicate across distances (such as between mountain ranges and across the distant plains). This was a much more effective way to communicate than shouting back and forth.

During Raids, War, and Hunting Parties

Sign language served a role in making and sharing battle plans secretly. Animals—such as deer—have a keen sense of hearing and signing was a way for hunters to communicate and alert each other in silence and not scare away the animals.

Deaf Family Members

When there were deaf members of tribal groups, sign language was a way to communicate with them and over time the sign language was expanded and handed down from one generation to the next—thus, it was linguistically enriched. In sum, Indian sign language served both intertribal and intratribal communication purposes. In the former case, individuals spoke different languages, but shared a common sign language; in the latter case, sign language was used within Native communities for seasonal stories, sacred rituals, or when certain members of the tribe were deaf.

NORTH AMERICAN INDIAN SIGN LANGUAGE TODAY

Compared to the traditional ways of signing described above, we find the following uses of sign language today.

Storytelling

Storytelling still plays a central role in the culture and cultural rules and norms are still followed. Today, a combination of ASL and Indian storytelling traditions has emerged; however in modern times, due to the influences of Hollywood movies and television, traditional storytelling is not as common as in previous times.

Christian Religious Texts

American Indians were often placed in special Indian schools and trained not to follow their Indian cultural ways—including Indian signed language. Although sign language as a natural form of discourse or for traditional storytelling was generally discouraged at Indian Schools, the "Lord's Prayer" and other religious songs or frozen texts were sometimes signed. Paradoxically, this was one way that signing continued to be transmitted to the next generations.

Native American Church (NAC)

Nowadays, NAISL is used in Native churches, although the emphasis is first on using and learning the Indian spoken language. Sometimes signed language is used as an alternate to spoken language, or to translate spoken language passages—that is, if members of the congregation know sign language.

Hollywood Depictions

Hollywood movies sometimes depict Indians signing in various ways (e.g., *Dances With Wolves* or *Bury My Heat at Wounded Knee*). Although a vast improvement from earlier films (produced in the Cowboy and Indian genre and John Wayne era), modern films still offer a limited portrayal of the ways American Indians actually signed. In most instances, only a few NAISL signs are featured. Typically, these signs are not shown in complete sentences, or without a full body view of the signer.

Deaf Family Members

Similar to the historical cases described above, Deaf Natives have played an active role in maintaining and expanding the use of indigenous signed language up until today. Thus, we still find contact signing between varieties of NAISL and ASL, including lexical borrowing, code-mixing, and code-switching. While including additional linguistic descriptions about distinct Native signed language varieties was beyond the scope of the present chapter, further research findings along these lines can be found in our previous published work (Davis, 2005, 2006; McKay-Cody 1997, 1998).

SUMMARY AND CONCLUSIONS

This chapter brought together our collaborative research and fieldwork about the traditional varieties of sign language used among North American Indians. We aimed to bridge some of the gaps in the literature about this subject. Our collaborative fieldwork and research is ongoing. It is informed by interpreting practices and multicultural work in general, and we hope this inspires further scholarship across multiple disciplines—especially Sign Language Linguistics, Interpretation/Translation Preparation, and Deaf Studies.

This chapter concentrated mainly on multicultural interpreting in AI/AN settings. This embraced Deaf Native perspectives and encompassed NAISL studies. Though our geographic focus has been Native North America, common themes have emerged globally among indigenous groups—such as the need to sustain cultural traditions and indigenous languages. In North America, for example, one outcome of intensive language and cultural contact has been a shift towards English as the dominant or primary language of most American Indians.

An alarming number of the languages of the world's indigenous cultural groups are currently endangered (Crystal, 2000; Nettle & Romaine, 2000). This all too common pattern of language endangerment also impacts indigenous signed languages (Davis, in press). Recognition of the rapid decline and loss of many indigenous languages globally has led to urgent calls for revitalization of endangered languages.[21] These matters are tightly intertwined, and rendered more complex taking into account the signed and spoken languages among American cultural groups (e.g., Deaf, American Indian, and Native Deaf).

Language revitalization is an ongoing and rigorous process based on discovering common ground among various stakeholders. Native community members, interpreters/translators, and linguists are among the key participants and allies in the arena of maintaining and revitalizing endangered indigenous languages and cultures.

The practices highlighted throughout this chapter are particularly critical to interpreting in multicultural and multilingual AI/AN settings. At the same time, they inform a wide range of interpreting work, which is inherently intercultural, that is, involving at least two languages and two cultures. Nearly one decade has passed since the conclusion of the NMIP, but its contributions remain highly germane to the work of interpreters today and in the future, both nationally and internationally. Fundamentally, the NMIP showed how interpreters can maintain and develop greater awareness and stronger multicultural backgrounds. To increase awareness about one's own cultural heritage is the first cornerstone. The formation of interpreting teams, mentorship, and alliances involving individuals from diverse cultural backgrounds and Native communities represent the other cornerstones. Thus, multicultural interpreting practitioners, educators, and other stakeholders, converge on the common ground of educational, cultural, social, historical, and linguistic domains.

21. In the United States, federal legislation (e.g., Bilingual Education Act), educational curriculum reform projects (e.g., NMIP), and research initiatives (e.g., National Science Foundation) have been mandated to prevent the further loss of native languages and to support the maintenance of bilingualism and multilingualism among American cultural groups.

ACKNOWLEDGMENTS

The authors of this chapter would like to acknowledge the support of a research grant (BCS–0853665) from the National Science Foundation's Documenting Endangered Languages Program. Any views, findings, conclusions, or recommendations expressed in this chapter do not necessarily reflect those of the National Science Foundation.

REFERENCES

American Indian/Alaskan Native curriculum modules. (2000). *National Multicultural Interpreting Project*. Retrieved from http://www.asl.neu.edu/ TIEM.online/NMIP/4B.pdf.

Busby, H. (2000). Preface to American Indian/Alaskan Native curriculum modules, *National Multicultural Interpreting Project*. Retrieved from http://www.asl.neu.edu/TIEM.online/NMIP/4B.pdf.

Campbell, L. (2000). *American Indian languages*. New York: Oxford University Press.

Christensen, K. M. (2000). *Deaf plus: A multicultural perspective*. San Diego: DawnSignPress.

Crystal, D. (2000). *Language death*. New York: Cambridge University Press.

Davis, J. E. (2005). Evidence of a historical signed lingua franca among North American Indians. *Deaf Worlds 21*(3), 47–72.

Davis, J. E. (2006). A historical linguistic account of sign language among North American Indians. In C. Lucas (Ed.), *Multilingualism and sign languages: Vol. 12. Sociolinguistics in Deaf communities* (pp. 3–35). Washington, DC: Gallaudet University Press.

Davis, J. E. (2007). North American Indian signed language varieties: A comparative historical linguistic assessment. In D. Quinto-Pozos (Ed.), *Sign languages in contact: Vol. 13. Sociolinguistics in Deaf communities* (pp. 85–122). Washington, DC: Gallaudet University Press.

Davis, J. E. (in press). *Hand talk: Sign language among American Indian nations*. Cambridge: Cambridge University Press.

Davis, J. E. & Supalla, S. (1995). A sociolinguistic description of sign language use in a Navajo family. In C. Lucas (Ed.), *Sociolinguistics in Deaf communities: Vol. 1. Sociolinguistics in Deaf communities* (pp. 77–106). Washington, DC: Gallaudet University Press.

Dively, V. L. (2001). Contemporary native Deaf experience: Overdue smoke rising. In Lois Bragg (Ed.), *Deaf world: A historical reader and primary sourcebook* (pp. 390–405). New York: New York University Press.

Dunbar, W. (1801). On the language of signs among certain North American Indians. *Transactions of the American Philosophical Society*, 6 (1), 1–8.

Gallaudet, T. H. (1848). On the natural language of signs; and its value and uses in the instruction of the deaf and dumb. *American Annals of the Deaf and Dumb*, 1, 55–60.

Gallaudet, T. H. (1852). Indian language of signs. *American Annals of the Deaf and Dumb*, 4, 157–71.

Goddard, I. (1979). The languages of South Texas and the lower Rio Grande. In L. Campbell & M. Mithun (Eds.), *The languages of native America: Historical and comparative assessment* (pp. 70–132). Austin: University of Texas Press.

Goff-Paris, D., & Wood, S. K. (2002). *Step into the circle: The heartbeat of American Indian, Alsaka Native, and First Nations Deaf communities.* Salem, OR: AGO Publications.

Gordon, R. G., Jr., (Ed.). (2005). *Ethnologue: Languages of the world* (15th ed.). Dallas: SIL International.

Groce, N. E. (1985). *Everyone here spoke sign language: Hereditary deafness on Martha's Vineyard.* Cambridge, MA: Harvard University Press.

Karttunen, F. (1994). *Between worlds: Interpreters, guides, and survivors.* New Brunswick, NJ: Rutgers University Press.

Kelly, W. P. (2004). History of the American Indian Deaf. In B. K. Eldredge, D. Stringham, & M. M. Wilding-Díaz (Eds.), *Deaf studies today! A kaleidoscope of knowledge, learning, and understanding* (pp. 217–23). Orem: Utah Valley State College.

Kelly, W. P., & McGregor, T. L. (2003). Keresan Pueblo Indian Sign Language. In J. Reyhner, O. Trujillo, R. L. Carrasco, & L. Lockard (Eds.), *Nurturing native languages* (pp.141–48). Flagstaff: Northern Arizona University.

Kendon, A. (1988). *Sign languages of aboriginal Australia: Cultural, semiotic, and communicative perspectives.* New York: Cambridge University Press.

Long, J. S. (1918). *The sign language: A manual of signs; being a descriptive vocabulary of signs used by the deaf of the United States and Canada* (2d ed.). Washington, DC: Gallaudet College.

Long, S. H. (1823). *Account of an expedition from Pittsburgh to the Rocky Mountains.* Philadelphia: Edwin James.

Mallery, G. (1881). Sign language among North American Indians. In J. W. Powell (Ed.), *First annual report of the Bureau of Ethnology of the Smithsonian Institution for 1879–1880* (pp. 263–552). Washington, DC: U.S. Government Printing Office.

Marschark, M., Peterson, R., & Winston, E. A. (Eds.). (2005). *Sign language interpreting and interpreter education: Directions for research and practice.* New York: Oxford University Press.

McCabe, M., Morgan, F., Curley, H., Begay, R., & Gohdes, D. (2005). The informed consent process in a cross-cultural setting: Is the process achieving the intended result? *Ethnicity & Disease 15*(2), 300–304.

McKay-Cody, M. (1997). *Plains Indian Sign Language: A comparative study of alternate and primary signers.* Unpublished master's thesis, University of Arizona.

McKay-Cody, M. (1998). *Plains Indian sign language: A comparative study of alternative and primary signers.* In *Deaf Studies V: Toward 2000—Unity and Diversity Conference Proceedings* (pp. 17–78). Washington, DC: Gallaudet University Continuing Education.

McKay-Cody, M. (1999). The "well hidden people" in Deaf and Native communities. *A Deaf American Monograph*, vol. 48 (pp. 49–51).

Miller, K. (2004). *Circle of unity: Pathways to improving outreach to American Indians and Alaska natives who are Deaf, Deaf-Blind, and Hard of Hearing.* Little Rock: University of Arkansas, Rehabilitation Research and Training Center.

Mithun, M. (1999). *The languages of native North America.* New York: Cambridge University Press.

Mooney, M. (2006). Interpreter training in less frequently taught languages. Changing the curriculum paradigm to multilingual and multicultural as applied to interpreter education programs. In C. Roy (Ed.), *New approaches to interpreter education.* Washington DC: Gallaudet University Press.

National Multicultural Interpreting Project Curriculum. 2000. Retrieved from http://www.asl.neu.edu/TIEM.online/curriculum_nmip.html.

Nettle, D., & Romaine, S. (2000). *Vanishing voices: The extinction of the world's languages.* Oxford: Oxford University Press.

Neundorf, A. (1987). *Bilingualism: A bridge to power for interpreters and leaders in the Navajo Tribal Council.* Unpublished doctoral dissertation, University of New Mexico.

Pritchard, E. T. (2002). *Native New Yorkers: The legacy of the Algonquin people of New York.* San Francisco: Council Oak Books.

Roth, A., Mooney, M., Nishimura, J., Aramburo, A., Davis, J., Dunbar, T., Hopkins, J., Bruce, J., & Zavala, Y. (2000). What factors decide who is best suited for an interpreting assignment? *National Multicultural Interpreting Project Curriculum.* Retrieved from http://www.asl.neu.edu/TIEM.online/NMIP/8B.pdf.

Sandler, W., Meir, I., Padden, C., & Aronoff, M. (2005). The emergence of grammar: Systematic structure in a new sign language. *Proceedings of the National Academy of Sciences, 102* (7), 2661–65.

Stuart, P. (1987). *Nations within a nation: Historical statistics of American Indians.* Westport, CT: Greenwood.

Taylor, A. R. (1978). Nonverbal communication in aboriginal North America: The Plains Sign Language. In D. J. Umiker-Sebeok & T. A. Sebeok (Eds.), *Aboriginal sign languages of the Americas and Australia: Vol. 2* (pp. 223–44). New York: Plenum.

Taylor, A. R. (1997). Nonspeech communication systems. In I. Goddard (Ed.), *Handbook of the North American Indian: Vol. 17, Languages* (pp. 275–89). Washington, DC: Smithsonian Institution Press.

Umiker-Sebeok, J., & Sebeok, T. A. (Eds.). (1978). *Aboriginal sign languages of the Americas and Australia: Vols. 1 and 2.* New York: Plenum.

Waldman, C. (2000). *Atlas of the North American Indian.* New York: Facts on File.

West, L. (1960). *The sign language: An analysis. Vols. 1 and 2.* Unpublished doctoral dissertation, Indiana University, Bloomington, Indiana.

Wurtzburg, S., & Campbell, L. (1995). North American Indian Sign Language: Evidence of its existence before European contact. *International Journal of American Linguistics 61,* 153–67.

Interpreting for Indigenous Australian Deaf Clients in Far North Queensland Australia Within the Legal Context

Karin Fayd'herbe and Ryan Teuma

Aboriginal and Torres Strait Islander (hereafter Indigenous Australian) Deaf people may not be receiving legal due process, as a result of marked differences in communication and cultural styles and specific language difficulties. We examine the concept of the interpreter as part of a team within legal contexts, issues around legal language competence, and the effects of language diversity among Indigenous Australian Deaf clients in forensic situations. Implications and outcomes for Indigenous Australian Deaf people who do not receive due process, and areas for further research are identified. Finally, guidelines and strategies for Auslan (Australian Sign Language) interpreters, legal professionals, and mental health clinicians working in a legal context are provided. An expected outcome is improved service delivery by the legal team, which includes a NAATI[1] accredited Auslan professional interpreter,[2] in order to achieve linguistic and cultural access that is consistent with basic human rights.

1. National Accreditation Authority for Translators and Interpreters (NAATI) is the government-owned body responsible for setting and monitoring standards for the translating and interpreting profession in Australia. It administers a system of accreditation. NAATI accreditation is the only credential officially accepted by employers for translation and interpreting professionals in Australia. See http://www.naati.com.au/at-index.html.

2. This is the first professional level and represents the minimum level of competence for professional interpreting. Interpreters convey the full meaning of the information from the source language into the target language in the appropriate style and register. Interpreters at this level are capable of interpreting across a wide range of subjects involving dialogues at specialist consultations. See http://www.naati.com.au/at-accreditation-levels.html.

Contemporary Australia is considered to be a multicultural nation, with a population that consists of many nationalities. Yet prior to 1788, Australia was inhabited solely by the Indigenous Australian peoples, Aboriginal and Torres Strait Islanders. Aboriginal people inhabited mainland Australia and Tasmania while Torres Strait Islanders inhabited the islands between the tip of Queensland and Papua New Guinea, now referred to as the Torres Strait (Australian Museum, 2004). There were a variety of communities, each with their own language, cultural practices, beliefs, and traditions. Life for Indigenous Australians prior to the colonization of Australia was very different to modern Australia. They primarily practiced a hunter-and-gatherer lifestyle and took great care of the land and its wildlife, ensuring that foods were not overhunted. Lands were divided up according to traditional areas, often marked by geographic boundaries such as rivers and mountains. Elders were responsible for passing on the knowledge of the traditional land and cultural practices to the younger folk through storytelling, dance, art, and song.

Today it is widely acknowledged that Aboriginal and Torres Strait Islander peoples are not a homogenous group, as their traditional cultural practices are diverse. To reflect this diversity, and to respectfully acknowledge the peoples who inhabited Australia prior to colonization, the nomenclature *Indigenous Australian/s* is used officially in all government, formalized, legalistic, and academic contexts to refer to the collective. For clarification, an Aboriginal or Torres Strait Islander is a person who is of Aboriginal or Torres Strait Islander descent, who identifies as an Aboriginal or Torres Strait Islander, and is accepted by the Indigenous community in which he or she lives (Australian Museum, 2004). The authors will hereafter use the capitalized term *Indigenous Australians* in this chapter to collectively identify persons who belong to Aboriginal and/or Torres Strait Islander groups.

The focus of this chapter is the Indigenous Australian Deaf population found in the Far North Queensland (FNQ) and Torres Strait Island regions of Australia and how they fare within the legal context. Our discussion is primarily aimed at Auslan interpreters, who should be considered as part of the team, alongside legal professionals and mental health clinicians, in the voluntary and statutory sectors. The ability to communicate effectively, to assert one's own defense in a legal sense, is a basic human right. It would appear to the authors that Indigenous Australian

Deaf people face greater obstacles in gaining equal linguistic and cultural access to the legal setting. This may increase their vulnerability and adversely affect their ability to develop a healthy offense-free lifestyle. Indigenous Australian Deaf people are at significant risk of not understanding their legal rights and subsequent criminal proceedings. They may be unwittingly denied their legal rights and therefore have limited or no access to due process.

Empirical research is much needed in this area; however the authors' respective professional experiences as an Auslan interpreter, trainer, and teacher of the deaf (Fayd'herbe) and forensic psychologist (Teuma) in working with Indigenous Australian Deaf people indicate that the risks of linguistic discrimination and cultural inequality are even higher for this group than for the general Australian Deaf population. This chapter aims to synthesize our own observations with relevant perspectives from research literature to draw attention to the position of Indigenous Australian Deaf persons in legal settings, and how interpreters and other professionals might tailor their practices to address their needs.

Quite often the sign language interpreter is the only person in an interpreted interaction with awareness of Deaf people and the likelihood of cultural and communication difficulties. The task of suggesting practices that will ensure fairness will inevitably fall on their shoulders. In these circumstances, we argue that interpreters must be able to recognize additional linguistic and cognitive issues affecting equitable communication strategies with Indigenous Australian Deaf clients. The interpreter may need to recommend culturally and linguistically appropriate communication accommodations within the forensic process. An interpreter may feel constrained by ethical boundaries; however, our position is that an Indigenous Australian Deaf client is extremely vulnerable in the legal setting and that the interpreter's ethical responsibility therefore encompasses monitoring issues in the communication process itself. Ultimately, Indigenous Australian Deaf clients within the legal setting have the same right as others to be fully informed and involved in proceedings concerning them.

When engaging with agencies relating to their offending behavior, Indigenous Australian Deaf people have the right to be treated equitably by police, court staff, and mental health clinicians. These professionals may not have a basic understanding of Indigenous Australian Deaf people and how best to achieve cultural and communication equality. For example, there is often a need for specialist expertise in the assessment of linguistic competency, and the provision of appropriate advocacy and communication access. Indigenous Australian Deaf people should be provided with allied professional support, such as an Auslan interpreter and a Deaf interpreter who is also Indigenous Australian. These specialists must work within a legal team paradigm where appropriate consultation and review is regularly expected among all parties. The aim is to ensure that Indigenous Australian Deaf people have the opportunity to fully and consensually participate in procedures relating to any legal matters.

INDIGENOUS PEOPLES IN FAR NORTH QUEENSLAND, AUSTRALIA

Within the state of Queensland, Far North Queensland is a very large region, containing many Indigenous Australian communities in remote and rural areas (see Figure 1).

According to the Australian Bureau of Statistics (ABS), in 2006 the Indigenous Australian population in the state of Queensland was 144,885 out of a total population of 4,090,908 (included in both figures are Indigenous Australian people who are of dual Aboriginal and Torres Strait Islander parentage). The Indigenous population proportion is 3.5%.

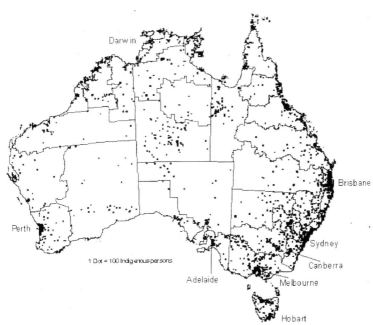

FIGURE 1. *Populations characteristics, Aboriginal and Torres Strait Islander Australians. Source: Australian Bureau of Statistics, 2006 (cat. no. 4713.0).*

There are an indeterminate number of Aboriginal communities made up of several hundred groupings identified by kinship, language, or a particular place or "country." Many still practice traditional ways of life. Aboriginal peoples have existed in Australia for over 60,000 years, and are considered one of the world's oldest living peoples (Lore of the Land, n.d.). In Queensland, Aboriginal peoples have strong connections to the land with clan groups holding traditional custodianship of their lands (Reconciliation Australia, n.d.). A variety of names may be used to describe groupings of Aboriginal peoples; for example, "skin-group" names are often used by peoples in central and northern Australia. Regional names that include descendents of all the language groups might also be used. Finally, Indigenous peoples may also refer to themselves by a chosen general name which in Queensland is known as *Murri* (Reconcilation Australia, n.d.).

The Torres Strait Islands are a group of at least 274 small islands in the Torres Strait of which only 17 are inhabited. The islands separate far northern continental Australia's Cape York Peninsula and Papua New Guinea. The traditional people of Torres Strait are of Melanesian origin. Two Indigenous Australian languages are spoken on the islands: *Kala Lagaw Ya* or *Kala Kawa Ya* (both dialects of the same language) is spoken in the Western and Central Islands and *Meriam Mir* is spoken in the Eastern Islands. Nevertheless, *Torres Strait Creole* is more commonly used throughout the Torres Straits (Torres Strait Regional Authority, 2007).

INDIGENOUS DEAF PEOPLES AND USE OF INDIGENOUS SIGN LANGUAGE IN FNQ

Hearing loss is a major epidemic in Indigenous Australian Communities in FNQ, with up to 40% of the community affected. (Howard, Quinn, Blokland, & Flynn, 1993). The level of ear disease and hearing loss among Indigenous Australian people is significantly higher than that of the general Australian population. Middle ear infections otherwise known as otitis media are widespread throughout the FNQ region. If left untreated in adolescence permanent sensorineural loss may result, manifesting in spoken language development impairments (Thomson, Burns, Hardy, Krom, Stumpers, & Urquhart, 2008). The FNQ Paediatric Outreach Service estimated the prevalence of *chronic suppurative otitis media* (persistent discharges from the middle ear through a tympanic membrane perforation for more than 6 weeks) in all Aboriginal children in the communities visited by the service in remote FNQ to be at 14.7%. Furthermore, they refer to a 1996 World Health Organization report, which states that a prevalence of over 4% for this disease is considered a public health emergency (Rothstein, Heazlewood, & Fraser, 2007). It was also reported that sensory impairment (sight, hearing, or speech) occurs in 10.2% of Indigenous Australian peoples in the 15–44 year age group across Australia. Of that, 23.3% results in a profound-severe core activity limitation (Australian Bureau of Statistics, 2005). Research has indicated that hearing loss among Indigenous Australians significantly affects linguistic competence and educational achievement, leads to social isolation, and is a catalyst for interpersonal difficulties in adult-hood (Howard et al. 1993).

Regardless of hearing loss, the existence of conventional gestures or sign language within Indigenous Australian communities is a phenom-enon that has been well documented in the literature. Roth (1908) found evidence of sign languages used among North Queensland Aborigines dating back to the early 19th century, and Kendon (1988) found that well-developed Indigenous Sign Languages in FNQ have evolved in asso-ciation with activities such as fishing and hunting (in order not to frighten the prey) and periods of mourning, in which women kin must observe silence. These Australian Aboriginal sign languages (AASL) appear most developed in areas where traditional cultures practice extensive speech taboos. These areas include the central desert of the Northern Territory (notably the *Warlpiri* and *Wurumingu Nations*), and western Cape York, FNQ. In addition, complex gestural systems have been reported in the southern, central, and western desert regions of the Northern Territory, the Gulf of Carpentaria, and in the Torres Strait Islands (Kendon, 1988; Kwek & Kendon, 1991). In relation to the use of sign language by Deaf people in Australia, Johnston and Schembri (2007) note that Australian Aboriginal forms of sign language exist but that there is no evidence to link these to the existence of deaf groups within Indigenous hearing com-munities. To date there is no empirical research available on the use of sign language by Indigenous Australian Deaf people living in FNQ, par-ticularly in remote Indigenous Australian communities. It is not known if the sign languages used by the FNQ Indigenous deaf population origi-nated from Indigenous community sign language, Auslan, or both.

The author's interpreter/educationalist observations and fieldwork in both FNQ and legal settings, suggest that a form of "Indigenous Deaf sign language" in addition to standard Auslan, is used among Indigenous Australian Deaf people in FNQ. Empirical research is required to substantiate this claim.

Furthermore we suggest that there appears to be a *spectrum of language diversity* within the FNQ Indigenous Australian Deaf population. The authors propose that the spectrum includes persons who are reasonably proficient in one or more of the following languages or modes—Auslan, Australian Aboriginal sign languages, Signed English, a spoken contact language such as Torres Strait Island Creole, and written/spoken English—through to persons who demonstrate significant literacy and sign language incompetence and educational failure. The latter group may not have acquired sufficient proficiency in any language to have been fully acculturated into either Indigenous hearing or Australian Deaf communities.

The subset of Indigenous Australian Deaf people with severe language deprivation may experience cultural exclusion, and multiple psychological and cognitive impairments. Consequently, they may have a profound incapacity to communicate in any language and present with limited cognitive processing abilities. We have observed that although many can competently write their name, address, and simple sentences with common nouns and verbs; most have great difficulty understanding texts of any length and depth containing unfamiliar concepts that are expressed in a non-literal form. O'Reilly (2005) similarly notes that some have severely restricted vocabulary and limited understanding of standard Auslan or English grammar. We will hereon refer to this as *language incompetence*. From the authors' observations in the field, such Indigenous Australian Deaf people appear to have no systematic means of communicating thoughts, feelings, and emotions through conventional sign systems such as Auslan, Aboriginal Australian sign language, Signed English, or a contact language such as Torres Strait Island Creole, or written/spoken English.

Although this spectrum of language diversity among Indigenous Australian Deaf populations has not been empirically researched, we hypothesize that it does exist. The research of Miller and Vernon (2002) in the area of linguistic diversity and language incompetency is relevant to the Australian context. Their studies of deaf criminal suspects in the United States of America find that language incompetence arises from language diversity profile, due to six inter-related sociocultural factors, as follows: (1) educational background; (2) age at which language acquisition starts; (3) age of onset of deafness and severity of deafness; (4) the region where the person grew up; (5) secondary impairments, and

(6) language deprivation. The authors propose that similar sociocultural factors determine language diversity within Indigenous Australian Deaf populations in FNQ. The following description of the characteristics of language diversity in this group draws upon the authors' professional experience, demographic data about Indigenous Australians, with reference to Miller and Vernon's (2002) discussion of sociocultural factors.

EDUCATIONAL BACKGROUND

In the early part of the 20th century, deaf children in Queensland attended the residential educational program at the Queensland School for the Deaf in Brisbane, the capital and southeast corner of Queensland. From 1948 to 1957, special education in Queensland underwent rapid change. In 1952, the Department of Education began appointing specialist teachers who received a year's training in Victoria before commencement (Logan & Clarke, 1984). In 1963, a major rubella epidemic occurred and facilities at the Queensland School for the Deaf were upgraded to cater for the vast increase in deaf children (Dept. of Education, Training and the Arts, 2007). Oralism was the predominant approach to teaching deaf students at this time. Many Indigenous Australian children with a moderate-profound hearing loss living in regional or remote areas were removed to attend the boarding facility attached to the school, often from as early as four years of age.

In the 1970s, a form of manual communication known as Signed English was introduced as a medium of instruction. Simultaneously, special education units began opening up in FNQ regional centers such as Cairns and Townsville. For Indigenous Australian Deaf students from remote FNQ areas, these new centers were logical placements. After the completion of their schooling, some Indigenous Australian Deaf people stayed in the regional centers while others returned to their home community. In addition, large numbers of Indigenous people with hearing loss received educational support through Education Queensland Advisory Teacher (hearing impaired) visiting services throughout the FNQ region. Indigenous Australian people are highly sociocentric; therefore, the experience of Indigenous children being removed from their community and family and sent to an all-white institution may have been traumatic and impacted negatively on educational achievement (A. Waia, personal communication, 2008; Cooke, 2002).

AGE OF LANGUAGE ACQUISITION

Without early intervention, deaf children will struggle to develop developmentally appropriate language and literacy abilities (Quigley &

Kretschmer, 1982; Quigley & Paul, 1984; Yoshinaga-Itano, Sedey, Coulter, & Mehl, 1998; Moeller, 2000). Furthermore, it is widely acknowledged that deafness occurring prelingually has a more detrimental effect on language acquisition, although any hearing impairment can affect language and educational attainment adversely (Quigley & Paul, 1984; Howard, 2006). Identifying hearing loss among Indigenous Australian deaf children living in remote communities in FNQ is of utmost importance in order to mitigate the effects of delayed language acquisition. Newborn screening and early childhood hearing impairment detection practices have certainly improved the rates of early diagnosis in recent years, with the first large-scale newborn hearing screening beginning in Australia in 2000 (Coates & Gifkins, 2003). However, for many adult Indigenous Australian Deaf people educated during the period 1948–1980, detection of prelingual hearing impairment in early childhood almost certainly did not occur.

AGE OF ONSET OF DEAFNESS AND SEVERITY

As mentioned previously, Indigenous Australians have a high incidence of middle ear disease and hearing loss. Hearing impairment is a common consequence of ear disease for Indigenous Australian children. Causes are numerous, including environmental factors (overcrowded housing and primitive water, sewage, and waste removal systems), poor nutrition, and limited access to medical treatment and services (Quinn & Rance, 2006).

REGIONAL EFFECTS

FNQ is a large and sparsely populated geographical area. Typically, Indigenous Australian Deaf persons grow up in remote communities isolated from technology, with inadequate or nonexistent educational facilities, and underdeveloped medical services. In addition, Indigenous Australian children are often more likely to be exposed to poverty, domestic violence, and neglect, and trauma from cultural and geographical displacement as a result of their people having being forcibly removed under former assimilationist legislation and policies (Human Rights and Equal Opportunity Commission, 1997).

Many Indigenous Australian Deaf people in FNQ associate and identity with the Deaf community in Cairns and communicate in Auslan or in an obscure and idiosyncratic form that mixes Auslan with Indigenous signs (O'Reilly, 2005; A. Waia, personal communication, 2008). O'Reilly's recorded consultations with the FNQ Indigenous Australian Deaf community, reveal that their Indigenous Deaf Sign Language has "evolved over time." O'Reilly further notes that there is considerable lexical variation or instability.

SECONDARY IMPAIRMENTS

Secondary impairments such as additional sensory, developmental, intellectual, or behavioral disabilities can all affect communication and linguistic competence. In particular, fetal alcohol spectrum disorders (FASD) are of concern for Indigenous Australian people. Statistics reveal that in Indigenous Australian communities 9.1 per 1,000 live births are affected by prenatal alcohol exposure (Green, 2007). FASD has negative developmental consequences, including poor cognitive and academic functioning, psychological disorders, behavioral problems, often leading to difficulties with independent living (ibid.). As such, any child affected by FASD will almost certainly have difficulties at school and for a deaf child, language incompetence may be an unfortunate additional outcome.

LANGUAGE DEPRIVATION

Early language deprivation is disastrous for effective social and cognitive development. Hearing loss and associated language deprivation can result in poor self-esteem, social exclusion, poor social skills, high levels of frustration and anger, and an inability to communicate basic needs. For many Indigenous Australian Deaf adults, language deprivation almost certainly occurred throughout childhood. Antisocial behavior and diminished social and emotional well-being are often heightened among Indigenous Australian Deaf populations (Howard, 2006).

INDIGENOUS AUSTRALIAN DEAF PEOPLE AND DETERMINING LANGUAGE INCOMPETENCE WITHIN THE FAR NORTH QUEENSLAND LEGAL SETTING

Language diversity and language incompetence among deaf criminal suspects in the United States has been identified as a serious concern (Miller & Vernon, 2002); however, there is a paucity of analogous research in Australia. According to Miller and Vernon, a failure to recognize that deaf criminal suspects may experience linguistic and functional incompetence still occurs throughout the United States. In such cases, the provision of standard accommodations such as interpreters may not be enough to ensure due process (Vernon & Coley, 1978; Vernon & Raifman, 1997;

Vernon, Raifman, Greenberg, & Monteiro, 2001). Vernon et al. argue that language diversity and incompetence among deaf suspects is problematic even for experienced and professional sign language interpreters. They further state that criminal case summaries have well documented the failure of law enforcement agencies to provide effective communication for linguistically incompetent deaf suspects (Vernon et al).

Without empirical research in Australia, the authors can only extrapolate from American studies. We hypothesize that the existence of the sociocultural conditions aforementioned has resulted in a spectrum of language diversity among Indigenous Deaf peoples in FNQ. Of major concern is the subset of language-deprived and uneducated persons who are most likely to appear in the criminal setting. Descriptions of such individuals in the United States show that many do have the capacity to use a form of sign language, however, their signing may be extremely rudimentary, consisting of idiosyncratic vocabulary relating to concrete and personal experiences (Richardson, 1996). They often demonstrate little advanced grammar, standard syntax, or higher-order thinking and processing skills. Furthermore, they may mix standard sign language, an obscure personal idiolect, and idiosyncratic gestures (Miller & Vernon, 2002)—and in the Australian setting, Indigenous signs. We propose that within the spectrum of language diversity among the FNQ Indigenous Deaf community, a subset of language-deprived individuals present similar characteristics.

Within sign language interpreting literature, deaf persons of such non- or semi-lingual status have been referred to as individuals with *Minimal Language Competency [MLC]* (Solow, 1988; RID, 1996), *High Visual Orientation* (Levitzke-Gray, 2006), and by a possibly controversial term *Primitive Personality Disorder (PPD)*, perhaps more appropriate to the realm of clinical psychology and mental health (Vernon & Raifman, 1997; Miller & Vernon, 2002). Although the term *PPD* appears on the surface contentious, Vernon and Raifman (1997) describe a set of diagnostic criteria for PPD, of which at least three must be present: (1) A meagre or total absence of knowledge of sign language, English, or a foreign sign language; (2) functionally illiterate, i.e., they read at grade level 2.0 or below as measured by a standardized educational achievement test; (3) a history of little or no formal education; (4) a persistent cognitive deprivation; and (5) a performance IQ score of 70 or above. Although interpreters and professionals in the legal setting should be familiar with these terms and the characteristics they encompass, the authors recognize that assigning labels to individuals can be problematic and potentially marginalizing, and should be done with caution or explanation. The important point to note is that these criteria *could* easily apply to the Indigenous Australian Deaf criminal suspect in the FNQ setting. If they do indeed exhibit some or all of these characteristics, it is likely they will experience significant disadvantage.

The diagnostic criteria described above can be highly useful for Auslan interpreters working within the legal setting in the FNQ region. Our observation is that Indigenous Australian Deaf criminal suspects with language deprivation often lack cognitive awareness of concepts and abstract thoughts outside their own personal reference. An identifiable crucial psychological and cognitive developmental milestone may not have been reached; conscious awareness of social interaction and insight into the thoughts and motives of oneself and others are referred to as Theory of Mind (ToM). The development of ToM is considered critical for effective communication, social interaction, and managing satisfying personal relationships with others (Baron-Cohen, 2000; Peterson & Siegal, 2000; Woolfe, Want, & Siegal, 2002).

ToM generally occurs in children at ages 4 or 5, easily identifiable by a *false-belief* task,[3] but typically develops later in deaf children who have *delayed* access to language. Peterson and Siegel (2000) found that deaf children with signing deaf parents achieve ToM milestones at age-appropriate stages, whereas most late-signing deaf children may not develop a ToM until their teenage years. Ultimately they may sustain life-long deficits in understanding the cognitive and emotional states of self and others (Marschark, Green, Hindmarsh, & Walker, 2000; Morgan & Kegl, 2006). Research conducted by Peterson, Wellman and Lui (2005) also included some late-signing Indigenous Australian deaf students from FNQ. They found that most of the late-signing deaf children, were still failing the standard false belief test at ages 8 to 10 years old (consistent with results from deaf children in other countries).

Without development of ToM, a language-deprived Indigenous Australian Deaf person will fail to understand that other people may have different motivations for behavior due to thoughts, values, and beliefs that differ from their own. In a legal setting, this limitation may significantly impede a criminal investigation; some Deaf clients may be cognitively unable to understand and therefore answer questions of motive or intent.

3. See Baron-Cohen (2000) for more detail.

We hypothesize that the aforementioned characteristics of language diversity, poor educational outcomes, and resulting interpersonal difficulties often associated with violence and criminal behavior, have quite likely led to an overrepresentation of Indigenous Australian Deaf people in the FNQ criminal setting. However, further research is required before these generalizations can be confirmed. Generally speaking, Indigenous Australian people are overrepresented in prisons. According to an Australian Bureau of Statistics report (ABS, 2006), there were 6,901 Indigenous Australian prisoners in Australia, representing 24% of the total prisoner population, whereas they comprise less than 2.4% of the total Australian population (as at June 1, 2001: ABS, 2007). Indigenous persons are 11 times more likely to be in prison than non-Indigenous persons after differences in age structure between the Indigenous Australian and non-Indigenous Australian populations are accounted for (ABS, 2005).

In the National Aboriginal and Torres Strait Islander Social Survey (2002), it was reported that 45.3% of Indigenous Australian peoples aged 15 years or over who were incarcerated had a disability or long-term health condition (ABS, 2006). The same study showed that Indigenous Australian people suffer high levels of family violence, with one in five Indigenous Australian people having reported being a victim of family violence and 24% of the over-15 year's age group having been a victim of physical or threatened personal violence. Unfortunately, there are no statistics available on the number of Indigenous Australian Deaf prisoners or the number of Deaf prisoners in Australia. One could extrapolate from these statistics that an Indigenous Australian Deaf person who is not afforded due process through linguistically and culturally tailored psychological assessments, and professional interpreting within the legal process has a very high risk of incarceration.

Based on the authors' experience in the field, a lack of understanding about language diversity and language incompetence among FNQ Indigenous Australian Deaf defendants may be systemic. It seems that little consideration is given to: (1) assessing their competency to be accorded due process, (2) how they should be questioned, and (3) provision of appropriate language and cultural accommodations. Within our hypothesized language diversity spectrum, an Indigenous Australian Deaf suspect may combine their signs from two languages (with various degrees of language competency)—Auslan and an Indigenous sign language.

The mixing of two sign varieties elsewhere has been described as a form of contact language (Lucas & Valli, 1992; Miller & Vernon, 2001;

see Quinto-Pozos, 2007 for studies of contact between signed languages in other locations). In the case of many FNQ Indigenous Australian Deaf people, we believe the term *idiolect* is more apt; i.e., idiosyncratic language use by an individual, due to unique circumstances of linguistic deprivation and/or isolation. As an example, a deaf child living in a remote FNQ Aboriginal community without other deaf people also residing in the community may improvise a sign system that is unique to the individual. The deaf child may not have fashioned this idiolect into a fully developed language for effective communication with others outside the immediate family.

An Indigenous Australian Deaf criminal suspect with language diversity or language incompetency may not be able to draw attention to their unique linguistic circumstances. Obviously this should be a concern for legal professionals. Often professionals wrongly (and naively) assume that all deaf people are able to read and write and even lip-read to some degree. It has been our experience (although awareness has increased in recent years), that interpreters are often not engaged at the first interview conducted by police. Therefore, initial interviews are often crudely and ineffectively conducted with pen and paper and/or English speech. If the deaf person is lucky, a family member might act as a pseudo "interpreter." As mentioned previously, in most cases the Indigenous Australian Deaf persons' literacy is often severely delayed and a reliance solely on written communication is unethical and unfair.

Specific Language Difficulties

The authors have observed that many linguistically and cognitively deprived Indigenous Australian Deaf people may exhibit several language difficulties. First, they may not know how to spell the names of people and/or places. They may instead use an improvised name sign or a gesture representing a physical feature and often used by others in the community. For example, one of the authors taught a Deaf teenager who referred to his remote home community as "FAR, FAR, AWAY": he could not name the place or describe where it was located. It may be impossible to interpret proper nouns without any visual reference, such as photos of people, the crime scene, or maps. Second, they may often experience considerable difficulty in comprehending professional or courtroom terms such as *offense, charge, bail, unlawful wounding, plea, verdict,* and *jury.* If sign equivalents for these terms are not re-conceptualized or explained beforehand with simplified language, the Indigenous Australian Deaf defendant may not understand the process. There are limitations in the lexicon of most signed languages with regard to equivalents for the "esoteric terminologies" of the legal system (Vernon, Raifman, Greenberg, & Monteiro, 2001). More often than not, an interpreter may demonstrate an overreliance on the use of fingerspelling (of the English word) for rendering legal concepts, vocabulary, and names (Brennan & Brown, 2004). Relying on fingerspelling would be a highly ineffectual interpreting strategy to use with Indigenous Deaf people with language incompetence, and accordingly an interpreter may need to be re-conceptualize, role-play, mime, explain, and approximate such concepts in a sign language in the absence of direct translations (Solow, 1988; Vernon & Raifman, 1997; O'Reilly, 2005). Third, they may not be able to understand hypothetical questions/scenarios and connective or qualifying words such as "if," "but," "because," "or," "at," "on or about" as these do not exist in their sign language or are not part of their conceptual understandings (see Theory of Mind discussed earlier). Conveying the implications of these common logical connectors can lead to misunderstandings.

To be effective in the legal setting, Auslan interpreters must be fully cognizant of the abovementioned issues. It is quite feasible that if interpreters and those in the legal system are not aware of such language diversity and incompetence, evidentiary mistakes and potential miscarriages of justice may occur, as has occurred in the United States (Miller & Vernon, 2002). They should also advise the legal team if language and communication strategies need to be modified to increase the ability of the client to participate more effectively and fairly in legal contexts. Readers are also referred to Russell and Hale (2008) for further discussion of sign language interpreting in legal settings. It would be sensible for Auslan interpreters to engage in professional development specific to working with Indigenous Deaf Australians. The following sections describe two actual cases to illustrate the effects of language diversity in Indigenous Deaf Australians in the legal setting.

CASE ONE: *EBATARINJA V. DELAND AND OTHERS*
In the case of the *Ebatarinja v. Deland and Others*, the question of linguistic and communicative competence of an Indigenous Australian Deaf

man was at stake. In Pether's (1999) summary of the case, she describes Roland Ebatarinja as an Aboriginal man from a remote community of *Arrernte*-speaking people in the Northern Territory, Australia. At three, he contracted meningitis, which left him deaf. Conley Ebatarinja, Roland Ebatarinja's father, stated in an affidavit that no one had been able to communicate with Roland Ebatarinja since; he had never completely acquired a language. Ebatarinja attended school in the regional town of Alice Springs, Northern Territory, until the age of 13 before returning to his family. When he was 17, Ebatarinja visited a house in the Larapinta Valley Camp in Central Australia with two other people. The following is a police account of what happened:

> Whilst at this Camp, the defendant grabbed hold of a female resident in an affectionate manner, which upset her husband and the victim in this matter. The victim walked up to the defendant and punched him twice in the head.
>
> The defendant ran from the area and returned shortly after with a brown handled pocket knife. He then attacked the victim stabbing him once in the back, once in the right upper thigh, and once in the right ankle. The stab wound to the thigh severed the femoral artery with the victim suffering massive blood loss.
>
> The defendant ran from the area . . .

Ebatarinja was subsequently arrested and charged with unlawfully causing grievous bodily harm and attempted murder before the Alice Springs Court of Summary Jurisdiction. Later that same day, the man allegedly stabbed by Ebatarinja died. Ebatarinja was then charged with murder. Evidence of eyewitnesses (who do apparently exist according to Pether) to the eventually fatal assault have never been presented to court. A question of alibi exists, but as Ebatarinja could not communicate, an alibi could not be obtained. Both prosecution and defense agreed that there was no method to enable Roland Ebatarinja to comprehend what was happening in legal proceedings. Mildren J, the Northern Territory Supreme Court judge accepted that Roland Ebatarinja "does not know of what he is charged [and] is unable to communicate with his lawyers" yet she proceeded to commit Ebatarinja for trial after staying an ex officio indictment.

In an appellant case to the High Court, it was argued that Mildren J had erred when she heard the application to have Roland Ebatarinja's ex officio indictment stayed and then committed him to trial.[4] The pleaded errors included Mildren J's refusal to grant the stays of the committal proceedings and her conclusions that:

> committals under the Northern Territory *Justices Act* required merely the opportunity to be heard; and that it was not the Magistrate's function at committal to inquire whether, or to decide that Roland Ebatarinja knew the case against him, was able to instruct counsel, or was able to give evidence.

The High Court decision in the *Ebatarinja* case, found that "a deaf, mute and illiterate defendant cannot be the subject of committal proceedings which s/he cannot understand or follow." Notwithstanding, it was found that if an accused cannot understand the language of the court, then they would be entitled to an interpreter. Ironically, the resulting judgment was useless for Ebatarinja, as no appropriate interpreter could be found who could faithfully understand his unique idiolect and resulting communication needs (Mildren, 1996). Before the High Court, the respondents expressed their hope that an interpreter might one day eventually be found (Pether, 1999). Paradoxically, and despite the High Court judgment, the right to an interpreter can still be waived by counsel and is too often the practice in Australian courts (Mildren, 1996).

CASE TWO: THE CASE OF ALBERT[5]

In 2004, author Fayd'herbe was asked by an Aboriginal legal firm to provide an initial language assessment of an accused Aboriginal man who was profoundly deaf. Legal counsel were seeking clarification as to whether an Auslan interpreter or an English notetaker would be necessary to assist in the communication of information at a criminal committal hearing, in order for the defendant to adequately defend a charge.

Albert lived in a remote Aboriginal community on the western side of Cape York, FNQ. He had been involved in an argument with a friend while both were intoxicated. Albert allegedly assaulted his friend, hitting him with

---

4. An ex officio indictment is a special indictment filed against a person to stand trial when a committal hearing has not taken place, or if insufficient evidence was found at a committal hearing to put a defendant on trial. The Director of Public Prosecutions may, in extraordinary circumstances, file such an ex officio indictment.

5. Not the defendant's real name.

an object. Albert was arrested and questioned by local police without an accredited interpreter. His cousin was present at the interview and provided basic 'interpreting' into the idiolect (of gestures/signs) that Albert used with her. Albert was charged with assault and remanded in custody. He was later transported to Cairns where he appeared before the court.

Upon meeting Albert, I began my interview for the purpose of an informal language assessment, by asking open-ended questions about his community and education. Albert told me that he had attended the former Queensland School for the Deaf as a boarder, where he mostly used fingerspelling and some signs. He was educated at the time when the extensive use of fingerspelling as an educational tool was favored. He did not complete school and returned to his remote community, where he has lived all his adult life. Albert did use a form of sign language, but had limited competency in Auslan. He appeared to use a highly idiosyncratic and mixed form of sign language, and slow, deliberate fingerspelling. He had difficulty answering questions that were not concrete or within his immediate frame of reference (e.g., answering questions about specific dates or locations outside his community). Given Albert's responses, I recommended to the court that further assessments, including sign language, language, and cognitive functioning, be conducted to ascertain his competency to stand trial. The presiding judge also had concerns about the ability of the accused to understand the case against him and granted a defense motion that further assessments be undertaken.

On my recommendation, all ensuing assessments with allied professionals were conducted with an Auslan interpreter and an Indigenous Australian Deaf interpreter present. After obtaining the results of the additional assessment, I was of the opinion that Albert did not have the requisite language or cognitive competence to linguistically satisfy competency to participate in court proceedings fairly and to respond to the prosecution case.

FNQ INDIGENOUS AUSTRALIAN DEAF PEOPLE: ADDITIONAL COMMUNICATION AND CULTURAL CONSIDERATIONS WITHIN A LEGAL SETTING

The Australian Institute of Judicial Administration Incorporated (2002) has produced two excellent publications for Western Australian courts, edited by Cooke (2002) and Fryer-Smith (2002), respectively. Both publications highlight cultural considerations for communication with

Indigenous Australians in the court setting, We believe that some of these considerations also apply to Indigenous Australian Deaf people and are therefore important knowledge for Auslan interpreters.

Conversational Cultural Styles

QUESTIONING STYLES

Direct, rapid-fire, and repeated questioning is often central to any forensic investigative process to illicit information. A traditional interview style following the question/answer (Q/A) approach is generally unfamiliar to Indigenous Australian Deaf witnesses and defendants, and rarely provides a good response or understanding. Author Fayd'herbe's extensive experience in police settings indicates that Indigenous Australian Deaf witnesses often have difficulty with direct questioning in interrogations that often includes linguistically complex questioning (e.g., trick questions, convoluted question forms, syntactically complex questions).

Diana Eades (1992, 1996) a foremost authority on Australian Aboriginal communication in the legal setting, has found that in general, Indigenous people are accustomed to less direct strategies to elicit information, including differences in the way silence is used and interpreted. The following is quoted from Eades's handbook, written to assist the communication of lawyers in Queensland:

> Aboriginal societies in Australia function on the basis of small-scale interaction between people who know each other and are often related to each other. Information or knowledge is often not freely accessible. Certain people have rights to certain knowledge. Direct questions are used in some settings, particularly to find out background details. E.g., "*Where's he from?*" However in situations where Aboriginal people want to find out what they consider to be significant or certain personal information, they do not use direct questions. It is important for Aboriginal people to respect the privacy of others, and not to embarrass someone by "putting them on the spot." People volunteer some of their own information, hinting about what they are trying to find out about. *Information is sought as part of a two-way exchange. Silence, and waiting till people are ready to give information, are also central to Aboriginal ways of seeking any substantial information.* (pp. 27–28) (Italics in original)

For Indigenous Australians, this style can lead to serious disadvantage in the legal setting. Indirect questioning is not a feature of courtroom questioning where, particularly in cross examination, lawyers are often both aggressive and direct in their questioning and usually demand direct and unequivocal answers.

The Australian Government's Commonwealth Evidence Act 1995 provides for narrative evidence in federal courts following application by counsel and direction from the court (section 29.2). While this Commonwealth legislation is not binding in other jurisdictions, the Queensland Criminal Justice Commission (Criminal Justice Commission 1996) reports:

> skilful counsel are able to elicit narrative from their witness in a natural and compelling way, but at the same time steer the witness away from inadmissible material (such as hearsay or prejudicial material). This controlled form of questioning is referred to as "guided narrative." (p. 49)

The authors find that a guided narrative style and an explanation of events is generally more effective in eliciting information from Indigenous Australian Deaf people, who will often gradually and indirectly express an opinion by describing events not necessarily related to the event but important in the mind of the Deaf person. Unfortunately, this style can cause significant crosscultural miscommunication and frustration for professionals in the legal setting who often seek explicit and precise answers. The authors have observed that it is often difficult for an Indigenous Australian Deaf person to provide explicit detail: For example, specifying the difference between 5:30 p.m. or 5:45 p.m. (which may be signed as "AROUND-SUNSET"); 500 km or 800 km (often signed as "FAR"), or 10 km or 20 km (often signed as "LITTLE FAR"), 15 or 25 people (often signed as "LOTS-OF PEOPLE/MOB").

Another form of questioning, problematic for Auslan interpreters, is the use of negative tag questions that require a "yes/no" response to confirm or refute a proposition, for example, "When he hit you on the head you couldn't see him, could you?" or "Isn't it the case that the man kicked you because you hit him, is that right?" This negative tag structure is not generally used in Auslan, and in translation, such questions can be ambiguous in terms of the appropriate response to express agreement or disagreement with the statement. Such question forms do not feature in the structure of Aboriginal English either, which Cooke (2002) notes as a problem for Aboriginal people in courts:

> It is interesting to note that the presence of an interpreter does not resolve the problematic nature of the negative question. The dilemma is thus: is

the interpreter to translate an affirmative answer to a negative question as "Yes" (because this is what the witness said in language) or "No" (because, in English, this is what the witness meant). (p. 27)

GRATUITOUS CONCURRENCE

Indigenous Australians (and interestingly many Deaf people) have a propensity towards *gratuitous concurrence* (Cooke, 2002). Cooke describes the term as referring to the inclination of indigenous peoples to nod when being spoken to. This behavior is culturally appropriate for it demonstrates that they understand the information being signed (spoken) to them. Unfortunately, non-signers often interpret this as an agreement or confirmation, which Cooke (p. 20) notes "does not necessarily signify the speaker's actual agreement with a proposition."

We have also observed Indigenous Australian Deaf people exhibiting "echolalia" (repeating or mimicking signed utterances or phrases) tendencies as they watch an interpreter signing. We believe this is a uniquely cultural phenomenon that assists them to comprehend the message and alerts the interpreter that they are attending. Paradoxically, this can be misinterpreted by non-signers as interjecting or privately conversing with the interpreter.

EYE CONTACT AND TRUST

In Indigenous Australian communities there are quite explicit norms regarding eye contact. For example, Indigenous Australians in general often avoid eye contact with persons with authority as a mark of respect (Fryer-Smith, 2002, p. 5). Client eye contact is of course vital to the interpreting process; however, this will almost certainly vanish if the interpreter does not attempt to establish rapport first. Eades (1996) explains that Aboriginal people frequently may not talk about important matters until they have a "relationship of trust" with a white person. To date, there are no NAATI-accredited Auslan interpreters in Australia who are of Aboriginal or Torres Strait Islander descent. In FNQ, there is only one experienced Indigenous Australian Deaf interpreter, Alma Waia. Waia works alongside Auslan interpreters (including author Fayd'herbe) to assist with mediating the spectrum of cultural and linguistic variations that exist throughout FNQ, Cape York, and Torres Strait Island communities. Non-Indigenous Interpreters are often viewed with suspicion at first by the region's Indigenous Deaf people. It takes some time, even years for Indigenous Deaf people to develop a sense of trust in a white Auslan interpreter (Fayd'herbe & Waia, 2007).

Non-verbal Communication

Non-verbal behaviors are also intrinsic to communication exchanges, for both hearing and Deaf Indigenous Australians. Fryer-Smith (2002) notes that "movements of the eye, head and lips may be used to indicate direction of motion, or the location of a person or of an event being discussed." The authors' have observed that Indigenous Deaf Australian greetings are also subtle: a head nod or eyebrow raise may occur before conversation is initiated. Often these signals are so subtle that non-Indigenous Australians may not even notice the exchange.

Kinship

Kin relationships have strict associated protocols of behavior. Obligations, rules of avoidance, and reciprocity play a significant role in the lives of all Indigenous Australian peoples (Reconciliation Australia, n.d.). As such, interpreters may find that some Indigenous Australians are reluctant to give evidence against family members for fear of straining relationships or guilt (Fryer-Smith, 2002).

IMPLICATIONS AND OUTCOMES FOR FAR NORTH QUEENSLAND INDIGENOUS AUSTRALIAN DEAF PEOPLE WHO ARE NOT AFFORDED DUE PROCESS

An incarcerated Deaf person, regardless of cultural background, is likely to endure communication discrimination in prison. As mentioned, the authors are not aware of research in the Australian context relating to Deaf prisoners' experiences in the corrections system. Yet if we generalize from the American studies of Miller and Vernon (2005), Deaf prisoners will be deprived of meaningful communication, are at greater risk of social isolation, and will have their mental health needs unrecognized. The authors are aware through clinical observation and conversations that a Deaf prisoner is at greater risk of violating rules and experiencing subsequent institutional penalties, particularly solitary confinement. Generally, Deaf prisoners are also at risk of being threatened for money, and are vulnerable to sexual abuse and violence by other prisoners. Consequently, a Deaf person in prison feels insecure and afraid of what is happening or what could happen to them. In prison, a Deaf person's experience is further complicated by deaf-unfriendly environments; that is, few or no conversational partners, difficulty following verbal instructions, no captions on television, no available TTY service, and difficulty requesting and accessing an interpreter.

STRATEGIES FOR AUSLAN INTERPRETERS WORKING IN LEGAL CONTEXTS WITH INDIGENOUS AUSTRALIAN DEAF CLIENTS

The following are recommended guidelines for interpreters, to assist Indigenous Australian Deaf clients achieve linguistic access and understanding of basic legal due process. Appended to this chapter are recommended strategies for legal and mental health personnel working in this context. The interpreter should:

- Meet with the rest of the legal team prior to engaging with the Indigenous Australian Deaf client to discuss the interpreting process and potential communication and cultural issues.
- Ensure that they have adequate time prior to an interview to establish communication and rapport with the client, especially if the interpreter has limited experience working with Indigenous Deaf clients.
- Immediately inform the rest of the legal team if there are any perceived concerns relating to the clients' psychological, cognitive, or communication deficits, that may otherwise go unnoticed by the untrained eye. An interpreter should be prepared to monitor the client's ability to understand what is transpiring and if necessary, advocate for a cessation of further interrogation until further assessments to establish whether the person is competent to be accorded due process and to (potentially) stand trial. This may include conducting very informal communication assessments and if required, advocating for professional standardized testing of language, psychological, and sign language skills (see Miller & Vernon, 2002 for more information).
- Ask that an Indigenous Australian Deaf interpreter also be engaged to assist with mediating communication (if not already present).
- Ask to see pictures/videos of the crime scene, diagrams, maps or ask to be taken to the scene (if applicable)—this is to be able

to effectively present the information in a visually appropriate manner for the client (Solow, 1998; O'Reilly, 2005).

- Consult with the client to determine the sign names of people relevant to the case, and any community signs they may use (Solow, 1998; O'Reilly, 2005).
- Build the linguistic context and adopt the client's own and/or improvised vocabulary.
- Show respect and consideration of the person's culture and language (Fryer-Smith, 2002).

DIRECTIONS FOR FUTURE RESEARCH

The foregoing discussion identifies several areas of interest that require further research. To assist interpreters, mental health clinicians, and legal professionals, we believe research should be undertaken in the following areas:

- The prevalence of Deaf signing persons among prison populations in Australia.
- The number of Deaf Indigenous Australians relative to Deaf non-Indigenous Australian prisoners in each state in Australia.
- The mental health needs and experiences of Indigenous and non-Indigenous Deaf Australian people within the prison system.
- The experiences of Deaf Indigenous Australians within the legal setting, including engagement with interpreters and mental health and legal professionals.
- The roles and collaborative practices of the Auslan interpreter, the Indigenous Australian Deaf interpreter, the mental health clinician, and the legal professional that contribute to maximizing cultural and linguistic access within a legal setting. (See Appendices 1 and 2 for our recommendations for counsel and clinicians.)
- The relevance of theoretical perspectives on the effects of language deprivation, specifically, Theory of Mind (Marschark, Green, Hindmarsh, & Walker, 2000; Woolfe, Want, & Siegal, 2002), Minimal Language Competency, and Primitive Personality Disorder (Vernon & Raifman, 1997; Miller & Vernon, 2005), in understanding how some Indigenous Australian Deaf adults have failed to develop a conventional language and compensate

with alternate forms of communication. Future research could investigate the relationship between Theory of Mind and Minimal Language Competency.

CONCLUSION

This chapter has presented the authors' professional insights and concerns about the communication characteristics and experiences of Indigenous Australian Deaf persons within Far North Queensland legal settings. Our discussion has highlighted the need for empirical investigation of the extent to which Indigenous Australian Deaf persons are afforded due process in the legal setting, given the gap between the forms of interaction expected in this context and their cultural, social, and linguistic characteristics as Indigenous and Deaf people. The observations, hypotheses, and professional practice recommendations presented here are in the formative stage and require rigorous debate, review, and development by professionals, researchers, and community members who have an interest in advancing the status of Indigenous Deaf people in the legal system in Australia and elsewhere.

REFERENCES

Australian Bureau of Statistics. (2002). *Indigenous Statistics for Schools*. ABS, Canberra. Retrieved November 4, 2009, from http://www.abs.gov.au/websitedbs/cashome.nsf/89a5f3d8684682b6ca256de4002c809b/0ea5f1e8a0 61c575ca25758b00020a98!OpenDocument.

Australian Bureau of Statistics. (2002). *National Aboriginal and Torres Strait Islander social survey (Cat. No.4714.0)*. ABS, Canberra. Retrieved February 17, 2009, from http://www.abs.gov.au/AUSSTATS/abs@.nsf/mf/4714.0/.

Australian Bureau of Statistics. (2005). *Australian social trends (Cat. No. 4102.0)*. ABS, Canberra. Retrieved February 17, 2009, from http://www.abs.gov.au/ausstats/ABS@.nsf/7d12b0f6763c78caca257061001cc588/72b476dd 4e468fdcca2570f300176b23!OpenDocument.

Australian Bureau of Statistics. (2005). *The health and welfare of Australia's Aboriginal and Torres Strait Islander (Cat. No. 4704.0)*. ABS, Canberra. Retrieved February 17, 2009, from http://www.abs.gov.au/AUSSTATS/abs@ .nsf/Lookup/4704.0Main+Features12005.

Australian Bureau of Statistics. (2006). *Law and justice statistics–Aboriginal and Torres Strait Islander People - A snapshot (Cat. No. 4722.0.55.003).* ABS, Canberra. Retrieved February 17, 2009, from http://www.abs.gov.au/ausstats/abs@.nsf/mf/4722.0.55.003.

Australian Bureau of Statistics. (2007). *Population characteristics, Aboriginal and Torres Strait Islander Australians, Australia, 2006 (Cat. No. 4713.0),* ABS, Canberra. Retrieved November 4, 2009, from http://www.abs.gov.au/websitedbs/cashome.NSF/4a256353001af3ed4b2562bb00121564/0ea5f1e8a061c575ca25758b00020a98!OpenDocument.

Australian Law Reform Commission. (1985). *ALRC 26 Evidence (Interim).* Retrieved February 17, 2009, from http://www.austlii.edu.au/au/other/alrc/publications/reports/26/index.html.

Australian Museum. (2004). *Dreaming online: Introduction to Indigenous Australia.* Retrieved February 17, 2009, from http://www.dreamtime.net.au/indigenous/index.cfm.

Baron-Cohen, S. (2000). Theory of Mind and Autism. In S. Baron-Cohen, H. Tager-Flusberg, & D. Cohen (Eds.), *Understanding other minds: Perspectives from developmental cognitive neuroscience* (p. 320) (2nd ed.). Oxford, UK: Oxford University Press.

Baron-Cohen, S., Leslie, A. M., & Frith, U. (1985). Does the autistic child have theory of mind? *Cognitio 21,* 37–46.

Brennan, M., Brown, R., & Mackay, B. (2004). *Equality before the law: Deaf people's access to justice.* Coleford, UK: Douglas McLean.

Coates, H., & Gifkins, K. (2003). Diagnostic tests: Newborn hearing screening. *Australian Prescriber 26* (4), 82–84.

Cooke, M. (2002). *Indigenous Australian Interpreting Issues for Courts.* Australian Institute of Judicial Administration Incorporated Publication Carlton, VIC: Retrieved February 17, 2009, from http://www.aija.org.au/ac01/Cooke.pdf.

Criminal Justice Commission. (1996). *Aboriginal witnesses in Queensland's criminal courts: Research Report.* Retrieved from http://www.cmc.qld.gov.au/data/portal/00000005/content/01317001200354523999.pdf.

Denman, L. (2007). Enhancing the accessibility of public mental health services in Queensland to meet the needs of deaf people from an Indigenous Australian or culturally and linguistically diverse background. *Australasian Psychiatry 15* (1), S85–S89.

Department of Education, Training and the Arts. (2007). *A chronology of special education in Queensland.* Retrieved February 17, 2009, from http://education.qld.gov.au/library/edhistory/state/chronology-spec/.

Eades, D. (1992). *Aboriginal English and the law: Communicating with Aboriginal English speaking clients: A handbook for legal practitioners.* Brisbane: Queensland Law Society.

Eades, D. (1996). Legal recognition of cultural differences in communication: The case of Robyn Kina. *Language & Communication 1* (3), 215–27.

Eades, D. (2000). I don't think it's an answer to the question: Silencing Aboriginal witnesses in court. *Language in Society 29*, 161–95.

Ebatarinja v. Deland and Others. [1998] HCA 62. Retrieved February 17, 2009, from http://www.austlii.edu.au/au/cases/cth/HCA/1998/62.html.

Farrugia, D. (1988). Practical steps for access and delivery of mental health services to clients who are Deaf. *Journal of Applied Rehabilitation Counselling 20*, 33–35.

Fayd'herbe, K., & Waia, A. (2007). *Interpreting for Indigenous Deaf persons in the legal setting.* Unpublished paper presented at the Association of Sign Language Interpreters Australia (ASLIA) National Conference: Sydney NSW.

Fiskin, R. (1994). *The Deaf in prison.* Unpublished ms.

Fryer-Smith, S. (2002). *Aboriginal Benchbook for Western Australian Courts.* Carlton, Victoria, Australia: Australian Institute of Judicial Administration Incorporated Publication. Retrieved February 17, 2009, from http://www .aija.org.au/online/ICABenchbook.htm.

Green, J. H. (2007). Fetal alcohol spectrum disorders: Understanding the effects of prenatal alcohol exposure and supporting students. *Journal of School Health 77* (3), 103–108.

Howard, D. (2006, March). Communication, listening and criminal justice. *NT Magistrates.* Symposium conducted in Darwin and Alice Springs, Australia. Retrieved February 17, 2009, from http://www.eartroubles.com/attachments/ presentation%20to%20magistrates.pdf.

Howard, D., Quinn, S., Blokland, J., & Flynn, M. (1993). Aboriginal hearing loss and the criminal justice system. *Aboriginal Law Bulletin 3* (65), 9–11. Retrieved February 17, 2009, from http://www.austlii.edu.au/au/journals/ AboriginalLB/1993/58.html.

Human Rights and Equal Opportunity Commission. (1997). *Bringing them home: Report of the national inquiry into the separation of Aboriginal and Torres Strait Islander children from their families.* Retrieved February 17, 2009, from http://www.humanrights.gov.au/social_justice/bth_report/report/ ch10_part3.html.

Johnston, T., & Schembri, A. (2007). *Australian Sign Language: An introduction to sign language linguistics.* Cambridge, UK: Cambridge University Press.

Kendon, A. (1988). *Sign languages of Aboriginal Australia: Cultural, semiotic and communicative perspectives.* Cambridge, UK: Cambridge University Press.

Kwek, J., & Kendon, A. (1991). Occasions for sign use in an Australian Aboriginal community. *Sign Language Studies 20* (71), 143–60.

Leigh, I. (Ed.). (1999). *Psychotherapy with Deaf clients from diverse groups.* Washington, DC: Gallaudet University Press.

Levitzke-Gray, P. (2006). *Teaming with relay interpreters: Enhancing interpreting possibilities.* Unpublished paper presented at the Association of Sign Language Interpreters Australia (ASLIA) Winterschool 2005, Perth.

Logan, G., & Clarke, E. (1984). *State Education in Queensland: A brief history.* Monographs On The History Of Education In Queensland No. 2. Queensland, Australia: Policy and Information Services Branch, Department of Education. Retrieved February 17, 2009, from http://education.qld.gov.au/library/docs/edhistory/stateedu.pdf.

Lore of the Land. (n.d.). Retrieved February 17, 2009, from http://www.loreoftheland.com.au/index.html.

Lucas, C. (2001). *The sociolinguistics of sign languages.* New York: Cambridge University Press.

Lucas, C., & Valli, C. (1992). *Language contact in the American Deaf community.* San Diego: Academic Press.

Marschark, M., Green, V., Hindmarsh, G., & Walker, S. (2000). Understanding theory of mind in children who are deaf. *Journal of Child Psychology and Psychiatry 41* (8), 1067–73.

Mildren, D. (1996). Redressing the imbalance: Aboriginal people in the criminal justice system. *Forensic Linguistics: The International Journal of Speech, Language and the Law V6* (1), 137–60.

Miller, K. (2001). Access to sign language interpreters in the criminal justice system. *American Annals of the Deaf 146* (4), 328–30.

Miller, K. R., & Vernon, M. (2001). Linguistic diversity in Deaf defendants and due process rights. *Journal of Deaf Studies and Deaf Education 6* (3), 226–34.

Miller, K. R., & Vernon, M. (2002). Assessing linguistic diversity in Deaf criminal suspects. *Sign Language Studies 2* (4), 380–90.

Moeller, M. P. (2000). Early intervention and language development in children who are deaf and hard of hearing. *Paediatrics 106*, E43.

Morgan, G., & Kegl, J. (2006). Nicaraguan Sign Language and Theory of Mind: The issue of critical periods and abilities. *Journal of Child Psychology and Psychiatry 47* (8), 811–19.

O'Reilly, S. (2005). *Indigenous Australian Sign Language and culture: The interpreting and access needs of Deaf people who are Aboriginal and/or Torres Strait Islander in Far North Queensland.* Cairns: Association of Sign Language Interpreters Australia (ASLIA) Winterschool.

O'Rourke, S., & Grewer, G. (2005). Assessment of Deaf people in a forensic mental health context: A risky business! *The Journal of Forensic Psychiatry and Psychology 16* (4), 671–84.

Office of the Queensland Parliamentary Counsel. (2000). Chapter 15: Investigations and Questioning. In *Office of the Queensland Parliamentary Counsel, Police Powers and Responsibilities Act 2000*, Reprint No. 5F, 350–56. Queensland: Government of Queensland.

Peterson, C. C., & Siegal, M. (2000). Insights into a Theory of Mind from deafness and autism. *Mind and Language 15*, 123–45.

Peterson, C. C., Wellman, H. M., & Liu, D. (2005). Steps in Theory-of-Mind development for children with deafness or autism. *Child Development 76* (2), 501–17.

Pether, P. (1999). We say the law is too important just to get one kid: Refusing the challenge of Ebatarinja v Deland and Ors. *Sydney Law Review*. Retrieved February 17, 2009, from http://www.austlii.edu.au/au/journals/SydLRev/1999/4.html.

Pollard, R. Q. (1994). Public mental health service and diagnostic trends regarding individuals who are Deaf or Hard of Hearing. *Rehabilitation Psychology 39*, 147–60.

Quigley, S. P., & Paul, P. (1984). *Language and Deafness*. San Diego: College-Hill Press.

Quigley, S. P., & Kretschmer, R. E. (1982). *The education of Deaf children*. Baltimore, MD: University Park Press.

Quinn, S., & Rance, G. (2006). *Investigation into hearing impairment amongst Indigenous Australian prisoners in the Victorian Correctional System*. Victoria: Department of Justice, Corrections. Retrieved February 17, 2009, from http://www.justice.vic.gov.au/wps/wcm/connect/DOJ+Internet/resources/file/ebc94945f1a30c6/REPORT_Hearing_Impairment_Indigenous_Prisoners.pdf.

Quinto-Pozos, D., (Ed.). (2007). *Signed languages in contact*. Washington, DC: Gallaudet University Press.

Raifman, L. J., & Vernon, M. (1996). New rights for deaf patients: New responsibilities for mental hospitals. *Psychiatric Quarterly 67*, 209–20.

Reconciliation Australia. (n.d.). *Share Our Pride*. Retrieved February 17, 2009, from http://www.shareourpride.org.au/pages//topics/culture/country.php.

Richardson, J. (1996). Court interpreting for Deaf persons: Culture, communication and the courts. *State Court Journal 20* (1): 16–22. Available at http://www.ncsconline.org/wc/publications/Res_CtInte_StateCrtJV20N1CtInterpForDeafPersonsPub.pdf.

Roth, W. E. (1908). *Miscellaneous papers*. Sydney: Australian Trustees of the Australian Museum.

Rothstein, R., Heazlewood, R., & Fraser, M. (2007). Health of Aboriginal and Torres Strait Islander children in remote Far North Qld: Findings of the Paediatric Outreach Service. *The Medical Journal of Australia 186* (10),

519–21. Retrieved February 17, 2009, from http://www.mja.com.au/public/issues/186_10_210507/rot10216_fm.html.

Russell, D., & Hale, S. (Eds.) (2008). *Interpreting in legal settings*. Washington, DC: Gallaudet University Press.

Solow, S. N. (1988). Interpreting for minimally linguistically competent individuals. *Journal of the National Association for Court Management 3* (2), 18.

The State of Queensland [Queensland Treasury]. (2008). Queensland Characteristics: A Statistical Division Comparison. Retrieved February 17, 2009, from http://www.oesr.qld.gov.au/queensland-by-theme/demography/population-characteristics/bulletins/census-2006/qld-characteristics-sd-comp-c06/qld-characteristics-sd-comp-c06.pdf.

Thomson, N., Burns, J., Hardy, A., Krom, I., Stumpers, S., & Urquhart, B. (2008). *Overview of Australian Indigenous Australian health status October 2008*. Retrieved February 17, 2009, from http://www.healthinfonet.ecu.edu.au/html/html_overviews/Overview_of_Australian_Indigenous_health_status_2008.pdf.

Torres Strait Regional Authority. (2007). *The Torres Strait*. Retrieved July 17, 2007, from http://www.tsra.gov.au/the-torres-strait.aspx.

Vernon, M., Steinberg, A. G., & Montoya, B. (1999). Deaf murderers: Clinical and forensic issues. *Behavioural Sciences and the Law 17*, 495–516.

Vernon, M., & Coley, J. (1978). Violation of constitutional rights: The language impaired person and the Miranda warnings. *Journal of Rehabilitation and the Deaf 11* (4), 1–8.

Vernon, M., & Miller, K. 1997. Obstacles faced by deaf people in the criminal justice system. *American Annals of the Deaf 150*(3), 283–91.

Vernon, M., & Raifman, L. (1997). Recognizing and handling problems of incompetent Deaf defendants charged with serious offences. *International Journal of Law and Psychiatry 20* (3), 373–87.

Vernon, M., Raifman, L., Greenberg, S., & Monteiro, B. (2001). Forensic pre-trial police interviews of deaf suspects: Avoiding legal pitfalls. *Journal of Law and Psychiatry 24*, 43–59.

Woolfe, T., Want, S., & Siegal, M. (2002). Signposts to development: Theory of Mind in Deaf children. *Journal of Child Development 73* (3), 768–78.

Yoshinaga-Itano, C., Sedey, A. L., Coulter, D. K., & Mehl, A. L. (1998). Language of early- and later-identified children with hearing loss. *Paediatrics 102*, 1161–71.

For Legal Professionals: Proposed Strategies and Guidelines for Effective Communication in Legal Interviews with Indigenous Australian Deaf Clients in FNQ

The following is a list of recommended practice guidelines for legal professionals, to provide Indigenous Australian Deaf clients with linguistic access and legal due process.

- Queensland law mandates that a police officer must not question or conduct an investigation without the presence of an Auslan interpreter if the [Deaf] client cannot speak with reasonable fluency (see Office of the Queensland Parliamentary Counsel, 2000).
- Ensure that the interpreter is experienced and NAATI qualified at the Professional Interpreter level. NAATI (the National Accreditation Authority for Translators and Interpreters) is the body responsible for setting and monitoring standards for the translating and interpreting profession in Australia. NAATI accreditation is the only credential officially accepted by employers for the profession of translation and interpreting in Australia.
- Allow the interpreter to make an informal assessment of the client's communication skills prior to interrogation or interview. Acknowledge that the interpreter may need a short time to converse with the client to allow for a building of rapport, trust, and safety. Any concerns about compromising interpreter impartiality by conversing could be addressed by having a second interpreter interpret the conversation into English for the benefit of non-signers present.
- Engage the services of an Indigenous Australian Deaf interpreter to work in tandem with the Auslan interpreter (O'Reilly, 2005), to enhance understanding of cultural and Indigenous sign language variations.
- Videorecord police interviews and ensure that both the interpreter's and client's faces and signing can be seen on the video. The videotape may be an important source of evidence

if subsequent questions arise about the client's communicative competence or the accuracy of interpretation during the interview.

- Conduct informal language skill assessments with the assistance of an interpreter, if there is any doubt about the client's language competency. Determining competency could be in the form of asking the client to describe and paraphrase the nature and consequences of the caution or the *oath*, administering the *Stephen's Test* (Australian Law Reform Commission, 1985), or asking simple comprehension questions. Arrange for professional standardized testing of literacy, IQ, and sign language skills if there are questions of competency.

- Be cognizant that under the Common Law there are ambiguities in regard to "competency" of deaf people: "Common Law, which applies in most jurisdictions, is deficient in permitting a deaf mute witness to be declared incompetent. No witness should be prevented from giving evidence who is able to communicate with human or mechanical help" (Australian Law Reform Commission, 1985).

- Use clear, simple, and slow speech/language (Fryer-Smith, 2002), minimize jargon (O'Reilly, 2005), and never assume a deaf person can read, write, or lip-read English proficiently enough to cope with a legal context, as this is rarely the case. Do not assume the witness can read with comprehension; if in doubt about their literacy, ask the witness to read a short newspaper article and then answer a few simple open-ended questions.

- Never check comprehension by using a yes/ no question such as "Do you understand?" It is best to have the witness re-state in their own language what they understand the question to be or re-phrase the cautioning and their legal rights. This strategy provides more evidence about whether the client does understand.

- Endeavor to use interview techniques that are culturally appropriate to Indigenous Australians, such as the indirect questioning style of guided narrative (Fryer-Smith, 2002).

- Avoid using "either-or," hypothetical, or negative questions (Fryer-Smith, 2002).

- Utilize pictures/photos/visual support of relevant crime scenes, landmarks, etc., to assist both the interpreter and witness (Solow, 1988; O'Reilly, 2005).

- Accept that the process will take much longer than a standard consultation and be prepared to offer regular breaks for both the interpreter and client's sake, as receiving and facilitating interpreted communication can be extremely fatiguing both mentally and physically.

APPENDIX 2

For Assessing Mental Health Clinicians: Proposed Interviews, Strategies, and Guidelines for Effective Communication with Indigenous Australian Clients

There is a high rate of psychological and psychiatric misdiagnosis of deaf clients in the United States, especially those who are prelingually deaf (Vernon, Steinberg, & Montoya, 1999). Errors are most often made in relation to the diagnosis for intellectual disability and mental illness. The diagnostic errors appear to be the consistent result of the Deaf client not having mastered the English language due to early onset of deafness, and/ or growing up in a non-English speaking community and culture, rather than being due to the result of brain damage, a psychological or psychiatric disorder. One might extrapolate from international data that the rate of misdiagnosis of deaf people in Australia might also be elevated.

As explained earlier in this chapter, by and large, Indigenous Australian Deaf people in FNQ may not grow up in a standard English-speaking community and may have great difficulty reading and writing in English. In Australia, Deaf clients are inherently discriminated against by the Western, hearing norms used by the mental health profession (Fiskin, 1994). By comparison, in the United States, Deaf clients have been given the legal right to equal access to psychiatric and psychological services via sign language and thus, court decisions based on expert opinion not meeting these legislative criteria would be subject to appeal (Raifman & Vernon, 1996).

The following is a list of recommended practice guidelines for mental health clinicians when working with a Professional Level 3 NAATI accredited Auslan interpreter. The objective is to enable the Indigenous

Australian Deaf client to participate with understanding in a legal psychological or psychiatric interview. For further insights readers should also refer to Leigh's (1999) volume, *Psychotherapy with Deaf Clients from Diverse Groups*.

- Talk to the interpreter before you meet in person about your experience (or perhaps lack of experience) working with interpreters. Ask the interpreter about their experience with facilitating mental health assessments. Establish a common understanding with the interpreter about the logistics of how the interpreted communication will work.
- Request any previous psychological, psychiatric, correctional, and educational assessments relating to the client.
- If possible, with the client's consent, talk to relevant case workers, doctors, teachers, parents, or extended family members to gain as much information as possible about the client's general functioning and communication strengths and weaknesses.
- Be aware that most psychometric assessment tools are not standardized on Indigenous Australian populations, or on Deaf persons. To avoid misdiagnosis, liaise with your local Deaf Society for advice about ensuring your testing is relevant and accessible for the client, and conduct a literature search on psychological assessments of Deaf persons.[6]
- On the day of the assessment, meet with the interpreter beforehand and discuss the nature of the assessment, the topics to be covered, the language to be used, potential risks, and sensitive information.
- Set up the room so that you, the interpreter, and the client have clear sight of each other. Ensure that the room is well lit, private from onlookers, and has good ventilation, comfortable chairs, and a table at a height that is practical for all concerned.
- Do not shout at the client; be aware of your facial gestures at all times. Speak clearly at an even pace. Regularly check in with the interpreter to see if you are speaking too fast or too slowly.

6. A Deaf Society is a non-profit benevolent organization in Australia that provides services, information, and support services for Deaf people, Hard of Hearing people and their families.

Pay attention to your register and choice of language as there are many terms in the discipline of mental health that have no corresponding signs.

- Explore with the client their previous experiences of a mental health assessment. Take time to build rapport and trust. Explain slowly and clearly what your role is and what you want to achieve. Explain why you have been asked to provide a psychological assessment. Ask the client if they have any questions before you start getting personal.
- Explain to the client your experience in working with Deaf people. If it is extensive this will greatly add to the client's sense of ease and comfort. If it is limited, say so. Ask the client to assist the process by seeking clarification.
- It is essential to conduct a basic language assessment and to determine how the client best communicates—whether they use standard Auslan, idiosyncratic signs, and whether they also like to use augmentative communication strategies such as lip-reading, hearing aids, mime, reading, or speech.
- Explore the client's perception of their Deaf identity and sense of affiliation with the Deaf community. It is not uncommon for a Deaf person to be ashamed about their deafness and feel isolated. When conducting a genogram ask if they are the only Deaf person in their family. Explore who their Deaf role models are. Explore whether other family sign fluently to them. Explore how they communicate with their family members who are not Deaf.
- Explore their education in detail. It is not uncommon for a deaf child to have been placed in mainstream schools with hearing children. Ask whether they were subject to bullying or ridicule because of their deafness. Explore their social circle and if they have any Deaf friends. Where did they go to school and what was their relationship like with their teachers? Who helped them with their homework?
- If the client does not respond to a question or seems to be having difficulty comprehending, try to re-phrase the message, instead of repeating it exactly.
- Avoid abrupt topic changes: explain when you are changing the topic or the focus of inquiry.
- Use visual aids whenever possible. Have a large notebook and thick markers so you can write down key words to guide your

inquiry. If the client can not read at all, draw a picture in a simple style. There are a number of pictorial cards that depict emotions, feelings, events, and behaviors; they are concrete, clear, and highly visual. These cards are usually used in the field of intellectual disability and learning disorders and are commercially available.

- Schedule breaks every 30 minutes and check in with the interpreter on how the client appears to comprehend the interaction. Discuss with the interpreter if your register and vocabulary is too difficult or too simplistic or if you are talking too fast or slow. Explore with the interpreter if they are comfortable with the level of detail (in questions) and if there are any confusing or ambiguous questions or responses.

- It is sometimes useful to explore details of an offense after you have gathered information about the client's social and developmental background, Deaf culture and identity, psychosexual development, drug and alcohol history, suicide and self harm behaviors, issues with aggression and violence, etc. This allows the client to feel that they are being understood as a person, not as a criminal. On occasion, the client may want to start the interview with the offense. In this situation, be guided by the client and then return to the offense after you have gathered all relevant background information to clarify specific details.

- Learn about a healthy psychological Deaf presentation in contrast to a healthy psychological hearing presentation (Pollard, 1994). Learn about Deaf adolescent mental health issues, for example: loneliness as a result of being left out of social interaction; social isolation, inferiority to hearing people; frustration from not being understood or listened to; aggressive behaviors; fear of rejection; low self esteem; shame resulting from being taught to behave and act like a hearing child; depression and despair that their life will always be a struggle; trauma from sexual abuse, rape, bullying, and ridicule; poor self expression from overly controlling parents; sexual development problems from delayed, confused, or poor sex education, Deaf gay/lesbian issues; suicide and self-injurious behaviors (ibid.).

- When formulating a diagnosis for a client for example, depression, obsessive compulsive disorder, post-traumatic stress disorder; do not rely on the *DSM-IV* (*Diagnostic and Statistical*

Manual for Mental Disorders) as it is culturally biased toward the Western hearing population (O'Rourke & Grewer, 2005). Misdiagnosis can lead to a number of problems, including an inappropriate treatment plan, inaccurate medication regime, client confusion and frustration, and further traumatization of the client. Inaccurate legal assessments have the potential to significantly disadvantage the deaf client. For example, overestimating the risk of re-offending or of danger to the community could lead to the client being detained in higher security cells unnecessarily, or imprisoned longer than is necessary (O'Rourke & Grewer, 2005).

- Learn some basic signs to express phrases such as "Hello, how are you?" "Would you like a break," "Coffee, tea, water?" This will demonstrate to the client that you respect them and have taken basic steps to understand their language. If you make a mistake, be prepared to express amusement at yourself and readily learn from the client and the interpreter's communication strategies (Farrugia, 1988)

Part 3 Globalizing: Interpreting in International Contexts

Developing Protocols for Interpreting in Multilingual International Conferences

Ted Supalla, Patricia Clark, Sharon Neumann Solow, and Ronice Muller de Quadros

Within the relatively new field of sign language research, an infrastructure or protocol for providing full access for Deaf researchers has been lacking. Moreover, there has been an unfulfilled need for a replicable mechanism to provide quality sign language access to major scientific conference content and networking, even at the national level in the United States where the Americans With Disabilities Act applies. The goal of the two-pronged strategy implemented at the 2006 Theoretical Issues in Sign Language Research (TISLR9) conference in Florianopolis, Brazil, was to provide full access to the conference for U.S. Deaf researchers in attendance and to develop an access protocol that could be replicated for other scientific conferences in the United States. This initiative was made possible by funding from the National Institutes of Health. The TISLR9 conference was selected because of its central role in scientific discussions related to sign language research, child language development, and deaf education as well as opportunities for Deaf scientists to gain recognition in this mainstream scientific community. The access protocol was developed and implemented, and a follow-up survey was conducted to assess the success of the protocol in providing American Sign Language (ASL) access.

The challenges of coordination and collaboration between signed and spoken language interpreters in this event are numerous. Effective interpretation between the official languages (ASL; the local sign language, Brazilian Sign Language (LSB); Brazilian Portuguese; and English), at TISLR9 was among the reasons for the success of the conference with the ASL coordinator and interpreting team playing a central role. The other language teams at the conference also benefited from the model protocol represented by the U.S. team.

The TISLR9 conference organizing committee carefully integrated conference format and interpreting needs at the outset of conference organization. This early consideration of the protocol by the TISLR9 organizing committee was an essential component of the mechanism promoting full access. It helped to mitigate the problem of interpreting as an ad hoc addition to a conference which has been planned, designed and funded with hearing people in mind, and which has not always been fully accessible to Deaf researchers.

As a scientific venue, the international TISLR9 conference was unique in the attention paid to language planning, with official signed and spoken languages providing access to Brazilian Deaf researchers for scheduled events. Unique also was the consideration shown to interpreters of non-official signed languages by attempts to make a "place" for them and allow access to the same preparatory materials that official language interpreters have had. In addition, the TISLR9 conference schedule was designed to avoid concurrent sessions, which would have made provision of interpreters at all events virtually impossible.

The TISLR9 planning, implementation, and evaluation processes are presented in this paper as a replicable model for future conferences. We outline the process undertaken to develop and execute an ASL Access protocol for U.S. Deaf and hearing researchers as well as report on the results of the post-conference survey of services provided. The paper will conclude with a recommended protocol (see Appendix 1) for ensuring full access of Deaf researchers to scientific conferences conducted internationally.

BACKGROUND

The TISLR Conference Series began in Rochester, New York, in 1986, as an outgrowth of U.S. and international workshops on sign language research beginning with the 1977 National Symposium on Sign Language Research and Teaching (NSSLRT) in Chicago, Illinois, and the 1983 International Symposium on Sign Language Research and Teaching (ISSLRT) in Finland. Subsequent meetings were held at Gallaudet University (1988 and 1998), Boston University (1990), the University of California, San Diego (1992), the University of Quebec at Montreal (1996), the University of Amsterdam (2000), and the University of Barcelona (2004).

The TISLR conference series is the recognized avenue for presentation and publication in the field of national and international sign language research. European conferences exist that are hosted completely in sign language, but they are regional and do not result in published proceedings. Attendance at the TISLR conferences has been an important means for Deaf scientists to gain recognition in the mainstream scientific community. However, since there has been no official organizational support for these conferences, it has always been incumbent on individual Deaf researchers to be proactive in providing for their own access needs, resulting in inadequate and inconsistent provision of access to conference proceedings. This is especially true for graduate students and non-tenured researchers who have had to rely on researchers who are funded sufficiently to bring their own interpreters. Indeed, in the United States there has been no direct funding mechanism for providing Deaf scholars interpreting access to international research conferences although there has been a mechanism for funding attendance at the same conferences. This missing component has effectively precluded Deaf and hard of hearing researchers from becoming involved in an increasingly global network of scholarly interactions. While recognizing this gap and subsequently funding the two initiatives that provided ASL interpreters for TISLR8 in Barcelona and TISLR9 in Florianopolis, the National Science Foundation and National Institutes of Health have yet to implement a distinct mechanism for addressing this issue of ASL access. At the 2000 conference in Amsterdam, a group of concerned Deaf researchers convened to discuss this very issue and drafted the Amsterdam Manifesto, which called for (1) the provision of sufficient funds to provide sign language interpreters ("officially designated" sign language[s]) for all sessions including social events of the conference; and (2) the inclusion of at least one Deaf scientist on the organizing committee to ensure necessary steps are taken to provide full access at TISLR conferences.

Toward the goal of implementing the recommendations of the Amsterdam Manifesto, co-author Supalla linked to the conference as lead project administrator and project liaison to the TISLR9 organizing committee. A project advisory committee of established Deaf and hearing scholars experienced in conference access was formed to consult with the ASL administrator on ASL access and evaluation before, during, and after the conference. An essential component of the ASL Access project was the networking with researchers who had previous experience with TISLR conferences such as those on the ASL Access advisory committee. Also crucial was the selection of a highly qualified ASL interpreting coordinator who worked with the administrator in implementing ASL interpreting during the conference and who served as the ASL interpreting liaison to existing conference subcommittees.

The ASL Access administrator, Ted Supalla, is an established Deaf scholar who has attended and presented at many earlier conferences, including the U.S. conferences that gave rise to the TISLR series. He has served as a mentor for numerous Deaf and hearing scholars nationally and internationally, and was one of the participants for the meeting that produced the "Deaf Action Plan" established by the National Institute on Deafness and other Communication Disorders.[1] The Deaf Action Plan promotes access and professional interaction leading to networking, sharing research, and the professional growth and leadership of Deaf scholars.

HISTORICAL CONTEXT

The 2004 NSF Award, "TISLR8: Enabling Full Access for Deaf and Hearing Americans and Increasing Representation of Deaf Americans" administered by Richard Meier of the University of Texas at Austin was a positive step toward providing ASL access to TISLR conferences held outside of the United States. In the past, such access was sporadic and dependent upon researchers bringing their own interpreters. This created a problem for researchers who did not have the resources to bring their own interpreters. Either they had to attend the sessions chosen by the researchers with their own interpreters or rely on the goodwill of those researchers to "loan out" their interpreters. The NSF Award allowed Meier to make six ASL interpreters available for all ASL-English users at the TISLR8 Conference enabling those without such resources to participate more fully in the proceedings. The process used to provide interpreters, however, had no framework for the interpreter selection process and relied heavily upon Meier's and his colleagues' in-house interpreters, therefore lacking a replicable protocol to ensure appropriate, qualified interpreters for this type of scientific conference.

In a logistics meeting following the TISLR8 Conference, co-author Supalla met with two other Deaf researchers to discuss issues surrounding the availability and quality of interpreters provided at TISLR conferences

1. The National Institute on Deafness and other Communication Disorders (NIDCD) is a branch of the National Institutes of Health.

and invited them to serve on the TISLR9 ASL Access Advisory Committee. They had attended the two previous TISLR conferences as well as the Amsterdam Manifesto meeting, and their experiences, insights, and suggestions related to interpreting services provided co-author Supalla with some of the information needed to develop a plan of action for improving the access situation for U.S. Deaf researchers. They also provided input regarding the selection of an interpreter coordinator.

During the same period, the three Deaf researchers were also able to meet with co-author Ronice Muller de Quadros, one of the lead organizers of the TISLR9 conference, and consult with her about the new plan. These meetings were crucial for determining the way that the conference was to be organized, since the goal was to incorporate a framework for an accessible conference involving multiple languages. ASL access, as well as LSB and Brazilian Portuguese access, were the guiding points for ensuring that the conference would be an accessible one. Also, although ASL was established as one of the official languages by the TISLR9 Organizing Committee, the ASL interpreters needed to be a team chosen by Deaf users of ASL. Supalla agreed to serve as the principal investigator (PI) for implementation of an ASL Access initiative for TISLR9. These meetings were part of the impetus for submitting the NIH proposal in December of 2005.

In March of 2006, during the Revolutions in Sign Language Studies, Linguistics, Literature, Literacy Conference hosted by Gallaudet University, Supalla hosted an informal discussion with a larger group of Deaf and hearing researchers about ASL access at the upcoming TISLR9 conference to gather further input about the plan and survey.[2]

Grant Award notification was announced in April of 2006 and in June Supalla (the project PI) met with co-author Neumann Solow (ASL team coordinator) to outline roles, responsibilities, and a plan of action for executing the NIH grant. Although email correspondence had been ongoing, the face-to-face meeting was the most productive way to ensure

2. Those people attending the ad hoc workshop on March 24, 2006, were: Patrick Boudreault (Canada), Paul Dudis (USA), Allan Fernandez (Costa Rica), Genie Gertz (USA), Joseph Hill (USA), Barbara Kanapell (USA), Gene Mirus (USA), Susan Mather (USA), Jane Norman (USA), Christian Rathman (Germany), Waldemar Schwager (Germany), Mark Zaurov (Germany). Others were present, but did not sign their names on the register.

mutual understanding of the goals of the grant, to review the work to be done, and to assign tasks and deadlines. Prior to receiving NIH award notification, recommendations were requested from the advisory committee and other researchers regarding interpreters they considered qualified to interpret in this venue. These recommendations were passed on to ASL team coordinator Neumann Solow.

PRE-CONFERENCE ORGANIZATIONAL COMPONENTS

Interpreter Coordination

Sharon Neumann Solow was selected as the coordinator for the U.S. interpreters because of her extensive experience in both interpreting and coordinating interpreters at national and international conferences (see Neumann Solow, 1985). Her overall responsibilities for the TISLR9 conference included recruitment of qualified interpreters, coordination and scheduling of ASL interpreting, development of interpreting protocols for working with conference organizers and presenters (see Appendix 3), troubleshooting issues that arose during the conference, and serving as liaison to coordinators of other languages at the conference.

In June of 2006, Supalla and Neumann Solow met to discuss an administrative plan, contractual arrangements and protocols to use before, during, and after the conference. Based on this meeting, Neumann Solow's duties were outlined, including duties discussed in the guidelines for consultant interpreters and conference organizers published by the International Association of Conference Interpreters (AIIC), the recognized organization for provision of highly qualified spoken language interpreters at international venues.[3] Immediately the ASL interpreter coordinator contacted Ronice M. de Quadros and the TISLR9 organizing committee to establish a procedure to ensure optimum performance during the conference. This connection was crucial to preparing the arrangements necessary for successful interpreting during the conference.

3. http://www.aiic.net/ViewPage.cfm/.

Appointment of Advisory Committee

In heading the NIH project, the PI collaborated with an advisory committee comprised of Deaf and hearing researchers who had been attendees and organizers at earlier TISLR conferences.

The ASL Access advisory committee was comprised of three Deaf members and two hearing members.[4] Once the award was announced, little time was left to fully utilize the expertise of the advisory committee in the interpreter selection process, but the committee was involved in providing input for the post-conference survey as it was being developed as well as providing assistance and advice during the conference.

Interpreter Team

A general call for interpreters for a scientific conference such as TISLR9 is an inefficient, time-consuming, and costly means of identifying and hiring qualified individuals qualified for this venue. A process that begins with input from Deaf professionals and previous conference organizers who have worked with interpreters in the relevant field is the optimum means of establishing an initial pool of interpreters from which to recruit.

Determining quality in international conference interpreting has been an ongoing challenge for spoken language interpreting since the Nuremburg Trials (Gaiba, 1998). The Nuremburg Trials are referred to in the literature as the first venue where the simultaneous transmission of information between spoken languages occurred. The motivation for ensuring accuracy in interpretation had serious ramifications leading to the establishment of the AIIC register of qualified interpreters. In the United States, signed language interpreting has its roots in the Rehabilitation Act of 1973, which mandates access to agencies and services receiving federal funding. The focus of interpreting, at that time, was on interpreting in community settings (occupational training, medical, mental health, and legal contexts). Quality assurance measures and recommended practices were designed to

---

4. The deaf members of the Advisory Committee were: Christian Rathmann, then of Ohio State University; Gaurav Mathur, then of Haskins Laboratories; and Carol Padden, of the University of California at San Diego. The hearing members were: Richard Meier, of the University of Texas at Austin and Diane Brentari, of Purdue University.

address these settings specifically. Another result of the original focal difference between signed language and spoken language interpreting is that the spoken language field has well-defined mechanisms for providing qualified interpreters to international conferences while the signed language field has the equivalent for community settings.

Another difference between signed and spoken language interpreting is that signed language interpreting has only recently turned its attention to the mechanisms and protocols necessary for quality in conference settings. Looking to spoken language studies of interpreting for conference-like events, a number of spoken language researchers (Kopczynski, 1994; Moser-Mercer, 1996; Buhler, 1986; Kurz, 2001; Pöchhacker, 2001) have discussed various approaches to assessing quality. Selection of research methods for looking at quality are based primarily on two factors: (1) the reason for the quality determination (i.e., pre-service, hiring, in-service, user satisfaction) and (2) the perspective of who is evaluating the quality of the interpreting (i.e., instructor, contracting entity, interpreters, users). Based on this research, the protocol incorporated specific steps and processes before, during, and after the conference to provide quality interpretation. In addition, the protocol was infused with multiple perspectives, including Deaf and hearing researchers, interpreters, and conference organizers.

Prior to award notification, suggestions of possible qualified interpreters for the U.S. team were obtained from the advisory committee. Neumann Solow contacted those individuals and obtained the commitment of several candidates. However, two of the six positions needed to be filled with as-yet unknown interpreters. A screening instrument was developed for selection of the final two interpreters for the team. In this pre-conference selection process, the goal was to evaluate the quality of interpreting in a setting that approximated the natural setting of a TISLR conference. Two Deaf and two hearing researchers were filmed presenting a brief 7–10 minute talk about one of their current research projects. During the national Conference of Interpreter Trainers meeting (2005), Neumann Solow recruited four individuals interested in the positions and had them film themselves interpreting the stimulus materials—the videos were then sent to the ASL Access administrator for final screening and approval.

Web Site Design and Management

In order to communicate effectively with Deaf and hearing participants prior to the TISLR9 conference, a web site about ASL access to TISLR9 was created to disseminate information. It provided information about NIH funding of ASL access to TISLR9, the names and credentials of the interpreters for the conference, contact information for making non-presentation interpreting requests, and a link to sign-up for ongoing updates as well as the post-conference survey.[5] In addition, information was provided about how to prepare a Deaf-friendly presentation and suggestions for working with interpreters (see appendices). Once the web site was ready, the link was provided to the TISLR9 organizing committee with an announcement to be placed on their web site about the new ASL Access web site. An announcement was also placed on the Deaf academics, sign language and general linguistic listservs, all of which reach an international network of scholars. Following the conference, the ASL Access survey was disseminated to all who signed up via the web site.

IMPLEMENTATION OF SERVICES

The AIIC Professional Standards, Version 2000, Article 7, Interpreter's Working Day states: "Given the constraints related to quality and health, the normal duration of an interpreter's working day shall not exceed two sessions of between two-and-a-half and three hours each."[6] According to this guideline, the maximum working day should be five to six hours comprised of two separate sessions. At TISLR9, the schedule included 48 presentations and two poster sessions that had to be covered over four days. Considering this schedule, the organization of the presentations was set in a way to have several breaks without sign language interpretation required. This was made possible by the insertion of entertainment breaks by Deaf performers presenting on themes related to the conference, but with no need of interpretation. The other factor that was important for the well-being of the interpreters was the provision of a special room for the interpreters to work and rest. The room contained computers and table space for talk preparation and meetings with speakers, as well as snacks and drinks and comfortable sofas for resting. Professional massages were also provided for interpreters to relax and be better prepared for their next

5. Patrick Boudreault of California State University at Northridge managed the ASL Access web site.

6. http://www.aiic.net/ViewPage.cfm/article122.

professional session. The room was reserved for interpreters to make sure that they would not be required to interpret in this environment.

Conference design called for no concurrent sessions. While this allowed for complete coverage of all sessions, the actual length of the interpreting day was about 10 hours. For an academic conference, this was a grueling schedule for only six interpreters. Each team of two handled 16 presentations, which left them little time to prepare or schedule interpreting for ad hoc meetings. In addition, for each presentation, one team was assigned as the lead team, one team served as a back-up team during the question-answer period following each presentation, and one team was "off-duty." In reality, the off-duty team most often was meeting with presenters to prepare for other presentations to which they were assigned. Fortunately, only two requests for ad hoc interpreting were made prior to the conference and two during the conference, and those requests were filled. Deaf and hearing conference attendees tended to make their own arrangements for networking interactions. Prior to the beginning of the conference, the interpreters were paired into three teams, provided with abstracts of all scheduled presentations, and asked which presentations they preferred to interpret. After receiving this information, the ASL team coordinator created the final schedule of assignments in order to allow the teams to focus preparation on their assigned presentations.

Although an international interpreter coordinator was hired to meet the needs of other language interpreters (LSB and spoken language interpreters), the other interpreting teams went to the ASL coordinator when issues arose and looked to the ASL team as the model for their work. This happened because of the ASL interpreter coordinator's extensive experience with this kind of setting. The LSB and spoken languages interpreters were learning how to manage the many variables specific to an international Deaf conference, an experience that was new to them. U.S. financial support for the ASL interpreters was another very important factor, since language interpretation is always very high when compared to overall conference budgets. If Brazil had to pay for interpreters from other countries, the conference would have been impossible to hold. The sign language interpreters from the United States, as well as all the other interpreters, benefited by the structure established by the conference; however, this would have been impossible had the conference been responsible for hiring sign language interpreters for all languages represented. This was particularly true for the cost of the ASL team since ASL was one of the official languages of this conference. These factors highlight the critical role U.S. governmental financial support and the ASL Access team had in contributing to a successful, accessible conference for Deaf and hearing participants and speakers.

Maximizing Access for Interpreters

A request was made to the organizing committee to allow the ASL Access administrator and coordinator of the U.S. team to visit the meeting room at least one day before the conference in order to review the logistics related to physical set up and troubleshoot potential problem areas for interpreting in a multilingual signing environment. Due to booking issues, access to the meeting room was not obtained until two hours before the conference began.

Sound and sight access for the interpreters became an issue on site. Fortunately the conference organizers were extremely helpful in attempting to find a quick solution to these issues. The two official sign language teams, LSB and ASL, were positioned on opposite ends of the stage with the presenter's podium mid-stage between them (see Figure 1).

The speakers were positioned in front of the stage meaning that the sound from the speakers would travel to the back wall before finally reaching the interpreters on stage, which would make it difficult to hear well or accurately. Small speakers were quickly located and set up in front of the interpreters on stage, which helped to resolve most of the sound issues. In order to interpret effectively, interpreters need access to all visual materials being used during a presentation, so monitors hooked up to the presenters' PowerPoint slides were placed on the floor in front of the interpreters so that they could see what the presenters were referring to while interpreting. This assisted the interpreters in establishing an accurate visual framework for the signed renditions they presented to the Deaf participants. These two adjustments made the work possible for the interpreters.

Maximizing Access for Deaf Eyes

The physical layout compromises described above were not as conducive to access for Deaf researchers, however. Having the interpreter, presenter, and PowerPoint display within the same sightline allows the Deaf researcher the opportunity to take in actions and behaviors from the presenter that approximates the experience of hearing researchers in the audience. The distance between the interpreter (both ASL and LSB)

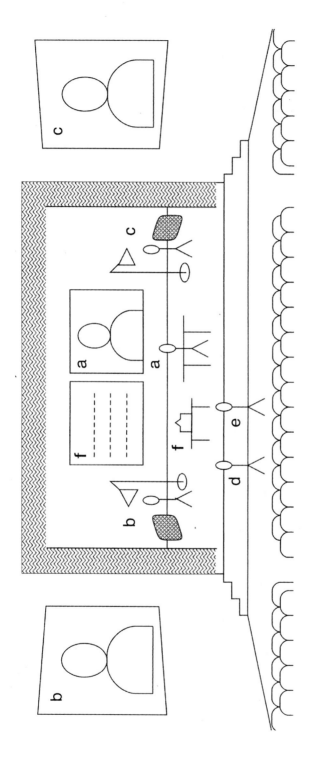

FIGURE 1. *TISLR9 stage arrangement*

A. *Speaker on stage and projected on screen*

B. *ASL-English interpreter on stage and projected on screen*

C. *LSB-Portuguese interpreter on stage and projected on screen*

D. *Danish SL-English interpreter on floor*

E. *BSL-English interpreter on floor*

F. *PowerPoint projection*

and the presenter was so great that those watching the interpreters were not able to easily observe the presenter or the PowerPoint display directly behind the presenter. Since the interpretation process by nature introduces a delay in transmission of information from the presenter to the audience dependent upon the interpretation, by the time the audience members receive the interpretation and thus the reference to the PowerPoint slide, the presenter often has already moved on to the next slide creating disjunction between the message and any supporting visual information.

Projection of PowerPoint presentations has also created an issue related to appropriate lighting for interpreters. The main reason for placing the interpreters so far removed from the presenter's position was to maximize whatever stage lighting was available for the interpreters while not washing out the PowerPoint slides. A compromise was reached resulting in less than optimal conditions for both viewing the interpreters and the PowerPoint presentations. In considering the challenges presented by modern technology, the authors have come up with some suggestions for future conferences that have the potential of resolving the issues discussed here while maximizing the use of technology currently available. These suggestions are discussed in Appendix 1.

MONITORING THE INTERPRETATION PROCESS

During the planning process, a concern based on experiences at previous conferences emerged, creating an opportunity to seek an innovative solution. Even with optimal preparation of interpreters and education of presenters about deaf-friendly talks, habits and conventions established over decades of conference presentations are hard to break. Speakers still speak rapidly, read their papers rather than present them, do not pause between major points to allow interpreters time to finish up the interpretation of one major point before moving into the next, fly through their PowerPoint slides without consideration of the time it takes to watch an interpretation before looking up at the slide, speak away from the microphone, and go over their time limit. Many scientific conferences appoint a moderator for each session whose responsibility is to watch the time and moderate any discussion following the session. However, the idea of appointing an individual to monitor (see Kalina, 2005 for a discussion of the role of the monitor) the pacing and volume of the actual presentation has not been considered.

This issue was presented to the TISLR9 organizing committee by the ASL Access administrator, recommending the appointment of a conference monitor whose responsibility would focus entirely on monitoring the accessibility of each presentation. The role of the monitor was to provide feedback to the interpreter teams, as well as to the organization that sponsored the conference and the technical team.

The organizing committee approved the idea and assigned the job to the international interpreter coordinator. An organizational chart of the flow of communication is shown in Figure 2.

Although the accessibility challenges were mediated somewhat, the fact that the international coordinator had two jobs to do during the conference sometimes took him out of the meeting room during presentations, leaving the interpreters without monitoring support. It is recommended that the individual appointed to this position commit to remaining in the conference room for all sessions and that no other responsibilities are assigned during sessions. It is also highly recommended that she or he know as many of the languages as possible including the official signed language as well as the official spoken languages.

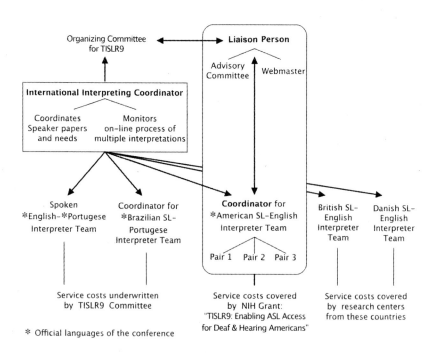

FIGURE 2. *Organizational chart for TISLR9*

Spoken Language Interpreters

One example of how conference monitoring was to work can be seen in the challenges presented by a multi-language setting (Gile, 2005). The conference languages were English, LSB, Portuguese, and ASL. The LSB interpreters were inexperienced in working linguistic conferences. In addition, many of them did not know English, not to mention the scientific jargon, and were therefore not able to interpret directly from English to LSB. Portuguese-English interpreters were hired to provide relay interpretation (AIIC term) for the LSB interpreters when an English or ASL speaker was presenting and then for the ASL and English users when a Portuguese speaker was presenting. The time that it took, for example, to convey the speaker's English message to Portuguese and then through a closed FM system to the LSB interpreters was extensive, necessitating even more time before the Brazilian Deaf people could look at the relevant slide. The appointed monitor was to watch the sign language interpreters with the greatest delay time, in this case, the LSB interpreters, and to signal the speaker when it was appropriate to change slides if the speaker was not self-monitoring.

Content preparation is a vital part of effective conference interpreting and in the AIIC "Checklist for conference organisers" it states, "Briefing: If the conference is very technical, it is advisable to organise a briefing between the interpreters and the speakers. Interpreters will thus be able to ask questions on terminology and procedure." The English-Portuguese interpreters' lack of experience with signed language research initially posed an issue for the LSB interpreters. Although the English-Portuguese interpreters were invited by the U.S. team to join the preparation meetings with presenters, their assumptions were that there was no need. By the end of the first day, the LSB interpreters expressed frustration with the misleading, inadequate interpretations they were receiving from the English-Portuguese interpreters and the international coordinator strongly encouraged them to begin attending the preparation meetings highlighting the importance of meeting with presenters before they speak.

International Sign Issues

Unique to an international conference including users of various signed languages is the fact that many Deaf individuals from other countries have some knowledge of ASL. As a result, many researchers from other countries who cannot afford to bring interpreters for their own signed language will watch the ASL interpreters to achieve access to conference proceedings. During question-and-answer sessions, these researchers often rely on the ASL interpreters to interpret their questions into English. However, the degree of competence with ASL that such individuals may possess varies greatly since it is often their second, third, or even fourth language.

Thus, another linguistic form that is commonly used at international Deaf conferences and at TISLR conferences is a lingua franca known as International Sign.[7] Those who use International Sign tend to adapt its use to their indigenous signed language, giving it a continuously varying look. At TISLR conferences, ASL interpreters may or may not have sufficient experience with International Sign to adequately interpret questions from such signers who often think they are using ASL but are actually using a mixed form approximating International Sign. No provision had been made to accommodate this form of communication at TISLR9. For future conferences, it is recommended that conference organizers arrange for one or more Deaf monitors/interpreters with expertise in interpreting into and from International Sign to accommodate the communication needs of those without access to their native signed language.

FORMAL EVALUATION OF ASL ACCESS PROVISION

This section will report on the results of the ASL Access survey designed and administered to TISLR9 participants who signed up on the web site. It is hoped that this pilot evaluation of conference access organization, practices, processes, and quality of interpreting will help in revising and building a model protocol for full access by Deaf scholars to professional academic conferences. Before discussing the survey results, we address one additional access service mentioned in the NIH proposal that did not occur. Some conferences provide open captioning or speech-to-text services for Deaf and hard of hearing participants. The TISLR9 organizing

7. International Sign functions like a pidgin language in cross-linguistic signed settings. It has evolved some standardized signs for use among signers at international meetings and conferences where no one signed language is known by all. See Supalla and Webb (1995).

committee considered it, but deemed the service too costly and therefore did not provide open captioning during the conference.

During the fall of 2006, an ASL Access for TISLR9 web site was established to provide information to both Deaf and hearing ASL users about access available during the conference. Also available on the web site was an opportunity to sign up to receive updated information about TISLR9 as well as the survey following the conference. During the conference, a bookmark with the ASL Access for TISLR9 web site address was distributed to ASL users who had not registered prior to the conference in order to allow them the opportunity to complete the post-conference evaluation.

The TISLR9 ASL Access Survey served as the basis for an evaluation and revision of the TISLR9 mechanism as a protocol for access of Deaf professionals to major scientific conferences. The evaluation was to help determine whether the model of access used for TISLR9 was a viable protocol for future conferences, national and international.

Development and Administration of Survey

The TISLR9 ASL Access Survey was developed based on the objectives outlined in the ASL Access grant and revised with input from the advisory committee. A final draft was then designed and uploaded to a secure, confidential web site to which TISLR9 participants could go to complete the survey anonymously.

As mentioned in the Interpreter Team section, user experience and a pre-conference screening instrument were used to select the U.S. team. For gathering post-conference information from users of interpreter services, the literature on spoken language interpreter quality assessment points to surveys as the preferred method. The survey covered four major areas of interest: quality of the U.S. interpreter team, value of the ASL Access web site, overall accessibility of the conference to Deaf and hard of hearing participants, and networking practices (Moody, 2002).

Demographic Information and Overall Interpreting Team Quality

Twenty-one participants signed up on the web site and all completed the survey. Twelve participants self-identified as Deaf and nine self-identified as hearing.

Participants were asked to rate their own sign language competence in two areas, their ASL competence, and their comfort in using International Sign. The rating scale for ASL competence ranged from 1 to 5 with 1 defined as novice level and 5 defined as native-like competence. Eight Deaf and five hearing respondents self-rated at 4 or 5, while three Deaf and one hearing respondent self-rated at 3. Only one Deaf person self-rated as a novice while three hearing people did. The question about International Sign showed that nine of the 12 Deaf participants felt comfortable with it while five of the nine hearing did. This may account for why only four requests were made to the interpreter coordinator for ad hoc interpreting. The participants utilized their own International Sign skills to communicate with colleagues who spoke other languages.

Information about individual interpreter performance has been shared with the individual interpreter and interpreter coordinator, but that information is not included here because the results have no direct bearing on the overall effectiveness of the protocol for access.

Access and the Conference in General

Of the 21 respondents to the survey, 16 (9 Deaf, 7 hearing) stated that they were presenters. Although reasons other Deaf and hearing users did not sign up on the web site are not known, it might be that presenters were more invested in the effectiveness of the interpreting team in the transmission of their message, and therefore were more likely to utilize the information about working with interpreters and to complete the survey. This may indicate that although web-based access information may not effectively reach all participants at a conference, it may be an effective means of reaching presenters. It also may be an effective means of gauging how web-based information is used. It is recommended that our findings be used as a baseline for future conferences to measure the overall effectiveness of this protocol.

For the question on overall conference quality and access, we looked at only the responses of the 13 Deaf and hearing respondents who assessed their own ASL competence at either level 4 or 5. The ratings of these Deaf and hearing respondents showed the same patterns, so these two groups were also collapsed. Their responses are shown in Table 1.

In general, participants seemed to rate conference access as effective. It is important to note that the item related to sessions and breaks showed a need for revision. Based on the comments made in this section of the

TABLE I.

Overall Conference Quality & Access	n=13
Check all that apply:	
No improvement needed	1
Sessions & breaks need revision	9
Content quality needs improvement	4
Voice interpreter quality needs improvement	3
Sign interpreter quality needs improvement	2
More interpreters needed*	3
* all 3 respondents were hearing	

survey, it was clear that participants who responded felt that factors such as the overall length of the conference day, number, and timing of breaks relative to the number of sessions were important in assessing the effectiveness of access to the conference.

CONCLUSION

Our goal in documenting the protocol for successful conference access for ASL users at TISLR9 is to show that full access *is* possible given the commitment to do so. These positive first efforts show, moreover, that such a protocol for access for Deaf and hearing academics in a sign language environment often improves conference logistics and access for *all*, especially in international settings, where non-native users of a language appreciate the extra time and care given to accurate, well-paced, multimodal exchange of academic ideas.

The value of the ASL Access protocol was recognized and adopted for use with other languages at the TISLR9 conference. The prior recommendations prepared by the ASL team coordinator were valuable to all interpreting teams. In Brazil, the organizing committee of the conference consulted with Neumann Solow for help with instituting a similar selection process for LSB and Portuguese-English interpreters. Although this was not a part of the ASL Access protocol, Neumann Solow worked with the organizing committee to establish a pre-conference training process to allow these interpreters to meet and exchange experiences. Also, conference papers were solicited from and provided by the presenters (speakers and signers) for all interpreters prior to the conference. These papers and the pre-conference training sessions were crucial for these international teams to be well prepared for the conference work.

Although not originally the goal of this funded project, it is important to consider the establishment of criteria for determining the qualifications of the principal investigator (PI) for future projects of this type. Ensuring that the PI has extensive firsthand experience utilizing the services of an interpreting team in this venue and understands the factors involved in quality interpretations are critical components for successful access.

We are taking the further step of sharing these results in the hopes of establishing a common foundation for conference access in professional disciplines. Presently, each discipline, and even each conference committee, attempts to design access anew, without an awareness of prior experience and efforts in this area. Hopefully, the insights and recommendations provided in this chapter will help professional discipline conference organizers to build upon this foundation, with the ultimate goal of increased communication and informed contributions from Deaf and hearing professionals.

ACKNOWLEDGMENTS

Our TISLR 9: Enabling Access for Deaf and Hearing Americans project team would like to acknowledge the National Institutes for Health for funding the R13 Grant #008507, which made this project possible. We express our appreciation to Betsy Hicks McDonald for her assistance in writing the R13 grant proposal and its subsequent editing. Without her invaluable contribution, the project would never have been funded. Besides thanking the members of the advisory committee for their support and feedback, we also want to thank MJ Bienvenu, chair of ASL and Deaf Studies for hosting the March 24th informal meeting in Washington, D.C.; Jennifer Gillis and Linda Cassidy for their superb administrative support; Aaron Rudner for his hard work as the international interpreting coordinator; and the presenters who supported access by providing preparatory materials and meeting with interpreters before each presentation.

Special thanks go to our ASL interpreting team members, Aaron Brace, Patricia Lessard, Brenda Nicodemus, Stacy Storme, and Dan Veltri, who set the standard for professionalism in skill, preparation, team support, and collaboration and made the ASL Access project a great success. We thank the many people in Brazil who supported the interpreting teams making the experience invaluable, enjoyable, and memorable.

REFERENCES

Buhler, H. (1986). Linguistic (semantic) and extra-linguistic (pragmatic) criteria for the evaluation of conference interpretation and interpreters. *Multilingua* 5(4), 231–35.

Coordinating Conferences. 2007. Retrieved August 27, 2007, from http://www.rid.org/UserFiles/File/pdfs/Standard_Practice_Papers/Drafts_June_2006/Coordinating_Conferences_SPP.pdf.

Gaiba, F. (1998). *The origins of simultaneous interpretation: The Nuremberg Trial.* Toronto: University of Toronto Press.

Gile, D. (2005). Directionality in conference interpreting: A cognitive view. *Communication & Cognition* 38(1–2), 9–26.

International Association of Conference Interpreters (AIIC). 2007. Retrieved September 4, 2007, from http://www.aiic.net/default.cfm.

Kalina, S. (2005). Quality assurance for interpreting processes. *Meta* 50(2), 768–84.

Kopczynski, A. (1994). Quality in conference interpreting: Some pragmatic problems. *Bridging the gap: Empirical research in simultaneous interpretation* (pp. 87–99). Philadelphia: Benjamins.

Kurz, I. (2001). Conference interpreting: Quality in the ears of the user. *Meta* 46(2), 394–409.

Moody, B. (2002). International Sign: A practitioner's perspective. In D. Watson (Ed.), *Journal of Interpretation* (pp. 1–47). Alexandria, VA: Registry of Interpreters for the Deaf.

Moser-Mercer, B. (1996). Quality in interpreting: Some methodological issues. *Interpreters' Newsletter* 7, 43–55.

Neumann Solow, S. (1985). The interpreting situation: ISSLR 1983. In *Proceedings of the III International Symposium on Sign Language Research, Rome, June 22–26, 1983.* Silver Spring, MD: Linstok Press.

Pöchhacker, F. (2001). Quality assessment in conference and community interpreting. *Meta* 46(2), 410–25.

Supalla, T., & Webb, R. (1995). The grammar of international sign: A new look at pidgin languages. In K. Emmory & J. Reilly (Eds.) *Language, gesture, and space* (pp. 333–52). Hillsdale, NJ: Lawrence Erlbaum.

Van Besien, F., & Meuleman, C. (2004). Dealing with speakers' errors and speakers' repairs in simultaneous interpretation: A corpus-based study. *Translator* 10(1), 59–81.

Recommendations for Scientific Conference Access

Recommendations have been developed based on the web-based participant survey, a post-conference focus group meeting with the ASL interpreters, and an internal review of the implementation of the TISLR9 protocol.[8] These recommendations, along with the protocol, will be passed on to the organizers of TISLR10.

CONFERENCE ORGANIZATIONAL ROLES

- The Organizing Committee (O) will have a Consultant Interpreter (CT) for non-official languages along with a Monitor (M).
- The organizational structure should include a Liaison (L) and Coordinator (C) for each language.

In the remainder of the recommendations listed below, the letter preceding the recommendation indicates the committee or individual responsible for implementing the recommendation.

CONFERENCE PLANNING

- **O.** For a large conference, hire an Interpreter or Access consultant with coordination experience[9]
- **O/M.** Design sessions to allow for breaks for both interpreters and Deaf and hard of hearing participants. Visual overload is a

8. See checklist for conference organizers: http://www.aiic.net/ViewPage .cfm?article_id=15.

9. See AIIC standards at http://www.aiic.net/viewpage.cfm?article_id=155 and RID Standard Practice Paper: "Coordinating Conferences." (http://www .rid.org/UserFiles/File/pdfs/Standard_Practice_Papers/Drafts_June_2006/ Coordinating_Conferences_SPP.pdf).

common occurrence when working in an environment that relies heavily on auditory processing.

- **O/L.** Provide links to web sites that provide information about interpreting access to conference organizers, speakers, and registrants.
- **L/C.** Ensure a timetable that will allow time to get the U.S. interpreting team selected and hired in order to set up the Access web site with interpreter information, to make travel arrangements, and obtain the proper travel visas necessary for the interpreters. In the case of the TISLR9 Conference, we allowed approximately one year beginning with the selection of the ASL Coordinator.
- **L/C.** Identify qualified interpreters for the conference by consulting Deaf scientists in the field and establishing a screening instrument with stimulus materials relevant to the conference theme and content. (O consults with Deaf scientists who assign L to manage this. Official signed languages should have their own L.)
- **C.** Utilize national rather than local networks of interpreters as the vehicle for recruiting qualified interpreters as demonstrated by CIT recruitment.
- **C.** Hire the appropriate number of interpreters to effectively provide access to all participants and presenters. This raises issues that organizers should be considering when planning such conferences—budgetary, space, personnel; for example, balancing the need for concurrent sessions with the budgetary demands of additional interpreters.
- **CT/C.** Provide interpreters with the program, titles and abstract of all talks, and information to directly contact conference presenters PRIOR TO the start of the conference, as well as knowledge of their individual presentation assignments.
- **CT.** Develop brief informational memos to send to all speakers about how to make their talks accessible, including the need to provide PowerPoint presentations in advance and to meet with the interpreters before their talks.
- **CT.** Set aside a place for interpreters to rest, meet with speakers, and prepare.
- **O.** Appoint an individual (M) to monitor speakers' pace and rate of speech, especially focused on transitions between slides.

- **L.** Establish a protocol checklist including these considerations and informational memos that can be provided to future conference organizers.
- **M/C/O.** With the technology available for the majority of participants to watch interpreters projected on the big screen, it is now possible to set up signed language interpreter booths at the back of the auditorium equipped with video cameras hooked into the projection system and dedicated sound to the booth. The AIIC web site provides information for rental of interpreter booths for international conferences as well as rental of other Simultaneous Interpreting hardware. This setup can:
- Enhance sound quality by (1) transmitting sound directly from the microphones to the interpreter booths; (2) filtering out extraneous noise in the auditorium that makes it difficult to hear the message; (3) reducing the distance that the message has to travel to the interpreters as well as the delay time in actually hearing the message.
- Enhance the lighting situation overall by (1) increasing light levels on the interpreters, making it easier to see (Deaf-friendly) without washing out the PowerPoint slides, and (2) reducing the washout effect on the PowerPoint slides by allowing the stage to be dimmed more than can be allowed when interpreters share the stage. The backdrop in the booths for the interpreters will need to be investigated to obtain maximum lighting contrast for visibility, but a booth makes this possible.
- Reduce the need for additional monitor hookups to the projections on stage because the interpreters can see the entire stage from the vantage point of the back of the auditorium.

Amsterdam Manifesto
(revised August 21, 2000)[10]

Since the TISLR2000 conference, there has been general consensus among participants, Deaf and hearing alike, that the conference has not been Deaf-friendly due to various reasons. Over 35 of us gathered outside of the conference on Wednesday, July 26, 2000, to address the problems that have come up during the conference. The following manifesto summarizes the main points we have agreed on during the meeting.

One main problem is that there has been no full access to academic discourse for the Deaf participants. This has partly to do with the selection of official languages that were declared for the conference. We know that around the world, the lingua franca within the scientific community, if not in the broader community, is English.

It is just as important to agree on a "lingua franca" for the scientific Deaf community, since the advantages are many: (i) using a lingua franca that is widely understood by the international scientific Deaf community will provide access to as wide a Deaf audience as possible; (ii) it will be financially more efficient to pay for a few interpreters to translate into one language, i.e. the lingua franca, which is understood by most of the audience rather than pay for individual interpreters from each of the many countries which would perhaps benefit only one or two participants; (iii) if one provides interpreters in one sign language that all people know, and provides interpreters in that same language for all sessions, Deaf attendees will not be constrained by the availability of interpreters and will have full freedom in choosing which session to attend, like their hearing peers.

It seems that BSL and ASL are the two signed languages which fit the criteria for a "lingua franca" for the scientific Deaf community, since they are widely understood by Deaf scientists from around the world. Thus we have agreed at the meeting that the official signed languages to be used for linguistics conferences should gradually include, over a span

---

10. Reprinted with permission of the original authors.

of 10 years, both BSL and ASL. Since this is an international setting, one should show respect and cultural sensitivity to the international audience by reducing the American (and British) culture-specific aspects of these signed languages and by making heavy use of the universal aspects of the signed languages.

The signed languages named above are mainly for TISLR conferences, but for a smaller international conference, it may make better sense to use another sign language that is widely understood by the audience, e.g., Swedish Sign Language if the conference consists mostly of participants from the Scandinavia area.

Note that these languages are for the purpose of linguistics conferences only, since there is a need to discuss technical material in depth and therefore a need to use a full signed language. We are not discussing whether to select a 'lingua franca' for other international Deaf-related events, like those focusing on sports, art, and/or culture (e.g., Deaf Way).

In addition to using the 'lingua franca' at scientific gatherings, we fully support providing access in the local signed language, since this serves to recognize the signed language on an international level and empowers the local Deaf community, the kind of support which is always sorely needed everywhere.

Thus, we strongly encourage future TISLR (and other conference) organizing committees to follow these guidelines:

(1) That the official languages of the conference should include English, the local signed language, BSL, and ASL; (in which case access through English should also be provided through computer-aided real-time captioning (CART) services);

(2) That the committee should ensure there are sufficient funds to provide sign language interpreters for *all* simultaneous sessions of the conference and for *all* social events during the conference.

(3) That there should be at least one Deaf scientist on the organizing committee to ensure that necessary steps are taken to provide full access for the whole scientific community.

One should keep in mind that most of sign language research is dependent on Deaf RA's (research assistants) and on data from native Deaf signers. If it were not for the hard work of these Deaf researchers, very little progress would have been made in sign language research! One must never forget to acknowledge their contributions, and one way to acknowledge their work is by giving something back to the signing community. The sign language researchers can easily do this by following the above guidelines and thereby making the conferences more Deaf-friendly. Participants who bring their own interpreters can afford to do so only because they are receiving grants or have salaried jobs. This puts Deaf students especially at a great disadvantage, since they do not have either, a situation which is unfair since the conference is also for linguists-in-training. If the conference can be made Deaf-friendly through the above guidelines, it will provide a platform on which prospective Deaf linguists can learn about the state of art in sign language research. Attracting more Deaf linguists this way can only serve to raise the overall quality of sign language research.

In sum, the ultimate goal behind these guidelines is to promote academic discourse among the Deaf and hearing linguists so that they can learn and benefit from one another's knowledge. Of course, the ideal type of interaction would be direct, in which all hearing linguists can sign along with everybody else. We hope that everybody will become more sensitive and accord one another respect.

Contact people:

Christian Rathmann (*rathmann@mail.utexas.edu*)

Gaurav Mathur (*gmathur@mit.edu*)

Patrick Boudreault (*pboudr@po-box.mcgill.ca*)

APPENDIX 3

Memo to Presenters

RE: SUGGESTIONS TO HELP INTERPRETATION GO MORE SMOOTHLY.

I am delighted to have been selected as the interpreter coordinator for the upcoming TISLR Conference. I am at your disposal if you have any questions or concerns before or during the conference. Interpretation should go almost unnoticed, but the only way for us to be unobtrusive is with your help and cooperation. Here are some pointers that have proven helpful in past conferences in keeping the information accessible to both the Hearing and Deaf participants. It is the organizing committee's goal at this conference that the content of all papers be accessible to all participants. For this reason please plan to "speak" from an outline or notes rather than reading a prepared paper. A read paper moves much too quickly, and typically is rhythmically so difficult as to be basically un-interpretable. Together we can create a satisfying and stimulating exchange for all interested participants.

1. Upon your arrival please come to Interpreting Headquarters.[11] We would appreciate the opportunity to arrange a meeting with your scheduled interpreters, to discuss your presentation. If you are using a term that may have a very specific usage or a novel application in your presentation, please inform the interpreters. Prior to the workshop you were asked to provide a copy of your presentation. Please let interpreters know of any changes or updates. Be sure to bring these and any demonstration materials (transparencies, illustrations, etc.) so the interpreters can become familiar with your presentation style. Interpreters will be preparing all day on _____ on site.

2. Interpreters may need to ask you to stop and repeat or slow down on occasion. This does not reflect a lack of competence but rather is intended to ensure that your presentation is interpreted accurately.

3. In your presentation please pause between whole thoughts, not between words.

4. It may help to mark your notes for places to pause and with reminders to "SPEAK SLOWLY."

5. If you plan to sign any portion of your presentation, a solid, contrasting blouse or shirt makes the signs more readable, especially from a distance.

6. Because your presentation will be interpreted, there will be a delay before your message reaches some of your audience. When using a visual aid or demonstration, please check that your interpreters have had time to complete your preceding message

11. If there is no one in the Interpreter room, please leave a note letting us know where you can be reached, your room number or local telephone number.

before proceeding. *This entire process takes time.* It cannot be rushed or a breakdown may occur.

7. Please keep in mind that complex numbers and items that must be spelled, such as proper names, are often most effective when they are repeated. It is very helpful to give your interpreters a list of such items ahead of time.

8. Interpreters will be available to interpret for audience questions or comments if they occur. At times it may be helpful for the presenter to repeat the comments or questions if the audience participant is not visible or audible to all.

THANK YOU!

Sign Language Interpreting in Multilingual International Settings

Maya de Wit

During the last decade, international exchange between national Deaf communities in Europe has increased. The increase of international exchanges between deaf people has had an impact on the kind of assignments sign language interpreters are asked to undertake. Interpreting in international meetings in Europe has become more common and interpreters are requested to interpret from a foreign spoken language into their national sign language and vice versa. The increase in international deaf interactions is due to factors such as increasing recognition of signed languages, the development of technology, the faster exchange of information in Western society (Nardi, 2008), and the higher levels of education that deaf people can now achieve due to available interpretation and other support services (Lang, 2002). These factors have affected the type and complexity of interpreting assignments for which sign language interpreters are requested, bringing new and different challenges to the sign language interpreting profession.

Sign language interpreters are typically trained to work between two languages and cultures; a signed language and a spoken language. But there are also settings in which deaf and hearing participants use more than two languages and cultures, such as international conferences, and deaf-related international events. Such complex settings require additional skills from the interpreter. This chapter explores aspects of interpreting between multiple sign languages and spoken languages, from a practitioner's point of view. This chapter does not report an empirical investigation of this topic; rather the aim is to provide ideas and suggestions based on my extensive interpreting experience in multilingual settings, mainly in Europe, with reference to relevant research literature.

THE COMPLEXITY OF INTERPRETING IN
MULTILINGUAL INTERNATIONAL SETTINGS

International settings are diverse and have different interpreting requirements. In this chapter, the phrase *multilingual international settings* refers to settings with languages and cultures additional to the two in which the sign language interpreter was primarily trained. These settings vary greatly and could be, for example, in the local community or in another country, but all entail the use of more than two languages and cultures. Additional challenges in such situations include: (a) the interpreter's level of fluency in the languages present in the situation; (b) increased demands on the interpreter's cognitive processing capacity; (c) interpreting for non-native speakers of one or more of the languages; and (d) the number of languages involved.

Currently, most sign language interpreter training programs focus on the interpreting process between a native spoken language and a national sign language,[1] with the latter in most cases being a second language for the interpreter. Until recently only a few educational programs have addressed the training of sign language interpreters to work in multilingual settings. In Austria and Spain, interpreters can be trained in more than one spoken and signed language. The University of Graz in Austria,[2] for example, offers a five-year master's degree, the highest level of all sign language interpreter (SLI) training programs in Europe (de Wit, 2008).

1. The combination of acquiring a second language and simultaneously learning the process of interpreting in the educational program seems to be a challenging task. Shaw, Collins, and Metzger (2006, p. 2) state, "It is unreasonable of us to expect students to learn both rudimentary language skills and interpreting skills at the same time. The mastery of basic skills in interpreting will always depend ultimately on an individual's foundation of solid linguistic skills and cultural adeptness." This implies that the program for interpreters should focus on the teaching of interpreting skills, knowledge, and abilities rather than on teaching the languages. The student should be required to be fluent in the two languages prior to entering the program.

2. http://www.uni-graz.at/itat/.

Of the nearly 50 SLI programs in Europe, this is one of the very few that addresses multilingual interpreting.[3]

International interpreting settings generally involve more than two spoken and/or signed languages. The interpreter's proficiency in the additional language(s) can range from near native to no familiarity with the language at all. For example, at a conference whose common languages are English and British Sign Language (BSL), hearing presenters at the conference may use French. A BSL interpreter whose mother is French has native fluency in French language and culture and might be able to interpret between French and BSL. But an interpreter who has no familiarity with French must rely on relayed interpretation from French into English provided by a spoken language interpreter. In either case, the interpreter has to work with a third language, either directly or through another interpretation.

Rendering a message from a source to target language in a two-language situation is complex. In multilingual international settings the additional language is an extra factor in the interpreted situation, which complicates the interpretation process. Successful interpretation relies on the processing capacity of the interpreter. Gile's (1997) effort model postulates that the interpretation process comprises several tasks, from comprehending the source message to the final production of the target language message, and that each task occupies a certain amount of the interpreter's processing capacity. If one task (such as comprehending the source message) requires the expenditure of more effort, then less processing capacity is available for another task in the process. I propose that in a multilingual interaction involving additional complexity, the interpreter uses extra effort and potentially more processing capacity due to the additional language and culture present in the communication. The interpreter must make choices on how to distribute the processing capacity available, which may affect the outcome of the interpretation, and thus the integrity of the target language message. In a study of the interpretation process between two languages, Leeson (2005) recommended that further research is needed to fully understand the processing

3. In January 2009 the first European master's in sign language interpreting started within a joint project of Humak University in Finland, Magdeburg University in Germany, and Heriot-Watt University in Scotland. One of the components of this program is interpreting in international settings.

demands on sign language interpreters and to identify successful strategies implemented by practitioners.

Understanding unfamiliar accents, facial expressions, and body language by speakers who are using a non-native spoken language is a challenge to the interpreter's processing in multilingual situations. Listening to idiosyncratic or accented language use by a speaker requires more effort than listening to a native speaker. In practice I have found that the non-native accent of a speaker is more readily comprehensible when the interpreter shares a native, or related, language of the foreign speaker; for example, a Dutch person presenting in English, and being interpreted by a German Sign Language interpreter. German and Dutch share many grammatical, prosodic, and idiomatic patterns, thus the average German interpreter recognizes the accent, choice of words, and grammatical usages of a Dutch-English speaker more readily than the average British interpreter. I have also observed that interpreters who are monolingual native speakers of English (e.g., many ASL interpreters) may have greater difficulty understanding non-native English speakers than the non-native English speakers in the audience. Non-native English listeners appear to have an enhanced ability to decipher non-native English speech, especially if the speaker comes from the same language family. Scholl (2008, p. 335) confirms this experience: "Even mistakes made, which would leave a native speaker completely clueless, do make sense to the interpreter because of their familiarity." Seleskovitch (1978) notes that proficiency in more than a single spoken language might contribute to a greater overall language agility, which assists the interpreter in coping with uncommon accents.

A similar difficulty arises when a sign language user presents in a second sign language. The sign language interpreter who is educated and fluent in one sign language usually has had little or no exposure to other sign languages. For example, if a Dutch Sign Language interpreter who has no knowledge of another sign language needs to interpret a non-native Dutch Sign Language user, the interpreter may have greater difficulty understanding than the interpreter who has been exposed to other sign languages. The latter has a greater active knowledge of the variety in sign languages that is available. Studying additional sign languages would therefore be helpful for the interpreter in international settings. Moody (2008), in a discussion of the learning and use of International Sign by interpreters at international events, points out that knowing more than one sign language increases an interpreter's flexibility to adapt to the vocabulary in use in different locations and different contexts (Moody, p. 28).

In multilingual settings the interpreter must also be aware of the risk that additional cultural differences may lead to misunderstandings between the participants. The deciphering of culturally bound facial expressions, gestures, and idioms may increase processing demands on the interpreter and thus may be potentially omitted or misinterpreted. For example, there is a gesture that is used by Dutch people, deaf or hearing, which means that something tastes good (LEKKER is the gloss used for this gesture). This gesture is typically Dutch and uncommon to other cultures. If a Dutch Sign Language user presenting in International Sign uses this particular gesture, the interpreter must be aware that this is a culturally bound, rather than a universal or transparent gesture, and interpret it correctly.

QUALITIES AND STRATEGIES REQUIRED OF AN INTERPRETER TO INTERPRET IN INTERNATIONAL SETTINGS

Providing interpreting services in multilingual international settings requires particular qualities and strategies on the part of the interpreter. These include additional language and cultural proficiency and the ability to use flexible interpreting techniques in response to extraordinary cultural and linguistic demands. The language and cultural proficiencies of the interpreter in the additional language(s) can vary, depending on the requirements of the situation. If the interpreter needs to work to and from a third language, it is expected that the interpreter has achieved language proficiency as high as the first two working languages. Anecdotal evidence suggests that there are currently very few sign language interpreters trained, native, or fluent in three languages who are available to work at the level of proficiency required (Scholl, 2008). Many interpreter training programs nowadays follow the Common European Framework of Reference for Languages (CEFRL).[4] The CEFRL is a framework for learning foreign languages, and could possibly be used in this context for learning an additional language as part of the curriculum of basic interpreter education. The CEFRL describes performance criteria in reading,

4. http://www.coe.int/t/dg4/linguistic/CADRE_EN.asp.

listening, speaking, and writing at each level. There are six levels in total, from A1 to C2. When a language learner is, for example, at A1, he or she can understand and use familiar everyday expressions. When C2 is reached, the language learner can understand with ease everything that is heard or read.

The more languages and cultures the interpreter is familiar with, the more flexibility the interpreter has, and the easier it will be for the interpreter to function. The basic interpreting skills used when interpreting from a first language into a second language provide the foundation for working in multilingual settings, but additional competencies are needed. A crucial skill is to be able to switch smoothly between more than two languages, without interlanguage interference. If, for example, a presenter in ASL needs to be interpreted into Dutch Sign Language, the interpreter should avoid linguistic borrowing from ASL in the interpretation into Dutch Sign Language. As Seleskovitch (1978, p. 73) says, "A few of those who have a gift for languages, in other words the gift to keep them apart, also possess the qualities necessary to be able to interpret."

The strategies I am suggesting here could be considered general interpreting strategies. However, one of the main points to be stressed is that extra attention is warranted when interpreting into or from a third language, either between a spoken and a signed language, or between two signed languages, in which the interpreter has not been formally trained. For example, a French Sign Language interpreter is trained in interpreting between French and French Sign Language. A third language for the interpreter could be English, in which case they could then work between French Sign Language (often their second language), and English (a third language). The issue of interpreting to and from one's third language in multilingual international settings is a recurring theme and one I will be addressing throughout this chapter.

An important interpreting strategy is the option of making the participants aware of the linguistic and logistical challenges of the interpretation process. Depending on the number of participants involved, the interpreters can choose to inform all or some of the participants. For example, if there is an interactive meeting with five participants and three languages, it is recommended to inform the participants that strict turn taking is essential for a full interpretation. Interpreters can only interpret one message at a time, requiring participants to communicate sequentially. Since there are three different languages, the interpreters have a relay function as well, working from an interpretation produced by another interpreter.

At a large conference it is necessary to inform the presenters that their message will be interpreted into multiple languages and, therefore, it will take a longer time to reach the listeners. In addition, speakers need to speak clearly into the microphone at all times. If audience members start posing questions to the presenters, they need to be informed that they should repeat the question into the microphone and make sure that only one person is talking at a time. Informing the audience on the interpreting procedure is the responsibility of the organizers of the event, not the interpreter's. The interpreter should be able to fully concentrate on the task at hand instead of on the logistics of the meeting (see Supalla, Clark, Neumann Solow, & de Quadros, this volume).

Such interpreting strategies should be used by the interpreter in combination with a sensitivity to the extraordinary cultural and linguistic demands involved in the international settings. This sensitivity is the ability of the interpreter to sense linguistic and cultural needs without an explicit request by the participants. The needs are implicitly present and something that the interpreter should sense. Consider the use of the respectful "Sie" (you) versus the familiar "du" (you) in German. When the interpreter interprets this into a language where there is no such distinction, the interpreter is responsible for conveying this culturally bound phenomenon. These kinds of cultural and linguistic adjustments are also present when working between two languages, but require an additional awareness by the interpreter in a multilingual situation with participants with different languages and cultures. This is especially so when there is a use of a relay interpreter, as explained further on in the article in relation to team interpreting.

An important part of the interpreter's sensitivity is knowing when to follow or to depart from regular interpreting practices in an international assignment. In consultation with clients and colleagues, the interpreter may, at times, vary standard practices without losing the quality of the interpretation. For example, clients from various countries using interpreting services at one event might have varying expectations of the role of the interpreter, depending on the status and practices of interpreting as a professional service in their own country. Clients from one country might expect the interpreter to interpret for them at all times, including break times and social events. Other clients have interpreters who are bound by the working times of their employer to minimize the chance of physical and mental stress. The interpreters must be flexible in working around the different cultural expectations, and create understanding among the clients of what can be expected of the interpreters present.

Team Interpreting

Interpreted interaction becomes more complex as the number of languages and cultures present increases. The interpreter must take into consideration the range of languages used by international participants, as well as the logistics of working with other spoken or sign language interpreters. In multilingual settings, each interpreter is responsible for working between their assigned languages, but must coordinate with other interpreters for whom they have a relay function. That is, the source message is interpreted by the first interpreter and from this interpretation the second interpreter renders it into a different target language. The second interpretation is thus fully dependent on the first interpretation. The first interpreter might, therefore, feel an additional responsibility of having to provide an interpretation that is understandable to the second interpreter and delivered at a rate that can be interpreted from.

Jones (2002) emphasizes the need for an explicit interpretation by the relay interpreter, so there is no room for any misinterpretation by the interpreters working from the relay. The relay interpreter must be aware that the relay interpretation might be in the non-native language or passive language of the secondary interpreter, who may have an imperfect knowledge of the relay language. The relay interpretation must therefore be clear in meaning, in grammatical form, and in pronunciation.

Cooperation between a team of interpreters requires flexibility and willingness to adapt, especially when working with colleagues of different nationalities. Prior to the assignment, the interpreters must meet to discuss jargon, logistics, and interpreting strategies. When working with spoken language interpreters it is useful to inform each other of the tasks of each interpreter. Spoken language interpreters with whom I have worked found it helpful to know that the sign language interpreters prefer that the spoken language interpreters match the flow, pace, and intonation of the speaker. This natural way of speaking makes a fluent interpretation into sign language easier. In addition, it is helpful that the spoken language interpreters announces the turn of a new speaker, since this is not always clear for the interpreters working from the relay language (Jones, 2002).

In this situation it is not necessary that the interpreter be fluent in the third language, but it is helpful to have some familiarity with it, since less concentration will be needed during the interpretation process. Seleskovitch (1978) mentions that it is impossible to know every language, but that it is useful to be able to recognize other languages and to become accustomed to the phenomenon of speakers presenting in a language other than their native tongue.

Working To and From a Third Language

In the situation where the interpreter has to work from a third language into a first or second language, the interpreter must have full fluency in the third language in order to provide a quality interpretation. The Association of Conference Interpreters (AIIC) has established classifications to rank working languages: the first is the A language, the interpreter's native language. The B language is not native, but is a language of which the interpreter has a perfect command, and into which s/he works from one or more of her or his other languages. The C language is a passive language of which the interpreter has good receptive understanding and from which s/he may work; Seleskovitch (1978, p. 65) writes that "with this language the emphasis is not on proficiency in expression but on understanding the meanings of words, turns of phrase and idiomatic expressions." Which languages the interpreter should work from or into is a matter of debate in the interpreting literature. Paneth (1957), for instance, cites Kaminker as someone who was convinced that interpreters should only translate into their mother tongue, except in the few cases where it is impossible to tell which of the two their mother tongue is. In short, it has long been considered best practice that interpreters work from their B or second language into their A or native language during conference interpreting. Along these lines, Seleskovitch (1978) proposes that successful interpretation into one's B language depends on several factors, such as the interpreter's familiarity with the content material and whether the interpretation is done consecutively or simultaneously. Consecutive interpretation potentially allows the interpreter more time to monitor and restructure the message into their B language.

If we consider how these ideas are applied to the field of sign language interpreting, we see different practices; sign language interpreters commonly work in dialogue situations that require interpreting in both directions. Anecdotally, it is sometimes observed that sign language interpreters have more problems when interpreting from signed into spoken language, which is most often their mother tongue. One of the reasons postulated for this is that interpreters more frequently work into sign language, thus having more practice in using signed language as the target language (Scholl, 2008). Furthermore, the majority of interpreters today are non-native signers (i.e., acquiring the language in adulthood), which create weaknesses in their comprehension of signed language as a source language. Another possible reason is related to modality: going from a visual-gestural mode of reception into an oral-aural mode of delivery means that the interpreter receives immediate auditory feedback on any errors made interpreting into spoken language. Interpreters might thus erroneously believe that their production into sign language is better, since their ability to critically monitor their output in sign language is less than in their native spoken language. In light of this, one might question whether sign language interpreters potentially make fewer or more errors when working into their third language. This may depend on the setting, content, and participants, and of course the interpreter's degree of proficiency in the third language.

ACHIEVING THE NECESSARY QUALITIES AND STRATEGIES

Interpreting in multilingual settings demands several qualities in the interpreter, such as a degree of proficiency in the second or third language, years of interpreting experience, and knowledge of the subject matter. In addition the interpreter must study and acquire relevant terminology and topics prior to the interpreting assignments (Seleskovitch, 1978). Not only spoken language interpreters but also sign language interpreters who match these requirements are needed to work in these multilingual settings.

Interpreting in international settings carries with it a certain prestige that appeals to many interpreters. Working with other nationalities, cultures, and languages is an extraordinary challenge for sign language interpreters. The European Forum of Sign Language Interpreters has received so many requests for educational opportunities to learn how to interpret between English, the international lingua franca, and a signed language, that they have launched special training to address these needs.[5]

5. http://www.efsli.org.

Earlier I discussed the qualities and strategies the interpreter needs to have in order to provide a quality interpretation in international settings. The crucial quality, the additional language proficiency, can be obtained by frequent exposure to different languages. Regular exposure to other languages helps the interpreter to develop not only language proficiency but also flexibility. Of course, learning a third language is not something that can be accomplished overnight. It takes great dedication and time to master a new language. But as recommended by Scholl (2008), it helps to train sign language interpreters to work in a third language, since the interpreters currently practicing in multilingual situations do not have specialized training to do so.

At the same time we must realize that for many, learning a third language has constraints, such as unavailability of training in interpreting or sign language, or minimal financial support. The low status of the profession in some European countries means few interpreters are willing and able to invest in learning additional languages. The status of the profession of sign language interpreters across Europe varies greatly. In many countries in Eastern Europe the profession is not recognized and is a voluntary, or low-paid profession. Although many European countries have not yet recognized sign language as an official language (Timmermans, 2005), it has hardly affected the implementation of interpreting services, training, or number of interpreters (De Wit, 2008). In countries that have achieved formal recognition of a signed language, this has generally occurred after the first training programs and services were established. In many countries the recognition of a signed language has, though, had an impact on the status of sign language, the quality of services, the right to an interpreter, and training programs.

Even though opportunities for sign language interpreters to learn a third language may be constrained, there is still a great need for interpreters with multilingual skills. When looking at the participation of deaf people in the main international European conferences, such as the European Union of the Deaf[6] and the European Forum of Sign Language Interpreters,[7] there is an urgent need for working interpreters to use English as a third language. English and/or International Sign are the working languages during these conferences; many deaf participants are

6. http://www.eud.eu.
7. http://www.efsli.org.

not fluent in International Sign and thus bring their own national sign language interpreters who interpret from English into their national sign language. Across Europe in the non-English speaking countries, there is only a small number of interpreters who are proficient enough to work between English and their national sign language. The scarcity of multilingual interpreters causes a barrier for deaf people in Europe to freely participate in any international event.

Not only do working sign language interpreters need more proficiency in English, but also interpreters who wish to participate as individuals in European professional interpreting conferences need more English skills. For example conference delegates from the Western and Northern part of Europe, with the exception of the French-speaking countries, generally have a good command of English. Interpreters from the Southern and Eastern part often do not participate or struggle with English when participating.[8] Regular participation in these European conferences helps greatly to improve the English skills of the participating interpreters, which can be applied later to working in multilingual interpreting settings.

The complexity of international interpreting assignments requires extensive international exposure in addition to formal training. Informal communication in both spoken and signed languages at international events has great benefits. Language learning through direct language contact is found to be one of the most successful ways of learning new languages (Appel, 1994). Attending international conferences, for instance, not only as an interpreter, but also as a participant, stimulates the development of specific terminology and jargon. These might be conferences related to the field of sign language interpreting, such as the conference of the European Forum of Sign Language Interpreters, or of international Deaf organizations. This experience also gives the interpreter the opportunity to become accustomed to additional languages and terminology in these languages related to the working environment of the interpreter. Traveling abroad also provides the interpreter with opportunities to learn about the political context and history of various countries. For instance, in the former Eastern European countries

8. To support interpreters with little or no available funding to participate in the conference of the European Forum of Sign Language Interpreters, the European Forum of Sign Language Interpreters has set up a Special Attendance Fund (SAF). See: http://www.efsli.org.

the recent history and political status of the country is often alluded to in everyday situations; understanding such allusions contributes to the quality of an interpretation.

It goes without saying that the interpreter should at first be careful in choosing these assignments. The interpreter should not test his techniques for the first time alone in a large conference setting with many languages. It is advisable to observe and work at first with experienced interpreters, who have had extensive experience in these settings. The client has the right to the best interpreting services available, which can only be guaranteed with an experienced interpreter on the team. The interpreter can then continue and build on the learned strategies and techniques with an experienced mentor in order to proceed to more complex and challenging assignments.

PRACTICAL CHALLENGES AND POSSIBLE SOLUTIONS

One major challenge is to foster the clients' awareness of the different interpreting issues faced by the interpreter in international settings. It is crucial to explain to clients the complexity of the multiple language situation and the consequences for the interpreting process, while, at the same time, avoiding overwhelming the client with too much information on the interpreting process. The interpreter in the end is responsible for a quality interpretation, and needs to be sensitive as to which information is of no interest to the client and may even frustrate a smooth interpreting process.

When the client is aware of the challenging interpreting conditions, the client will have more patience when a problem in the interpreting process arises. For example, for people who were born deaf, the difference between an interpreter being able to hear and to understand spoken language is not always obvious. For example, I have had a client tell me to please continue to interpret since the presenter was continuing to speak. In this situation, the presenter's speech was barely intelligible due to heavily accented English. As discussed earlier, any interference in perceiving the source message decreases the cognitive capacity available for the interpreting process, and quality of the output. Since accents cannot be changed, I have found it helpful to inform the client of the presenter's strong accent; the client is then aware of the interpreter's and the audience's difficulty in understanding the message.

To avoid some difficulties, it is essential to communicate with the client about their needs and goals for their participation in the event. In a regular assignment, the interpreter should do this as well, but it is particularly important in international settings where the situation is complex, and the interpreter needs to take account of the purpose of the client's presence. The client may be participating in the event with less interest in the formal presentations than in networking and making new contacts; or the client may want to know more about one of the topics and may want the interpreter to focus on the terminology in a particular presentation. Interpreting for one deaf client from English to Dutch Sign Language, the client asked me to fingerspell the precise English terms used in the presentation, so he could familiarize himself with this terminology and use it when reading about this topic in the future. Even without knowing this specific wish of the client, the interpreter should be aware of any technical terminology in another language that is central to certain concepts. The terminology might appear in a presentation as loan words in a different language.

Consultation is an important strategy to clarify and find equivalence for jargon or culturally embedded terminology used by a deaf presenter. The word *handicapped*, for example, is a loan word from English used in Dutch and other European spoken languages and signed languages. However the word *handicap* has since acquired different connotations in the English speaking community. Some languages, though, still use the word *handicap* in relation to people with disabilities, and do not have an alternative synonym, or may use another term with a slightly different meaning. The interpreter cannot use a literal translation, since this is considered a pejorative term by native speakers of English, but must seek cultural and linguistic equivalence with the intent of the speaker and the culture of the target language. It is a complex process to achieve the interpretation that is acceptable to all parties involved in a multilingual context. On the other hand, participants in an international meeting context may share a relatively large body of terminology and references related to their common agenda and background experience, which assists the interpreter's task.

Communication in international settings may at times involve codeswitching to a language that the interpreter does not know and where no other interpretation is provided. This happens, for example, when quotations from another language are used in a presentation. If the presenter does not give a rendition of the content of the quotation or a translation, the interpreter might want to inform the presenter of the impossibility to interpret the quotation. Another approach could be to inform the client, who can decide if the presenter needs to be interrupted or not.

An important aspect of providing a quality interpretation is preparation for the assignment. The content of an assignment in international settings can be highly variable. The assignment can be anything from interpreting at an international conference, or interpreting for a group traveling abroad. This means that the content can be highly specialized, demanding knowledge in one specific domain, but it can also be general information on one topic.

By obtaining materials for the assignment in advance, the interpreter can familiarize herself with such elements as content, names of presenters, and terminology. Good preparation has a qualitative effect on improving the interpretation (Stone, 2007). The interpreter benefits from having the client make the full presentation available in writing beforehand. During the interpretation the interpreter does not read the presentation, but uses it for guidance, for instance, with regard to the English terminology the client prefers to be used in this context. Word choice and terminology can be highly political and potentially contentious in international settings involving different cultures. The interpreter should be extra alert to this. Discussing these possible risks with the other interpreters prior to the event can reduce the use of culturally or politically incorrect terminology.

CONCLUSION

The sign language interpreter must realize that each international interpreting situation poses its own challenges and develop the flexibility to deal with these professionally. Interpreting in international settings must not being taken lightly or seen as something exotic that can be tried out at will. The interpreter carries a great responsibility to mediate the multiple languages and cultures in a sensitive and accurate manner.

The interpreter can only succeed in an international assignment after obtaining the necessary additional language proficiency and mastering interpreting strategies specific to multi-language interaction. The level of language fluency in additional languages will determine the language combinations that the interpreter can work between. Learning additional languages is not a simple task, but can be accomplished by frequent exposure and active use of the languages in relevant contexts.

A successful interpretation in the multilingual international setting also depends on a good cooperation between the interpreter and the client. The interpreter can create a larger awareness on the part of the client about the additional challenges the interpreter faces in multilingual environments. The client will then have a better understanding of problems that arise, and can assist the interpreter to provide effective interpretation by, for example, making sure that the interpreter receives preparation materials prior to the assignment.

This will all take time, experience, and practice, but concrete steps can be taken to achieve the skills and strategies needed in international settings. Through extensive experience and team work with clients and interpreters, the interpreter can be successful in rendering a smooth and quality interpretation in international settings.

REFERENCES

Appel, R. (1994). *Tweede Taal verwerving en Tweede Taal onderwijs*. Bussum: Coutinho.

Gile, D. (1997). Conference interpreting as a cognitive management problem. In J. E. Danks, G. M. Shreve, S. B. Fountain, & M. K. McBeath (Eds.), *Cognitive processes in translation and interpreting* (pp. 196–214). Thousand Oaks, CA: Sage.

Hermans, D., Dijk, R. van, Christoffels, I. (2007). *De effectiviteit van gebarentaaltolken in de communicatie tussen dove en horende mensen*. Utrecht: Pontem.

Jones, R. (2002). *Conference interpreting explained*. Manchester: St. Jerome Publishing.

Kamiker, A. (1955). Conférence de M. André Kamiker. *L'Interprète 4–5*, 9.

Lang, H. G. (2002). Higher education for deaf students: Research priorities in the new millennium. *Journal of Deaf Studies and Deaf Education 7*(4), 267–280.

Leeson, L. (2005). Making the effort in simultaneous interpreting: Some considerations for signed language interpreters. In T. Janzen (Ed.), *Topics in signed language interpreting: Theory and practice* (pp. 51–68). Amsterdam: John Benjamins.

Moody, B. (2008). The role of International Sign interpreting in today's world. In C. Roy (Ed.), *Diversity and community in the worldwide sign language interpreting profession: Proceedings of the second WASLI conference* (pp. 19–33). Gloucestershire, UK: Douglas McLean.

Nardi, M. (2008). To boldly go. abroad!? In C. K. Bidoli & E. Ochse (Eds.), *English in international deaf communication* (pp. 279–303). Frankfurt-am-Main: Peter Lang Verlagsgruppe.

Paneth, E. (1957). An investigation into conference interpreting (with special reference to the training of interpreters). In F. Pöchhacker & M. Shlesinger (Eds.), *The interpreting studies reader* (pp. 30–40). London: Routledge.

Pöchhacker, F. (2004). *Introducing interpreting studies.* London: Routledge.

Pöchhacker, F. & Shlesinger, M. (2002). *The interpreting studies reader.* London: Routledge.

Scholl, S. (2008). A twisted brain: Interpreting between sign language and a third language. In C. J. K. Bidoli & E. Ochse (Eds.), *English in international deaf communication* (pp. 331–42). Bern: Peter Lang AG.

Seleskovitch, D. (1978). *Interpreting for international conferences.* Washington, DC: Pen and Booth.

Shaw, R., Collins, S., & Metzger, M. (2006). MA to BA: A quest for distinguishing between undergraduate and graduate interpreter education, Bachelor of Arts in interpretation curriculum at Gallaudet University. In C. B. Roy (Ed.), *New approaches to interpreter education* (pp. 1–21). Washington, DC: Gallaudet University Press.

Stone, C. (2007). Deaf translators/interpreters' rendering processes: The translation of oral languages. *The Sign Language Translator and Interpreter* 1, 53–72. Manchester, UK: St. Jerome Publishing.

Timmermans, N. (2005). *The status of sign language in Europe.* Strasbourg, France: Council of Europe Publishing.

Wit, M. de. (2008). *Sign language interpreting in Europe* (4th ed.). Baarn: M. De Wit.

Contributors

Stephanie Awheto, of Ngati Ruanui/Taranaki descent, is the senior NZSL-English-Māori interpreter in New Zealand. She holds a diploma in sign language interpreting and a B.SocSci in Māori Development. She has been a professional interpreter since 1996. Ms. Awheto is active in supporting Māori Deaf development activities and in mentoring trilingual Māori interpreters.

John Bichsel received his master's degree in English as a Second Language from the University of Arizona in 1987. He spent 3 years at the University of Veracruz in Mexico training teachers in language testing methodologies and collaborating with the British Council to develop the accredited Exaver English language testing program. He is currently a Senior Research Specialist at the University of Arizona National Center for Testing, Research and Policy, where he has 20 years of experience in the fields of translation and interpretation curriculum development, interpreter training, and interpreter test development, administration, and validation.

Kristie Casanova de Canales, CI/CT, NIC is a trilingual (English/Spanish/ASL) interpreter. She is originally from Ohio, although she presently resides in Ciudad Azteca, Mexico. She is nationally certified as an English-ASL interpreter and as a sign language transliterator by the Registry of Interpreters for the Deaf (RID). In addition to working as a trilingual VRS interpreter, her experience includes interpreting at state and national conferences and presenting on the subject of trilingual interpreting. She holds an associate's degree in American Sign Language interpreting and transliterating and is currently working towards her bachelor's degree in Communication at the University of Phoenix.

Patricia Clark, MA, is a CODA and RID certified (CSC) interpreter of ASL and English. Patricia has worked as an interpreter and interpreter trainer for over 30 years. At the University of Rochester, she works as staff interpreter and research assistant in the Sign Language Research Center, and instructor in the ASL Program. Her research interests are in translation, as a result of her research on older forms of ASL, and in the application of spoken language models for interpreting.

Jeffrey E. Davis, has worked as an interpreter, teacher, and researcher in the fields of sign language linguistics and interpretation for more than 25 years. He is a nationally certified (CI/CT; SC:L) ASL-English interpreter. Jeffrey holds master's and doctoral degrees in linguistics and has held academic positions at Gallaudet University, the University of Arizona, and Miami-Dade College, and has been at the University of Tennessee since 2000. In 2006, he was awarded a Fellowship from the National Endowment for the Humanities and National Science Foundation for Documenting Endangered Languages at the Smithsonian Institution to research North American Indian Sign Language. He has published and presented extensively on his research relating to sign language and interpreting.

Karin Fayd'herbe, BTeach, BED, MA, NAATI, resides in Cairns, Far North Queensland, Australia. Karin is a qualified teacher of the Deaf and professional Auslan interpreter. She works in a number of roles including: Project Officer—Transition to Auslan Project, Queensland Department of Education Training and the Arts; Convenor/Lecturer, Postgraduate Certificate in Auslan Studies, Griffith University; and as a freelance Auslan interpreter/trainer. Karin's interests are legal interpreting and indigenous deaf consumers, bilingual pedagogy, and linguistics. She is currently secretary of the Australian Sign Language Interpreters Association (ASLIA).

Paul Gatto holds a C.Phil. from the University of California, San Diego. He is the senior program coordinator at the University of Arizona National Center for Interpretation Testing, Research and Policy. During his 10-year tenure, he has been involved in various interpreter curriculum and certification projects, including materials and test development, administration and validation, and projects to use translation and interpretation studies as a mechanism to improve the academic outcomes of Latino school students. Paul is the co-pincipal investigator with Dr. Roseann Gonzalez for the Texas Trilingual Initiative, a project that resulted in the development of trilingual ASL/Spanish/English certification exams.

Roseann Dueñas González, PhD, professor of English at the University of Arizona, is the director of the National Center for Interpretation Testing, Research and Policy, founded in 1979 when she served as the lead government expert for federal court interpreter certification. The National Center is a major repository of the theoretical and practical aspects of specialized interpretation, including its cognitive underpinnings, ethical parameters, and the policy guiding its practice and assessment. Dr. González's research focuses on applied linguistics, bilingual education, and language policy. Her numerous language service initiatives are responsible for training and assessing tens of thousands of professional and aspiring interpreters.

Melanie McKay-Cody, of Cherokee-Choctaw descent, graduated from Gallaudet University with a BA, and earned a MA from the University of Arizona, Tucson, in sign language studies with a concentration in the linguistic study of North American Indian Sign Language. Since the mid-1990s she has worked and researched in the field of American Indian/Alaska Native/ Deaf Native Studies and has conducted multicultural training activities nationwide. She also was an American Indian consultant for the National Multicultural Interpreter Project (1995–2000). Currently, Melanie is an assistant professor in the American Sign Language Interpreting Program at William Woods University in Fulton, Missouri.

Rachel Locker McKee is program director of deaf studies at Victoria University of Wellington, New Zealand. Trained in the first cohort of NZSL interpreters (1985), she also holds RID (CI) certification as an ASL interpreter, and a PhD in Applied Linguistics from the University of California, Los Angeles. In collaboration with her husband, Dr. McKee has established programs to train sign language interpreters, Deaf teachers of NZSL, and introduced NZSL as an undergraduate subject. She has published research on various aspects of NZSL, interpreting, deaf education, and the NZSL community.

Ronice Müller de Quadros holds a PhD in linguistics and is a full professor at Universidade Federal de Santa Catarina in Florianopolis, Brazil. Her research activities focus primarily in sign language studies. She has published on sign language acquisition, sign language grammar, bilingualism, deaf education, and sign language interpretation.

David Quinto-Pozos, received his BS in sign language interpretation/ religious studies from the University of New Mexico and his MA and PhD degrees in linguistics from the University of Texas at Austin. He has directed the ASL programs at the University of Pittsburgh and the University of Illinois at Urbana-Champaign, and he is a nationally certified (CI/CT) ASL-English interpreter. His primary research topics include: interaction of language and gesture, register and language contact, and signed language disorders. Dr. Quinto-Pozos is on the faculty of the Department of Linguistics at the University of Texas at Austin where he teaches courses on linguistics and bilingualism and conducts linguistic research on various aspects of sign languages.

Sergio Peña is an LSM-ASL-English-Spanish interpreter who works in the United States and Mexico. He holds a BA from San Diego State University in education with a linguistics specialization. He is RID-certified, NIC level, and a founding member of both national and state-level Mexican interpreter associations, *Asociación Nacional de Intérpretes en Lengua de Señas* and the *Asociación de Interpretes y Traductores de Lengua de Señas de Baja California A.C.* He is active in the professional development of sign language interpreters in Mexico, in particular development of certification standards. He founded and coordinates an interpreter education program at *Universidad Autónoma de Baja California* in Tijuana.

Claire Ramsey has worked as a translator of Spanish and French, an ASL-English interpreter holding the former CSC (RID) certification. She holds a PhD in language, culture, and literacy from the University of California, Berkeley. Currently, she is an associate professor of education studies at University of California, San Diego. She conducts research on the sociolinguistics of sign languages, in particular processes of transmission and continuity among LSM signers in Mexico City.

Sharon Neumann Solow is an interpreter, interpreter coordinator, performer, lecturer, and consultant in the United States and internationally. She has extensive experience coordinating conference interpreters in a variety of formats and venues. Sharon has received the national Virginia Hughes Award, the President's Choice Award from the National Alliance of Black Interpreters, and the President's Award from the Registry of Interpreters for the Deaf.

Ted Supalla, PhD, was born Deaf to Deaf parents and a consumer of interpreting services at international conferences. Dr. Supalla is associate professor of brain and cognitive sciences and linguistics at the University of Rochester. He is the director of the University's American Sign Language Program, which offers a bachelor's degree in ASL. His research involves the study of signed languages that have emerged naturally within communities of deaf people; he is also interested in online psycholinguistic and neurolinguistic processing research in relation to visual-gestural languages.

Ryan Teuma is a senior forensic psychologist for the National Indigenous Intelligence Task Force of the Australian Crime Commission. He has worked with incarcerated offenders and victims of crime in Australia for the last 10 years, and has experience working with members of the Deaf and Deaf-Blind community, Deaf Indigenous Australians and Deaf Maori people from New Zealand. He presented at the World Federation of the Deaf, Madrid, 2008, on the forensic needs of Deaf offenders. Ryan has worked with Deaf clients who are also autistic, have Asperger syndrome, or are living with schizophrenia, and is passionate about the mental health needs of Deaf offenders and their right to an accessible and equitable justice system.

Rafael Treviño, NIC:Adv., is a trilingual (English/Spanish/ASL) interpreter in Miami, Florida. He is RID-certified as an English-ASL interpreter. His experience includes working as a trilingual interpreter at state, national, and international conferences and helping to launch Spanish Video Relay Services for providers in the United States. He is currently in the process of completing his bachelor's degree in Spanish translation and legal interpreting at Florida International University, and he is also pursuing a specialist certificate in legal interpreting from RID.

Maya de Wit, is an RID-certified ASL interpreter (CI), and a graduate of the bachelor's program for Dutch Sign Language Interpreting in the Netherlands. She interprets between Dutch, English, German, Dutch Sign Language, ASL, and International Sign. She is currently enrolled in the European Master of Sign Language Interpreting (EUMASLI) program. Ms. de Wit has given international presentations on the status of sign language interpreting in Europe. She was the policy maker of the Dutch Association of Sign Language Interpreters (NBTG) from 1998–2008, and has been president of the European Forum of Sign Language Interpreters (EFSLI) since 2006.

Index

Figures, tables, and notes are indicated by f, t, and n following the page number.

interpreters
   in American Indian settings. *See*
      American Indian/Alaskan
      Native (AI/AN) settings
   for Australian indigenous
      people. *See* Far North
      Queensland, Australia,
      Indigenous Deaf people of
   certification of. *See* certification
   differences between signed
      and spoken language
      interpreting, 204
   four-language interpreters on
      border. *See* Mexico-U.S. border
      and sign language interpreting
   low status of, 236
   at multilingual international
      conferences. *See* European
      conferences, multilingual
      interpreting at; Theoretical
      Issues in Sign Language
      Research (TISLR9)
   role of. *See* professional
      role of interpreters
   teams of. *See* teaming of
      interpreters
   training of. *See* education and
      training of interpreters
   trilingual, 48–49. *See also*
      trilingual interpreter
      certification; trilingual
      video relay services (VRS)
interpreting-as-interaction
      paradigm, 86
interpreting teams. *See* teaming
      of interpreters
Interstate Telecommunications Relay
      Service (TRS) Fund, 30, 31–32
intertribal communication
      of American Indians/
      Alaskan Natives, 149
Intertribal Deaf Council
      (IDC), 140, 144

intimate register and trilingual
      VRS use, 38–39
Inuit. *See* American Indian/Alaskan
      Native (AI/AN) settings

Johnston, T., 163
Jones, R., 233

Kala Lagaw Ya or *Kala Kawa Ya*
      (Australian Indigenous
      dialects), 162
Kaminker, A., 234
Karlin, B., 110, 113
Kendon, A., 163
kinship, 179
kinship connection, 112

language deprivation, 167, 168
language incompetence, 164,
      167–75
language proficiency for trilingual
      interpreter certification, 62
Latin American signed languages
      and Spanish dialects, 35, 37
legal settings and signed languages.
      See criminal proceedings
      and deaf suspects; Far North
      Queensland (FNQ), Australia,
      Indigenous Deaf people of
Leigh, I. W., vii, 191
Lengua de Señas Mexicana (LSM).
      See also Mexico-U.S. border
      and sign language interpreting
   ASL-LSM hybrid, use of, 20–21
   authors' learning of, 9, 14
   certification as trilingual
      interpreter and, 68
   certification in LSM/Spanish
      interpreting, 12
   deaf parents or family members
      in Mexico and, 20
   education of deaf students
      and, 18–19